For Betty. a wonderful
friend — and neighbor.
    May your future path
have no Banana Peels —
only the Rose petals you
deserve —
                much love
                    Fran

4/16/ '93

Waiting
for the
Banana Peel

by

Frances Adams Kearton

R&E Publishers
P.O. Box 2008, Saratoga, CA 95070
Tel: (408) 866-6303   Fax: (408) 866-0825

Book Cover and Illustrations by Kaye Quinn
Typesetting by elletro Productions

ISBN 0-88247-977-6

Designed, typeset and totally manufactured in the United States of America.
Library of Congress No.92-50859

Dedication

My heartfelt appreciation and love to Reg, Al, and Editors Thelma Shaw and Ruth Paya. And to the many pleasant memories of those 'live'ly days with Dick Van Dyke.

CHAPTER 1

WE DID IT LIVE!

"Aw, c'mon Fran... Saturday's mine this time."

"I beg to differ...and why so eager? You always groan over weekend personal appearances."

Dick Van Dyke and I, the so-called stars of Atlanta's WLWA-TV's daily hour-long variety show, were having our usual ongoing argument. Either Dick or I would have to forfeit a work-free Saturday for yet another personal appearance promotion dreamed up by Bill Colvin, our public relations man. Today's wrangle, however, was taking an unexpected turn. Instead of our habitual efforts to weasel out of Saturday duty, this time we *both* wanted it. I had my reasons but had no idea what Dick's might be. Let me explain.

After the two and half frenetic years we'd been on live television, the *TV Guide* for the week of April 3, 1953 was listing our show thus: "Channel 8's *Music Shop*, featuring Fran Adams and Dick Van Dyke, with music, comedy, fun and pantomimes. 4 to 5 p.m."

Now, in this decade, the fifties are often referred to as the Golden Age of Television. The "B Age" would be a better name: BC, BV, BT—Before Cable and Color, Before Videotape, Before TelePrompTers and laugh machines. In our own case, three more B's must be added for Bare Bones Budget.

We did have something which the stars of today seem to prize—"artistic control". Dick and I had that in abundance on the *Music Shop*, but to us it was an euphemism for an incredible amount of work and only meager assistance. We were given a time hole and told to fill it. One hour of air time, five days a week, takes a heap of filling.

We longed for less control in that domain and more control over such daily mishaps as falling scenery, guests who failed to show, guests who did and we wished they had not, sound failure when we were lip-synching a record, upside-down commercial slides and a million—or so it seemed—other pitfalls associated with a freewheeling ad-lib operation put together with masking tape, Elmer's glue and a lot of nerve on our part.

In those pioneering days, our audience had fun WAITING FOR THE BANANA PEEL—the slips came daily. The show was one long obstacle course. Full of youthful optimism and energy, we were too naive to realize it couldn't be done. But we did it, and we had fun...well, most of the time.

In the early fifties, before coaxial cable linked the East and West coasts, networks transmitted their programs by means of filmed kinescopes taken directly off a cathode tube. Present day viewers might well think that the locale for all kinescoped shows was San Francisco in a heavy fog.

Our station, WLWA-TV (now WXIA-TV) hadn't been on the air as long as the other two Atlanta stations, which had already acquired the stronger networks of NBC and CBS. We were left with ABC, the straggler. The scant 15 hours a week of such forgettables as "Boston Blackie" with Kent Taylor, "Rocky King, Detective" with Roscoe Karns, and Bert Parks' "Break the Bank" were all classed by us as "suspense" due to their unreliable arrival times. Once while we desperately filled airtime for one of ABC's no-shows, Dick's comment to me was, "ABC must ship those films by a stagecoach hitched to turtles."

So it was necessity that forced the station's management to develop local shows. Carter Sever, the manager of our underdog station, was elated when the Nielsen rating system indicated that the *Music Shop* was the most popular show in town... besting the likes of our network competition at the same hour—Arthur Godfrey and Kate Smith.

When we heard a rumor that ABC was considering the show for national distribution, Dick said, "Even if they pick it up, Fran, I don't think we have a chance with this same show ... it's too Atlanta and southern for a national audience."

I agreed with him. "It'd be like French table wine...vinegar by the time it got to Queens or Kansas."

"Still..," Dick brightened at the idea, "maybe the attention might goose Carter into giving us some help."

"Optimist," I gloomed. "If I had a secretary, I could rule the world. We've begged for help since this show began...so what do we get—more promotional appearances."

Typing the daily format, the comedy skits, and answers to the daily fan mail, all fell into my lap because remnants of the touch system learned in a high school typing class, enabled me to type faster than Dick's search and destroy method. Somehow we managed to share the chores more or less evenly with a minimum of friction.

That minor miracle spoke well of us as our working day was usually 10 to 12 pressure-filled hours. Dick's wife, Marjorie, an attractive brunette, complained that I saw him far more than she did. Television did offer improvement in his family life—in comparison to the previous constant travel with the "Merry Mutes", his night club act with former partner, Phil Erickson—yet it was not the hoped-for routine of 9 to 5 with regular weekends free to be with Marjorie and their two preschoolers, Chris and Barry. With a young son of my own, I sympathized but not enough to surrender any of my treasured Saturdays.

On rare occasions, a sponsor would request both of us, otherwise, we alternated. A hardship case sometimes resulted in a trade-off but it was out of character for either of us to joyfully volunteer. Therefore, Dick's eagerness to accept Saturday's assignment instead of venting his usual unprintable howls of anguish raised my eyebrows. Especially since this one involved some dumb idea about auditioning parakeets!

Intent upon solving the mystery, I continued my third degree. "Why the switch? Kay's Jewelers aren't giving us diamonds to tangle with a bunch of parakeets on a Saturday morning."

Waving long bony fingers at our sizable wall calendar, he answered, "Number one, it really is my turn...and number two ...hey, where's that memo from Bill?"

He began pawing through piles of paper on his desk in our jointly shared office space. Our office was comparatively spacious in our reconverted radio station due to the removal of a dividing wall. The top floor of the *Atlanta Constitution* building on Forsyth St. was considered ample for a former radio station, but it was tight quarters for the visual media.

Our one room served as a storehouse for props, costumes, fan mail, contest entries, stacks of 78 and 45 RPM records, and as a rehearsal hall for our 'merry mad-cap antics"—publicity's description of our hectic efforts to feed with ingenuity our insatiable Venus flytrap of a program. As a result, extensive hunts through chaos were routine.

Dick began his search with his typical question. "I don't have Bill's memo, is it on your desk?"

"Which memo?" I began poking around in my pile. "The Snowplow dumped at least fifty here this morning."

Long ago the sobriquet of *Snowplow* attached itself to our rotund, ruddy-faced bantam of a publicity man, Bill Colvin. He was always in constant motion spraying forth mountains of white paper memos instead of snow. Station personnel spent much time plowing through his energetic distributions.

"Here it is." Dick triumphantly waved the memo over his head. "It says, Kay's Jewelers will pay $1000 to the parakeet who can most clearly say, 'It's Okay to Owe Kay'—the parakeet to be selected by three impartial judges at auditions this Saturday at the Kimball House. Two judges will be Paul Jones, the *Atlanta Constitution* drama and television critic, and Big John Whitney, WQST radio's disc jockey. Bill says one of us will be the third judge."

"You have yet to answer main question. Why your interest?"

"Elementary, my dear Watson. It can't take very long to hear a few parakeets squawk 'It's Okay to Owe Kay', and I'll be home in time for tennis with Marge. The poor gal's been cooped up with the kids all week and needs air."

In spite of my vigorous head shakes, Dick continued, "Also, who knows what horrors lurk around the *next* promotional appearance corner. Premonition tells me it might be worse than this piece of cake."

I shook my head with finality and told Dick that I too wanted this Saturday for a good reason. My son's school carnival was Saturday week and I'd promised to take him. I couldn't risk being tied up next weekend. "You have a good memory, but it's short," I said. "In February we traded Saturdays when you took Barry to the dentist. You had the last one so fair's fair, it's my turn."

Unfolding his Ichabod Crane frame from his desk chair, Dick walked over to the huge wall calendar—which we used to keep our frantic schedule from becoming hopelessly snarled—and flipped back to February.

The calendar's original purpose for orderly coordination with other departments had not been altogether lost. By searching like scholars poring over Egyptian hieroglyphs, we could find a clue to our past and future activities among the messages, reminders, phone numbers, comedy sketch ideas, and jokes that seemed to collect like algae, not only on the calendar but trailing off on to the seasick green colored wall in all directions.

"Look at the last Saturday in February," I said with conviction. "A day I wish I'd been spared. Bill said it was for the Doraville Mall's grand opening...oodles of prospective sponsors. It rained all day and I stopped so many times for directions, I was soaked. It was a grand opening all right—Mancini's Meat Market."

"You didn't tell me that," Dick said, still peering at the calendar.

"By Monday I'd forgotten. Mancini's soggy red ribbon bled on my blue taffeta raincoat...the red and blue added a patriotic touch to the ceremony. And for all that effort, Mr. Mancini didn't even offer me a small T-bone."

"Don't tell me your troubles...it's a pain. The beauty contests are the worst...infinity. Aha! Here it is." Dick pointed victoriously to Saturday, then did a double take. "Awrr, damnation, you're right. I'm scratched that day."

He walked back to his desk and sat down in time to avoid a collision with Bill Colvin, who sprinted into the room in his usual out-of-breath state. Depositing another batch of memos on our desks, he rushed out—saying over his shoulder, "Don't forget about the parakeet auditions...you and Fran work it out...and don't forget, one of you has to judge the Miss Atlanta tryouts...a week from this Saturday."

The silence he left was punctuated by my continued typing. "Hum", I said. "Your premonition came straight from that Delphic Oracle, Bill Colvin...you rat."

Dick gave me his caught-in-the-cookie jar look and began his Stan Laurel crying imitation, which never failed to make me laugh.

"Don't cry, maybe only one Miss Boll Weevil will enter."

He grinned, sailed the wadded up parakeet memo past my ear, gathered up his pile of commercial scripts and notes for today's show and said, "Well, Saturday's a long way off...still three more shows to go this week. What's our double for today?"

Our pantomimes to popular records were a much-in-demand staple. As a rule, we each had a solo, then finished with a duet. Boy/girl records were so scarce that we asked the record shops to be on the alert for them. Our fragile 78 RPM collection of such duos as Buddy Clark/Dinah Shore, Garland/Rooney, and Bing Crosby/Mary Martin were kept wrapped in cotton like Tiffany's jewels.

I chewed on my pencil. "Look on the record list and see when we last did the Fred Astaire/Jane Powell one."

"The one with the long title I like?"

"Yep, we get a lot of requests for it."

I looked down at the show's format I had typed.

"A Bosco film commercial and then the Swingbillies give us six minutes to change into costume."

"Okay." Dick took the record we would use out of its cotton nest. "I'll give it to the boys in the control room." He left, singing the title of the record: "How Could You Believe Me When I Told You That I Loved You When You Know I've Been a Liar All My Life."

A glance at the clock brought my thoughts back to my typewriter and the show. One hour until deadline.

I typed it all down: 1) Announcer Ed Capral will say, "WLWA-TV presents The Music Shop, starring Fran Adams and Dick Van Dyke." 2) an opening slide will appear on the screen with our theme music, "Ain't We Got Fun", fading in and out. 3) From the control booth, Martin Magnus, our director, will give the go-ahead signal into Red O'Brien's headset for camera number one of the two cameras on the floor. 4) Red will dolly into position, flick on the red light—and we'll be on the air for an hour.

Warts and all—ready or not.

CHAPTER 2

HISSY FITS

In spite of our squabbles over Saturday duty, Dick was easier to work with than my former co-host. In its inception, the *Music Shop* featured Fran Adams and Lee Alexander. Lee was a conventionally handsome, six foot, thirty-year-old man bearing a slight resemblance to Cary Grant, a fact he pointed out himself if someone failed to notice.

In addition to good looks, his deep, impressive voice gave the proper amount of dignity to sponsors' products. He could make the statement "Laboratory tests have proven that DrainAway is today's safest, fastest-acting agent for unclogging kitchen sinks" sound like a Shakespearean sonnet.

Although the *Music Shop* was an immediate public favorite, Lee felt such frivolous fare beneath his talents. Some of our classic Buster Keaton-type comedians have been wooden dead-pans, but in Lee's case, his wooden facade matched his disposition. His feet-dragging, complaining attitude affected all of us.

After one show, when Lee stormed out of the studio over some imagined affront to his ego, Junebug, the guitarist with our five-piece country music band, the Swingbillies, carefully laid his instrument down on the piano and sighed, "I swan, Fran, I feel like I've been to Dee-troit and back carryin' a load of stove wood when that man throws them hissy fits."

I agreed with him. "Junebug, I'll go you one. I feel like I've climbed Stone Mountain with an anvil in one hand and a polecat in the other...and I have bruises to prove it."

During our few months of partnership, I'd collected some black-and-blue spots before learning to stay twenty paces behind Lee when he strode through Studio A's swinging doors. He had a habit of letting those doors snap back, with never an over-the-shoulder glance. I'd be trailing behind him—with paraphernalia piled so high in my arms that I couldn't see over it—and the closing doors would send me sprawling, bruising my anatomy and my pride as well.

A collective sigh of relief was heard from the cast when management offered Lee his own show—a half-hour of interviews of Georgians prominent in medicine, politics and education. In Lee's estimation, these subjects were dignified enough for a man with his abilities.

Lee's *Exchange Viewpoints* had all the sparkle of a funeral directors' seminar on casket sealing, and sank of its own weight within a few weeks. Shortly afterward, Lee took his morose-colored glasses to Macon, Georgia's newly opened WETV. Since he'd be the only announcer with television experience, we hoped his disposition would improve with his seniority. The bruises he'd unintentionally given me had healed and I sincerely wished him well.

Dick Van Dyke was a different personality altogether. Not long after he joined the *Music Shop*, a guest graphologist, Professor H. L. Watling of London, gave us both a reading on the air. It's difficult to view one's own character traits with an impartial eye so I can't vouch for the accuracy of my analysis. On the other hand, I thought the Professor was on the mark with Dick's.

After studying Dick's handwriting for a few moments, he said, "This shows you to be enthusiastic, direct, versatile and restless. You have a love of sports, animals, nature and travel. You're generous, inclined to be moralistic, have an eye for dressing well, keep a great many things to yourself, and sometimes suffer from foot-in-the-mouth disease."

Dick shook his head in amazement. "How can you tell all that....what's the secret?"

Professor Watling said, "Many things, look at your t crossings—the bar slants almost straight up. Very unusual...indicates an overabundance of hopefulness and optimism... also a touch of exhibitionism...a good thing for an actor."

"You haven't told me anything bad...must be faults in there somewhere."

The Professor was an actor also. He intrigued us by saying, "Dick, I'd better discuss other traits later. You have a strong private streak—you wouldn't relish a complete reading in public."

We teased Dick unmercifully for several days after that but he never would tell us what the Professor told him after the show.

CHAPTER 3

AUNT SUE'S DISAPPROVAL

Friday evening I forgot to set the alarm for an early morning wake-up, but my lively tow-headed six-year-old Al, christened Allison Hoyle Adams, Jr., served as a good substitute. We had adjacent bedrooms in the roomy, old-fashioned, white wood-frame house that we shared with my mother in Ansley Park.

Ansley Park, an older residential section developed in the early 1900's, has kept its original ambiance due to a Park-supported historical organization which has to approves any remodeling or building. The streets meander in such confusing fashion that the natives think Mr. Edwin Ansley, the developer, must have planned it after enjoying mint juleps.

Older settlers tell each newcomer to the Park a story about a cat-hating doctor who, a week after moving into Ansley Park, decided to get rid of an unwanted tabby by driving it to the country with the intention of leaving it. Upon returning to the Park, he became hopelessly lost, had to retrace his route, find the cat, and follow it home.

Many long-suffering visitors have complained that Atlanta streets make no sense. It's possible to become lost just driving around the block. Said block may turn into triangles, Y's, curves, or every geometric design possible except for a sturdy, straightforward square.

The same inconsistency falls over into street names, which have a fickle tendency to change along the same route. Some historical basis accounts for the eccentric paths of the main streets. They evolved from cow-paths or Indian trails, winding through the woods toward the Chattahoochee River, or the small streams that branch out from it.

On the other hand, Mr. Ansley didn't have to follow cow-paths to lay out his dream development in 1904, so it's curious to note that the most tangled skein of streets in Atlanta was planned. The effect is charming, though, and residents fortunate enough to live in the Park wouldn't have it otherwise.

With the exception of a few childhood years when my late father's nostalgia for rural life beguiled him into gentleman farming, and again during a short marital period, I lived in Ansley Park most of my life. With our church, a good grammar school, and several small parks within a radius of a few blocks, I was pleased to raise my son in such an ideal setting. But if you asked Al why he liked Ansley Park, he would say, "'Cause Turner, my bestest friend, lives here."

That Saturday morning when I was condemned to parakeet judging, Turner's mother, Marian Callaway, had invited Al to spend the whole day at their house twenty blocks away. Al, my substitute alarm clock, went into action. His excitement was too great for him to stay in bed past 6 a.m., and at that hour, I felt a gentle tug at my blanket. I opened one blue eye to see two more like it staring me closely in the face.

"Mother, what time is Mrs. Callaway coming for me?"

"Dear Heart, not until nine o'clock. Go back to bed and let Mother sleep."

Ten minutes later the same gentle tug and a whispered, "Mother, is it nine yet?" led me to abandon hope of any more sleep. I was relieved, furthermore, to be rescued from a bizarre dream which had me perched on a swing in an enormous silver cage and had me dressed in a Las Vegas-type costume of pink feathers and rhinestones. From the stage, the black-tie audience seemed appropriate for a first night opening until I realized that they were all parakeets.

Hurriedly putting on a navy silk dress with a wide white collar, I made a mental note to add a touch of color with a red camellia from a bush that grew beside the wrap-around porch of our house. I made another note to refurbish my personal wardrobe, which had received no attention since my television debut because of Rich's Department Store's loan of various outfits to be modeled on my show and to be worn in personal appearances. However, in this case, I didn't want to expose the store's clothing to some stage-frightened, accident-prone parakeet.

Pausing by Al's door to check on his choice of attire for the day, I discovered him putting on his new Sunday School trousers in honor of the occasion.

"Well, sport, what are the big plans today?"

"Turner says his mother's letting us dig a cave in the backyard."

The terraced clay bank rising behind the Callaway property was made for cave digging by small boys. I suggested blue jeans might be easier on his knees as cave digging was hard work. It was also hard work to wash out virtually indelible red clay. Less flamboyant shades of earth are anemic by comparison and Georgia's clay is beautiful to my eyes—but not on Al's Sunday britches.

Our cook, Cora Lee Downing, was in the kitchen and Al hurried down for breakfast. I followed him down the wide staircase as far as the landing. There I found Mother (affectionately known as "Peace"—her married name but it suits her) seated at the phone table. She was holding the earphone at arm's length with a resigned look on her face. When I leaned over with a good morning kiss, she glanced up, pointed to the phone and silently mouthed, "Aunt Sue."

An extension phone wasn't needed to hear Aunt Sue's conversations. She held the firm belief that phones work on a hollow tube principle, and a subscriber's voice raised to the maximum volume, insured the phone company's survival. I heard my name mentioned so curiosity prompted me to listen in on the old martinet's daily message.

My great-aunt Sue, Mrs. Archibald Topliff Davis, was often described by two newspapers, *The Atlanta Constitution* and *The Atlanta Journal*, as a "prominent and beloved figure in religious, civic and social circles." That description was translated by me into "a juggernaut with incredible drive and intelligence."

Personnel at those papers called her Mrs. Genghis Khan, Jr. behind her back, because she swept all before her in conquest and had never been known to lose a battle.

Peace's mother, Fanny Maria Brooks, died of pneumonia when Peace was eight years old. Fanny Maria's deathbed request to her younger sister, Susan, to watch over her daughter Margaret Brooks, Mother's maiden name, had been honored in Aunt Sue's own fashion. The daily spoonfuls of advice and criticism which accompanied the many kindnesses shown to Peace and her two daughters during our growing up years, make me appreciate Aunt Sue more now than then. She seemed to feel that my long-suffering mother's incredible string of misfortunes—the untimely death of two husbands and Peggy, my younger sister, the loss of our house and all our possessions by fire, the disappearance of a considerable fortune through dishonest stock brokers—was more the result of some flighty whim or character flaw on my mother's part—rather than inexplicable bad luck.

Since the death of Judge Davis ten years ago, Aunt Sue had lived alone at 1490 Peachtree Street. Her house, a handsome pink brick structure with two stone lions guarding the entrance to the driveway, was not far from ours on Fifteenth Street.

In a later era, Aunt Sue might have concentrated her formidable leadership ability, and domineering instinct on running a corporation or on filling a political office. Instead, she had to content herself with worthy causes. She belonged to the Colonial Dames, Daughters of the American Revolution, the Atlanta Woman's Club, the Red Cross, Daughters of 1812, the Atlanta Historical Society—the list was interminable. Fortunately, she thrived on dedicating plaques and championing causes.

Her physical appearance and her inner character were a dichotomy. By rights, she deserved a Junoesque figure instead of a diminutive five feet. Until she spoke, Aunt Sue's cobalt-blue eyes and her quick movements were the only outer indications of her inner drive. Her voice was a surprise...like hearing the tones of Westminster Abbey's bells coming from a small silver serving bell.

The only car she learned to drive was a small electric one, used for jaunts around the neighborhood. Otherwise, she relied on Grant, a tall, kindly black man, to chauffeur her Packard. He played the role of the Highlander, John Brown, to her Queen Victoria. The sole person who wasn't awed by her to some degree, Grant watched over her with an indulgent eye. If she wanted to make one too many calls in a day, he'd been known to say politely but firmly, "Now Miss Susan, we's both too tired."

The well-preserved, dark-blue, 1933 Packard, formerly belonging to the late Judge and kept for sentimental reasons, was a familiar sight around town. A *too* familiar sight perhaps. A glimpse of the Packard with Grant at the wheel, and a hatted-and-gloved Aunt Sue perched on the back seat like a small plump partridge caused many a politician, business man or City Editor to hurriedly schedule an out-of-town meeting. When the duo pulled into a driveway or up to an office building, the cowards could think of no other way to avoid her gracious bullying. When pursuing funds or publicity for her projects, her dignified browbeating bordered on genteel blackmail; she rarely came away empty handed.

On this particular morning, Aunt Sue's call promised to be longer than usual, so I settled myself on a step within easy overhearing distance.

"Margaret, I wish you'd speak to Fanny. Her undignified clowning on that idiotic television show is becoming a source of great embarrassment to me. Whatever would the Judge say?"

While alive, the Judge was the most taciturn of men at home, whether from inclination or the lack of opportunity to speak, I don't know. I doubted he would rise from his grave to deliver a ruling on my choice of employment.

"Aunt Sue, you told me that television was a passing fad and you had no intention of wasting your time on such trash...so how do you know about it?"

"My friends can't wait to tell me about Fanny's latest ridiculous antic on that show...along with some silly young man, Dick somebody or other."

By this time, Peace and I were laughing so hard we thought she'd hear. No such luck for she continued, "haven't you any influence over her? Why doesn't she marry some nice young man again? Or at least settle down to something serious and stable. Why'd she resign from the Coca-Cola Company?...she only lasted a few weeks."

I flinched when I heard that last remark. Two years ago, when Aunt Sue had visited the office of Burton Frazier, a Coca-Cola Company executive, to collect his pledge for the church building fund, he told her that his long-time secretary was retiring; he needed a replacement. Aunt Sue immediately offered my services and Burton accepted.

My touch-typing and shorthand from one semester in school were covered with dusty neglect, but neither Burton nor Aunt Sue discussed such minor details as secretarial skills.

My efforts to earn a living for a young son and myself were hampered by a grasshopper tendency to become bored with routine tasks. Although I'd been a model since my teen years, I was realistic enough to know that wasn't an answer for the long pull. And as for re-marrying, all my white knights so far had come in too many shades of tattle-tale gray.

Burton's offer came during August, a vulnerable month for older fashion models. The stores were promoting back-to-school clothing and the sight of rosy-cheeked college freshmen filling the fashion offices strengthened my misgivings. Before I knew it, I was sitting in Burton Frazier's office with a shorthand pad upon my knee.

Peace shifted the phone to her other ear before tackling her aunt's last question. "Fanny won't talk about why she left."

Aunt Sue insisted Peace must know something, but Peace stuck with her denial. "Nope, someday maybe she'll tell me, but so far, it's a mystery. Once I broached the subject to Burton at an altar meeting, but he skittered away mumbling something about restless modern young women."

Hoping to divert the conversation away from my shortcomings to a different subject, Peace asked, "Did you get by Mrs. Frobisber's last week...I know you want your spring hats before Easter."

Aunt Sue wore hats both indoors and out as often as possible—probably to compensate for her lack of height. Aunt Sue's hats from Mrs. Frobisher's custom millinery shop were a bellwether for the changing seasons. Fall brought forth felts, velours, and pheasant feathers—winter, velvet turbans and fur trims—and spring, shiny straws or Panama's, garnished with silk flowers, artificial fruits or grosgrain ribbons.

One time Aunt Sue appeared at our house wearing a particularly startling headpiece trimmed in black net and egret feathers. After she'd left, Peace remarked, "She must have an automatic pulley system that plops the hat-of-the-day on Aunt Sue's bead."

But this Saturday morning, our elderly relative was not to be diverted from the subject of my desertion from the Coca-Cola Company, and kept such an iron grip on the theme that Peace lost patience. Peace's sweet disposition holds most of the time, but when defending her young, she's no doormat.

"Listen, Aunt Sue, Fanny is a single parent with a small son to raise. I can't treat her like a baby...now wait a minute... let me finish. Furthermore, you'd be surprised at what they pay her for, as you put it, making a fool of herself...the money's a big help." Then Peace ended the conversation by saying, "I thought you had an Historical Society meeting this morning; and Fanny and Al are ready to leave so I'll have to call you back later."

She placed the ear piece back on its hook and said with an exasperated sigh, "Sometimes Aunt Sue drives me wild...she's the last link with my mother and I love her, but, but...."

"Never mind, Peace, you'll recover." I patted her on the shoulder. "I'm on my way...actually, judging parakeets will be easy to me after a bout with Aunt Sue."

In our out-of-date oversized kitchen, I found Al seated at the round Tate, Georgia, pink marble-topped table simultaneously trying to swallow his cereal and tell Cora Lee about his cave-digging plans. Hugging them both, I grabbed a piece of Al's toast and ran out the back door, pretending not to hear Cora Lee's scolding voice, "Miss Fanny, come back and eat somethin', you heah."

Yes, I heard. Cora Lee had been part of the family since I was a baby and still treated me as one. But I'd wasted too much time eavesdropping on Aunt Sue to spend any time eating. I could get coffee at the Kimball House while I listened to the parakeets warble the magic words, "It's Okay to Owe Kay."

CHAPTER 4

MY BRIEF SECRETARIAL CAREER

or

A SQUARE PEG IN A ROUND BOTTLE

While driving my green '48 Nash down Atlanta streets to my appointment with the parakeets, I mused over Aunt Sue's written-in-indelible-ink memory. Would she never cease carping on my brief attempt to settle for a down-to-earth job with the Coca-Cola Company—guaranteed to give me a gold watch and a pension upon retirement.

When I accepted Burton's secretarial offer, I knew it would be difficult for me to exchange the more glamorous occupation of modeling clothes in fashion shows for a 9 to 5 routine. Yet I convinced myself that it was a mature decision, one bolstered by Burton's assurance that I would advance rapidly in the company. I never thought to ask, "Advance to where?" Their lone woman executive was the personnel officer, Miss Troutman.

Therefore, in spite of my reluctance, one crisp fall day in the late forties, I reported to work for a company venerated by a multitude of Atlantans as the cornerstone of their wealth. The architectural style of many Atlanta "finger bowl" section houses has been dubbed "rococola."

That morning in the modest six-story building on North Avenue, (a far cry from the present vast Coca-Cola headquarters), my first duty was a trip to the office supply room. The clerk welcomed me to the company and asked, "How many steno pads do you want?"

"Gee, I guess a dozen for now...and a dozen pencils."

If I'd known that my secretarial career was going to be so brief,

I would have ordered only one pencil and one lone steno pad for Burton's dictation.

Burton Frazier was one of the company's many junior executives. It's said he'd been hired during World War II sugar rationing days because of *whom* he knew rather than *what* he knew. His former Harvard roommate had powerful White House connections so the company hoped that this friendship would provide a sugar supply that could keep the coke syrup up to its sweet standard. Sugar rationing finally went but Burton stayed.

He was an average-looking man with no particular distinctive features. Although he tended to blend into the landscape, Burton filled his post of deacon of our church in a diligent, pleasant manner and was held in esteem by the congregation, including Aunt Sue and Peace.

As a Coca-Cola Company employee, I soon learned that serving the famous beverage to office visitors was top priority. On heavy traffic days, I felt more like a fast-food counter girl than a secretary.

When I wasn't serving Coca-Cola, I spent my time decoding my own creative version of Gregg's shorthand ciphers and putting through Burton's phone calls. The latter assignment sounds like an easy task, but due to the lack of automatic dialing then and remnants of a childhood stammer, I contacted the company's switchboard with timidity. When Burton said, "Get me Eastern Airlines", I wished that he preferred Delta because I had difficulty with words that began with an E. In time, the compassionate operators grew familiar with my handicap. When the operator on duty heard a voice say, "May I have E-E-E ... " followed by a long silence, she'd say, "Hold on, Fran, I'll get Eastern for you."

My days with the company would have been even briefer without my fairy godmother in the guise of Eleanor Blaine, secretary to Mr. Norwood, a senior vice president.

Secretaries in large corporations tend to take on the rank of their boss. Some were as haughty and touchy about the pecking order as any ambassador from an obscure country.

If I hadn't been so green, I would have known that the lower ranking office always delivers messages to the one above, and in the hierarchy, Eleanor ranked high indeed. The day she called Burton's office to ask in a chilly tone of voice why a certain requested letter wasn't on her desk, I answered by sobbing over the phone, "I don't know", and hung up.

Within a few minutes, an attractive brunette in her early thirties came into the office. It was Eleanor Blaine. Instead of dressing me down as expected, she said, "What's the matter, sugah?"

I blubbered, "I can't read my shorthand, I can't ask for E-E-Eastern Airlines on the phone...I grabbed my steno pad and pointed at the salutation, "and I know this man's name's wrong, nobody's named Pichegru Foolwalk."

For some reason, it struck Eleanor as funny that Burton had hired a secretary with phone and shorthand trouble. She laughed. I managed a smile, and our friendship began.

When my artistic but incomprehensible chicken scratches failed to lend subject-matter clues, and the Pichegru Foolwalks of the world were too much for me, Eleanor lent a helping hand, but she couldn't spend all her time rescuing me. However, my failures in business communications didn't prevent another type of communication.

After a few weeks of my scant improvement in reconstructing Burton's dictation, he called me into his office and gently closed the door. Instead of sitting behind his desk as usual, he walked to the window and looked out. I held my steno pad in readiness, but when he turned around, he said, "Put your book away...I've something to tell you that's off the record."

"Uh, oh," I thought, "here it comes...I've taxed this poor man to the breaking point." Secretly I was relieved. It hadn't taken me long to realize how thoroughly I detested secretarial work. The confinement was so unbearable to me that during the day I'd slip out of a side door in order to run around the block. I'd done my best to emulate Eleanor, the perfect secretary, but alas, my square pegs didn't fit into those round bottles.

Burton's waffling throat-clearing speech didn't have my full attention. My thoughts were occupied with the calls I'd make to various fashion offices announcing my full time availability. Burton droned on and I wished he'd give me my two weeks notice and be done with it.

At last, he walked over by my chair, put his hand on my shoulder and said, "And so, Frances, I wanted you to know how I feel...you've crept into my heart and I wondered if we could have a quiet dinner somewhere soon to talk it over."

That astounding statement *did* get my attention. Crept into his heart indeed...and now I was supposed to creep into his lap. It was so unexpected that all I could do was put my hand over my mouth to suppress a giggle, and say the first thing that came to mind, "Aunt Sue would have a fit, and Al's Sunday School teacher, your wife, Cornelia, wouldn't be too crazy 'bout the idea either."

Unlucky Burton. He may have lost a potential lap sitter but he could have found a more efficient secretary at the dog pound. For many a Sunday when he passed the collection plate along Aunt Sue's pew, his hand shook. Time and my silence finally steadied it.

Needless to say, I parted from the Coca-Cola Company to once more search for the perfect job which I knew was waiting somewhere. And it was—my job at the television station.

I found that I looked forward with eagerness to going to work each morning, even on controversial Saturdays when birds waited for my under-qualified judgment.

Over time, Dick and I learned that a television personality with five workable senses apparently made us authorities on any and all subjects. We'd judged dog and cat contests, horse shows, most identical twins, most freckles, art shows, amateur nights, and beauty pageants, plus sewing contests and bake-offs.

And now, it was to be parakeets. I gave silent thanks that Aunt Sue couldn't know about this one. She wouldn't consider judging a parakeet's ability to enunciate a jewelry store slogan to be in the same league as dedicating an historical plaque. Perhaps she'd relax her prejudice against the new medium if she'd realize how helpful television could be to her causes.

CHAPTER 5

MUM'S THE BIRD

On the way toward Peachtree street and downtown, I passed by one of the many small parks that lie within the Ansley Park area and caught my breath at the sight. Once more, spring in Atlanta, and the Iris Garden Club, had combined to outdo themselves. The park was a bewitching mass of color with its jeweled shades of azaleas and clouds of white dogwood against a Kodachrome blue sky.

Past the park, I made a left turn onto Peachtree and was on my way to the Kimball House where a lucky parakeet would soon earn an extra cuttlebone from its grateful $1,000 dollar-richer owner. Since the simple Kay's slogan should be a snap for a breed of talking birds, I puzzled as to what other criteria could be used to elect the future Laurence Olivier of the parakeet world.

When I walked up to the entrance of the turreted, iron-balconied Victorian Gothic hotel, I remembered a bit of its history. It was the most opulent hotel in town and first choice for visiting Presidents and Atlanta society when it opened in 1870. After the original hotel burned in 1885, this even handsomer hotel was built. Now the old grand dame had declined into seedy elegance.

When I entered its lobby, the sound of my heels clattering across the marble floor gathered curious glances from several men dozing in the shabby lounge chairs. Some of the Kimball House clientele looked as if they'd been recent guests of the nearby Decatur Street police station. I wondered at Kay's location choice until I thought of Aunt Sue's current publicity drive in support of the Historical Society to save the old building from the wrecker's ball.

At the desk, I was preparing to ask the clerk for directions when I felt a tap on my shoulder and a voice behind me said, "Pardon me, Miss, but is this yours?"

I whirled around to see the familiar face of disc jockey Big John Whitney, "John, you startled me...running that gauntlet of lobby-lizards made me nervous."

Big John grinned and dangled a silk stocking in front of me.

"Why're you waving that around...it isn't mine," I said, taking a quick peek down at my slightly bowed but stockinged legs.

"Oh, yes it is, it was caught in your coat belt...I surmise that you dressed in a hurry, me proud beauty." John gave a melodrama villain's leer and twirled an imaginary mustache.

Snatching the stocking out of his hand, I hurriedly stuffed it in my coat pocket. "With your sense of humor, I'm surprised you didn't let it trail behind me the rest of the day."

He laughed. "To tell the truth, I was torn between seeing the expression on your face or letting the parakeets have a three-legged judge. I take it you're here for this damn-fool thing too."

"Yes, but I don't know where to go."

"Follow me, sixth floor ballroom."

During the slow-moving ride in the European-style gilt cage elevator, I congratulated Big John on his recently being chosen by *Radio and TV Mirror* magazine as Atlanta's favorite disc jockey. I added, "But John, if you keep playing records like that Elvis Presley fellow you've been pushing lately, you won't win again. He's terrible."

John gave me an indulgent look. "There's room for all kinds of music—but thanks for the congrats. How about celebrating with me, say like dinner at Emile's next week?"

"Now, John, don't start that again."

"The reason for your last turn down doesn't exist anymore ...my divorce is final."

"How sad," I said with sincerity, "both for you and Dorothea, but...well, I'll let you know about dinner later." In fact, I was already thinking about it and what the results might be.

In the conservative fifties in a middle-sized Southern city, a working woman with or without a high profile had a running battle to stay out of trouble. As the term "sexual harassment" had yet to be coined, I don't know what we called it then.

The Madonna/whore syndrome flourished. Sometimes a friendly dinner date became transformed with the telling, into a torrid affair. Such untruths often led to a Hydra-headed monster of unflattering and unwanted invitations. As a result of that fine line to be walked, the no-dating-men-at-work rule was a sensible one. On the other hand, my rule wasn't so rigid that it included *everyone* in the same type of business. John was an attractive man so I'd probably take my chances and accept his dinner suggestion.

As we walked off the elevator, we ran into Mr. Hammond, manager of Kay's Jewelers store. Paul Jones, the third judge, was with him. Paul looked tired, and I guessed that he'd stayed up too many nights lately catching new shows. Paul, the movie and theater critic for the *Atlanta Constitution*, was also the recently assigned television critic.

The hall was filled with people, including two staff photographers from the papers, who began posing us for shots with Kay's officials and various owners and their birds.

Once the photographers had left, Mr. Hammond led us into the Grand Ballroom. Age and neglect couldn't diminish the beauty of that room: French windows, parquetry floors, old ivory woodwork combined with gold leaf, an Italian mantelpiece and three Waterford chandeliers. To replace something irreplaceable with a projected parking garage seemed a crime.

My reverie of imagining Scarlett and Rhett dancing in this very ballroom was interrupted by Mr. Hammond. "Judges, your judging equipment," and he pointed to three flimsy straight-backed chairs directly under the largest chandelier. On each chair was a list of the thirteen entrants. On a table in front of the chairs sat a birdcage-size glass box.

"What's that?" the three of us chorused.

"That, John, Paul, and Fran, is Kay's guarantee of an honest contest."

Big John gave me a nudge and whispered, "He makes us sound like a vocal trio."

Mr. Hammond threw him a disapproving glance. "I designed this box myself...sound and ventriloquist proof...with a microphone inside. If this trial run is successful, my idea will be used in every store in our chain."

He explained that his box eliminated any chance of the contest turning into a bird-world scandal—like some of the quiz show scandals of the fifties. A congressional investigation revealed that the richest of them all, *Twenty One*, was rigged.

What seemed like just a lark to me was obviously weighty business for the Kay Company, for Mr. Hammond finished his speech by adding that all birds were insured by Lloyd's of London for the duration of the contest. The owners were to bring in their bird by turn and transfer it to the glass box. Each bird was to be scored on clarity of the spoken slogan, repetition and personality.

Paul seemed to be taking the instructions in stride, but John and I looked at each other and simultaneously dissolved into laughter. Wiping his eyes, John said, "And to think my mother wanted me to take over Dad's medical practice."

"John," I shushed him. "This is serious. Not only is Kay's coughing up a thousand bucks, but the owners have turned their birds into Frankenstein monsters. Imagine hearing that dumb slogan all day every day."

We'd pulled ourselves together, however, by the time Mrs. Raiford brought in the first parakeet, Cuddles. The blue and white parakeet in some ways resembled its owner, an elderly, sweet-faced woman, who shyly confessed that Cuddles was her best company these days. Since reading about the contest, she'd rehearsed him daily. Mr. Hammond gently transferred the bird from his cage, filled with such comforts as swings, mirrors, bells and birdseed, into the austere glass box.

After fifteen minutes of bird silence which went by with all the speed of a very old glacier, Mr. Hammond called time. The disappointed Mrs. Raiford put Cuddles back in his cage and chided him: "Naughty, naughty bird." Cuddles mutely admired himself in his little mirror.

The other twelve birds repeated the scenario. One by one, Perky, Woodles, Baby Doll, Jojo and the rest clammed up in the glass box. At noon, sandwiches were brought in. After a conference with the bird owners, Mr. Hammond said, "The owners complain that the glass box scares the birds. We'll start over without it."

I refrained from asking Mr. Hammond why he hadn't consulted a parakeet authority before building his precious box. John and Paul left to make phone calls canceling their appointments for the rest of the day. I was thankful that Al's carnival was *next* Saturday.

We began again. One by one the birds came in...and went out...all in sullen silence. Despite pleas, promises, kisses, radio country music, mirrors and an occasional swear word, the birds wouldn't budge. John commented that was why budgerigar was another name of the stubborn fowls.

We all perked up when one owner said that her bird, Baby Doll, always talked outside its cage. Desperate by then, Mr. Hammond, sounding like a king granting a pardon, commanded, "Let Baby Doll out."

Upon release, Baby Doll flew up to perch on the chandelier above us. Blinking beady little eyes, she quietly let out a few derisive wolf whistles.

John said, "Hurry, somebody get a ladder...we can't hear her up there."

Baby Doll was still on the chandelier when Mr. Hammond came back with a ladder, which he and John held steady while dignified Paul mounted the steps. Those years of critiquing Atlanta's road company dramatic fare came to the fore. Baby Doll was Juliet on her balcony and Paul was Romeo on the trellis below. The thought of spending eternity at the Kimball House made Paul's delivery of the magic words, "It's Okay to Owe Kay", a moving plea. But Baby Doll's cold heart wasn't touched and Paul climbed down the ladder a defeated man.

Then nine-year-old Bobbie Lee Barber brought in her bird, JoJo. In previous tries, JoJo hadn't covered himself with any more glory than the rest of the miserable flock. Mr. Hammond told Bobbie Lee that the rules had been somewhat relaxed. Relaxed wasn't quite the word—they had collapsed, been stomped on, been bundled up and thrown out on Decatur Street. In the hall, the owners were threatening mutiny and law suits; the judges were restrained from joining them solely by Kay's large advertising budget.

By now, Mr. Hammond had been reduced to a speechless shell of man, incapable of anything but strange whimpering sounds. I assumed that he was preparing his explanation to the head office as to why his expensive glass box idea had been shot down by a handful of tiny birds.

I tried to console him by saying, "Mr. Hammond, be happy this isn't on live television...although it's about par for the course."

During the time I was ineffectually cheering Mr. Hammond, John gleaned interesting information from Bobbie Lee on JoJo's fragile talent. The bird was most garrulous while outside his cage listening to her play "Suwanne River" on a toy flute.

The four of us knocked heads at the cage in our haste to let the bird out. With the cage opened, JoJo hopped out on Bobbie Lee's finger, made a pit stop on the chandelier, then flew out of the window. Bobbie Lee screamed, and Mr. Hammond must have forgotten his Lloyds of London insurance because he turned even paler. We all stampeded to the window.

JoJo was resting on the ledge, preparing for flight into the wild blue yonder.

John conferred briefly with Bobbie Lee, then pushed the bird's cage into my hands. "Fran, maybe this'll work. Since you weigh the least, Paul and I'll hold your ankles so you won't fall...you can reach around the ledge and coax the bird back into the cage."

"Are you out of your cotton-pickin' mind?" I looked at him in amazement. "Anyway, why me? It's Bobbie Lee's bird and she weighs a lot less than I do."

"Don't whine...Bobbie Lee has to play the flute. If JoJo hears his favorite tune, he might get back into the cage."

Bobbie Lee blew a practice scale and seemed remarkably calm considering it was her bird about to take off.

By that time, the sight of so many people leaning out of the sixth story window of the Kimball House had collected a crowd on the street below. I held the cage, John and Paul grabbed my ankles and Bobbie Lee tootled. Glory Hallelujah! The plan worked. JoJo hopped back in his cage. While I was carefully bringing him back to Bobbie Lee's waiting arms, JoJo squawked out a triumphant, "It's Okay to Owe Kay." The pump had been primed and he repeated the phrase over and over.

After that, Mr. Hammond recovered enough to think that his idea was a winner after all. He thanked everyone for their patience, and promised the losers and the judges a substantial discount on their next Kay's Jewelry store purchase.

I remember muttering to John, "Nothing short of the Hope Diamond would be enough for this day."

CHAPTER 6

KEEPING
DICK IN THE DARK

At Sunday morning breakfast, before I could tell Peace and Al of Kay's Jewelers attempt to turn me against our feathered friends, Al asked a question, "What's splunking?"

Words didn't intimidate Al. He'd wrap his tongue around any unfamiliar word he heard, including some we wished he hadn't. He was his mother's child in that respect. Peace called me Mrs. Malaprop long before I knew why.

A favorite family quote was my character summation of our neighbor, Mrs. Wexler, a chronic complainer. One day I remarked, "Mrs. Wexler certainly has a lot of faucets to her personality." Peace's eyebrows shot up but she agreed that indeed Mrs. Wexler did run hot and cold. Another gem was when the word *nirvana* cropped up in the dinner table conversation. I thought it was a small town near Valdosta, Georgia, and for all I know, I may have been right on that one.

Al had us stumped though with his *splunking* until be said, "Yesterday Turner's daddy helped us dig our cave and he promised to take us splunking some day."

Peace said, "Al, you mean *spelunking.*"

"Thas what I said, "splunking'."

"Al, honey, don't talk with your mouth full," I said. "S-p-e-l-u-n-k-i-n-g, it means to explore caves...we can't do that today but I know something almost as much fun...gold panning."

"Gold." That idea caused Al to jump out of his chair and run around the room.

Peace gave me a skeptical look and asked how I was going to keep my word.

"We'll drive up to the mountains today. We interviewed a man from the Dahlonega Chamber of Commerce last week and I've wanted to take you and Al there ever since."

"What's in Dahlonega that's so special?"

"It was a gold rush town in the early 1800's. Now they have a different type of gold rush...tourists. We can rent some equipment for gold panning. Al will love it."

Peace looked interested. "Say," she said, "I wouldn't mind panning some of that myself."

We had ourselves an adventuresome day—filled with beautiful north Georgia mountain scenery, and a tour of the Gold Museum with its nuggets, gold dust and mining equipment.

We lunched at a restaurant, the Golden Pan, that had a nearby stream with a sluice trough. Al's pleasure in panning for pyrite or fool's gold was as much as if he'd found the real thing.

The three of us drove home in high spirits, singing silly songs. Al's favorite: "I wish I was a little piece of soap, I'd slippity and slidey over everybody's hidey, I wish I was a little piece of soap."

Happily, parakeets were forgotten until Peace asked me to finish the story I'd begun at the breakfast table. That was a mistake. Al bounced up and down in the back seat, chanting the Kay's Jewelers slogan.

"Al, *don't* sing that anymore."

"But Mothurr-r, why can't I?" and he continued. "It's Okay to Owe Kay."

"Dear Heart, it gives Mother a headache and if you don't stop, you'll have an ache where you sit. Be quiet and count your gold rocks."

The rest of the ride home was quiet.

Monday morning, Aunt Sue's usual call arrived. Peace motioned for me to listen. At times, she felt more capable of dealing with Aunt Sue if she had a hand to hold.

"Margaret, where were you all yesterday? I didn't see you in church."

Without waiting for an answer, Aunt Sue hastened on. "Margaret, tell me I'm imagining things these days."

"Why, I've seen no such signs,"

"Saturday afternoon, Catherine Ottley and I were standing outside the Kimball House. Suddenly Catherine grabbed me by the arm and said, 'There's your niece, Fanny!' I asked her where and she pointed. 'Up there, see, hanging out that window like a bat.' I looked up and saw a woman on the window ledge, with some people trying to pull her back in. I thought she was some unfortunate soul trying to jump out."

Stalling for time, Peace asked, "What on earth were you doing in that part of town Saturday?"

"We were on a tour of the Kimball House for the Historical Society. But the sight of Fanny—at least Catherine thought it might be her—upset me so, I don't remember if we decided we could save the building. The people pulled the woman back in, so we knew she was all right ... but what a shock."

Peace said, "Let me explain...."

"Catherine and I finally decided that it couldn't possibly have been Fanny."

Ignoring my negative semaphores, Peace admitted, "Aunt Sue, that *was* Fanny you saw at the Kimball House, she was there on business."

"Business? What sort of business could she have in the Kimball House on a Saturday, or any other day for that matter?"

Peace explained that it involved my television job and that she'd drop by Aunt Sue's for afternoon tea, with more details.

That didn't satisfy Aunt Sue. "I keep telling you to make her quit being such an embarrassment. How a shy child with a speech impediment ever got mixed up with such crazy people is beyond me."

By this time, Peace was tapping her foot and twisting a strand of hair around her forefinger—danger signals if you knew her. "Aunt Sue, you'll have to admit that Fanny was considerate of you that day."

"How can you claim that?"

"Suppose she'd actually fallen or jumped out of the Kimball House window?" and Peace paused before giving her coup de grace, "You'd have loved those big black headlines reading *Hysterical Star Lands on Historical Galaxy.*"

The silence from Aunt Sue's end of the line indicatd that for the moment, dear Peace had the last word.

At work, later on that morning, Dick and I were opening fan mail. We both enjoyed that part of our work so the office boy put half the pile on Dick's desk, the other half on mine.

The more interesting letters were thrown into our emergency box for 'panic time'. Near the end of our hour, we dreaded to see our floor director give a taffy-pulling stretch gesture, which meant that there was a delay with the next program. Our improvisation skills and gossamer-thin material were already wrung dry by then so those unplanned few minutes could seem insupportably long. Our panic-time letter box had more than once rescued us from a television performer's nightmare—dead air time.

Dick usually opened his mail with his teeth. He claimed that it was a safer way than risking a mangled finger with the kitchen knife I used. He stopped to remove a piece of envelope stuck on his tongue before he said, "By the way, how'd Saturday go?"

The thought of having Dick cock-a-doodle over my insistence on keeping last Saturday's date made me choose my words carefully. "Uh, er, okay, not much to it. Some little girl's parakeet won...a real pro, he was still 'okaying" going down the elevator."

Dick began to tear open another letter and said, "Well, I'm envious ... sounds like an easy one. You got home early?"

"Yes, yes, early." Early evening but he didn't have to know that.

I'd been concentrating on reading a letter during this conversation because I lie better to someone if I don't look at the person. When I finally glanced up, Dick was rubbing his forefingers together. "Shame, shame on Fran. You weren't going to tell Uncle Dick, were you? Didn't you see the paper this morning?"

"Nope, no time."

"*Big* write-up...pictures with the title 'No Peeps From 'Keets'. Now I know what you want for your birthday...a parakeet all your own."

Mass murderers who go undetected for years and con men who bilk the public for decades make me wonder at such expertise. The one person I preferred to keep in the dark about my Keystone-Kop comedy day already knew the story. Those blasted birds weren't so mum after all.

Once I realized that the story was out, I couldn't wait to describe in detail the Saturday absurdities, and Dick listened sympathetically for awhile before he yawned. "Fran, your parakeets are beginning to remind me of the penguin story."

"Why? Parakeets aren't a bit like penguins."

"You've heard that old chestnut. Barry can't read yet but I'll use him for local color...Son Barry checked a book out from the library. When he returned it, the librarian asked him how he liked it. 'I'm sorry, ma'am,' he said, 'but it told me more about penguins than I wanted to know.'"

"Okay, okay. I get it. Never mind, now you know how I suffered, you'll agree that Saturday was worth two normal ones ...so I'm ahead."

Dick was almost out of the door when the impact of that statement reeled him back like a big-mouthed bass. "Now wa-a-ait a minute, just a tin-horned minute. That's not fair...we can't work it that way...."

And we were off and running with our continuing argument ...and, like mashed potatoes and gravy, never coming out even. Several decades later, I *still* think Dick owes me a Saturday in there somewhere.

CHAPTER 7

AN UNHAPPY BIRTHDAY PRESENT

My birthday, April 24th, brought a warm spring rain along with the fresh smell of wet daffodils and budding trees—a welcome relief from the cold rains of winter. Rescuing the *Atlanta Constitution* from our front steps before going into breakfast, I glanced at the headlines: IKE RENEWS VOW OF ALL-OUT KOREAN PEACE QUEST.

At the breakfast table, Peace had put a bowl of yellow tulips by my plate with a loving card addressed to her 'Saturday's child.'

"You never told me I was born on a Saturday."

"And a rainy one too, like today."

"How does that rhyme go?" I said, and repeated it. 'Monday's child is fair of face...don't remember any more till 'Saturday's child works hard for a living.' Peace, why didn't you hold out 'til after midnight so I'd be Sunday's 'full of grace'?"

By now, Al could no longer restrain his eagerness to get to the main event. He thrust a clumsily wrapped package in my hand and commanded, "Open it, open it."

I oh'd and ah'd over the collage he'd made, with gold foil for rocks—a scene from our day in the mountains, and dedicated to "The best Mother in the whole world." I hoped that he'd always keep that uncritical six-year-old opinion of Mother.

When it was time to go to work, I kissed them both good-by and headed downtown to celebrate my birthday at the station.

Due to Dick's on-the-air mention last week of my upcoming birthday, the fan letters had been filled with greetings.

"Here, Birthday Girl," Dick said, dumping his share of the mail on my desk, "you might as well open them, probably more cards."

Our daily visits into the living rooms of our audience made them feel as if we were 'family'; most of our letters were filled with ego-boosting comments. Many said our show was superior to many network programs, and they enjoyed our brand of unpredictable humor and clean fun which they could allow their children to watch.

Of course, we had our detractors. For example, Jerry Adair from Franklin, Georgia, wrote on August 12, 1953:

> "Dear Sirs: I want to complain about the program, *Music Shop*. The boy and girl (Dick and Fran) are so silly we can hardly bear to look at them. I really don't see how they got on television. Please excuse the pencil."

Only a handful of the hundreds of letters we received were like Mr. Adair's mildly disparaging and funny comments, so when I opened one particular letter on this birthday morning, the ugliness of it leaped out. The letter was typewritten on heavy, expensive-looking stationery, but the 'Fran Adams' address on the envelope marked *Personal* was in longhand. Deciding not to share it with anyone, I hastily hid it in my desk drawer.

During the afternoon show, Dick and the cast surprised me with a chocolate cake. It had ten candles on it, to be, as they said, "on the safe side". And true to Dick's threat, I received a green parakeet, in a cage that contained all parakeet comforts. Dick said, "We're color-coordinated now—green bird, green office."

After the show, I spent an hour with Algernon, the bird's newly acquired name, trying to teach him to say "Happy Birthday." But with no success. Algernon showed the same reluctance for speech as his cousins at the Kay's Jewelers contest. Unless he talked, he was of no use to the *Music Shop*.

That problem was solved by Junebug, the Swingbillies' guitarist. He volunteered to be Algernon's alter ego via an off-camera mike. From then on, our *talking* bird was a popular cast member. Although we explained that Algernon's extensive vocabulary, spoken in a thick southern accent, was an illusion, parakeet owners continued to request our remarkable speech-training technique.

Sadly, however, the pressure of show business, plus the hot lights, may have proven too much for Algernon. After only a few weeks, his meteoric career was cut short. One morning, I found his stiff, cold body lying on the floor of his luxurious home.

I mourned the little bird for days; but my grief was augmented by an underlying cause. Algernon's departure coincided with the fourth anniversary of the death of my younger sister, Peggy, at age 20. Each year, Peace, our mother, rivaled the April weather in outbursts of tearful showers; nothing could comfort her.

Peggy had been the beauty of the family with classic features, honey-blonde hair and turquoise eyes, and she'd also cornered most of the common sense genes. Whenever I needed some good advice, I had an imaginary conversation with Peggy. This year, my inner Peggy voice reminded me that Peace was always cheered by a Technicolor movie. The Loew's Grand Theater was featuring a good one that week, so I took her to see it. The remedy failed and I could hear the Peggy voice saying, "Fanny, didn't you realize that *Gentleman Prefer Blondes* was not a good selection to get her mind off blondes?"

She was right. Peace cried all the way through the comedy because all those blondes reminded her of Peggy.

My business associates on the show didn't know the reason for the impact of Algernon's death. Consequently, a week later, Dick said, "Fran, I do respect your grief, but for God's sake, it was a bird—not a close family relative. Enough sniffles...here." He handed me two pages of script. "I wrote this last night...let's try it...needs no scenery, our regular counter can be the department store counter...I'll start."

Here is the script Dick wrote: Dick approaches Fran (sales girl in the stocking department) with a let's-get-this-over-with look on his face and a piece of paper in his hand. He says firmly, "Miss, I want a pair of nylon stockings, size nine, medium length, in pale tape? tupe? (peers uncertainly at paper)...I think that's a color."

Fran: "Yes sir, something in a little gift? Have you seen these darling marabou-trimmed garters?"

Dick: "I don't want a gift...just a pair of...."

Fran: "How about these needle-point taxi whistles with the...."

Dick: "Look lady. the only thing I need is a pair of nylon...."

Fran interrupts: "Nylon! Oh, we have some beautiful nylon hand-embroidered sequin toe covers that will simply thrill ...."

Dick holds up his hand in a *stop* gesture, "No, no, young lady. Let's get this straight...I came in here to do a simple errand for my wife. The last thing I'm interested in is silly knick-knacks."

Fran looks crestfallen and meekly replies: "Yes sir, nylon stockings coming up."

Dick: Size nine, medium length...pale tupe."

Fran bats her eyes: "Pardon sir...but I think she meant *taupe*. It's a new fashion color...so new I've just learned it myself. (Fran leans over the counter with a helpless look.) "Sir, you've no idea how hard it is to keep up with all the new colors, weaves, and sizes. And sometimes the women get so mad at me...you wouldn't believe some of the things I've been called...right here in stockings."

Dick: "You understand, I didn't mean to be rude...it's just that the wife was down to her last pair and wrote out these instructions..."

Fran: "Of course I understand. Honestly, it's a pleasure to wait on a man who recognizes true value in women's wear...we don't get one in six months with your artistic eye. Not many men would have the good sense to even glance at these lovely combing jackets that just came in."

Dick looks puzzled: "Homing jackets?"

Fran: "Combing jackets. Exactly what every woman needs when she combs her hair, and so few men think to buy one. Isn't it the cuddliest thing...so sheer and yet so...here, feel it."

Dick: "Well, I...that is...you...er...."

Fran: "And a real bargain at $79.98."

Dick: "Actually, come to think of it, the wife does have a birthday coming up soon...well, six months isn't exactly soon. That is kinda cute though...guess you can't have too many of whatever it is."

Fran: "I'll gift wrap it for you...and would you like the stockings gift-wrapped too?"

Dick: "Stockings, what stockings? Oh yes, by all means, the stockings."

Fran: "I do admire a man who knows his own mind. Sir, will that be cash or charge?"

End of script.

I agreed that it was a natural for us, and added, "But Dick, the children liked Algernon so much, I think we need another pet on the show."

After Algernon's untimely death, we'd given out a lame explanation that the homesick bird had flown back to Athens, Georgia. Judging by the number of inquiries about the bird's absence, I wasn't the only person who missed him.

"It's too soon for another bird," I continued, "but we could get something else live."

"How about a nice copperhead? No, Fran, no...Algernon was a fluke...we have our hands full without a zoo."

"Honest," I said, making a cross-my-heart sign, "I'll be responsible...you won't have to do a thing."

"Ha!, that's what my kids say when they watch me feed the latest pet mongoose."

CHAPTER 8

A TRIP
TO THE PET STORE

In spite of Dick's reservations, I thought the pet idea was a good one. I decided to discuss the matter with a new friend, Sheila LeClaire, who worked in the next-door office. Sheila was a recent addition to the staff but we'd already struck up rapport. Her *Shopping with Sheila* was the obligatory daily woman's show featuring a melange of bargains, gifts, household hints and recipes.

In the early TV days, many on-the-air roles were not considered suitable for women by the local stations—for example, those of newscaster or weather reporter.

Television's weather-women were the first wedge into that realm. The barrier was broken when some innovative program director discovered that a pretty young woman moving plastic clouds on a weather map caused no hurricanes, only more viewer appeal.

Consequently, WLWA-TV employed only three women in the talent department—Sheila; Mary Reins, who produced a Department of Education children's show; and me. As the secretaries had their own clique and the lone saleswoman, Martha Lord, stayed out of the office selling, I'd been lonely for a female buddy. Hence, in Sheila, I was delighted to have a compatible someone who sympathized with the problems of getting a daily show on the air.

She was reading a cookbook when I came into her office. "Damn!" She slammed the book shut in disgust. "All these recipes begin with 'run down to your nearest Chinese grocer'. My audience thinks a marshmallow-mandarin orange salad is the height of sophistication."

"Furthermore," I added, "you'd have to run all the way to New York or San Francisco."

"Which would suit me fine if the station would spring for the trip—as unlikely as finding a Chinese grocer in Atlanta. Say, glad you stopped by, I have a hot tip."

I perched on the edge of her desk. "What about?"

She threw the cookbook over on her stockpile and said, "My Rich's spy says all their better dresses up to $29.98 are on sale tomorrow at half-price...if we choose some today, she'll save 'em for us."

"Oh, Sheila, I hate to miss that...but no time. Be a lamb and pick out a couple of size eight's for me...your taste is better anyway."

"I doubt that, but I'll do my best," and she got up from her desk. "I'm through here so I'll trot on over to Rich's now."

As she started toward the door, I thought once more how much I admired Sheila. She was everything I wasn't. The willowy five-foot-nine brunette had dark brown hair and matching eyes, plus creamy ivory skin, which gave her a faintly exotic Latin appearance. Most of all, I envied her university-drama-major trained speech with its perfect diction and low pitch. My own flat Georgia drawl was a constant source of dismay to me and I longed for improvement.

"Wait a minute." I caught up with her before she reached the door. "This won't take a second...the real reason I came in was to ask your advice. Dick says no, but I think we need a live pet to take Algernon's place...what do you think?"

Sheila agreed with me, suggesting I see one of her shopping sources, a Mr. Lummock at the Peachtree Pet Store. Unless I wanted a whooping crane, he'd probably oblige for a few free commercials.

I was tempted to share the contents of the disturbing letter I'd received that morning, but before I could mention it, Sheila was on the way to the elevators. But her suggestion was welcomed and I decided to visit the pet store today to settle the matter.

At quarter to twelve, Candy Higgins, our receptionist, said I had a call from Doris Lockerman, an associate Editor of the *Atlanta Constitution*. "Fran, Celestine and Anne, and I are having lunch at Luigi's today, can you join us?"

Work be damned. I weakened at the prospect of the company of Doris; Celestine Sibley, well-known author and columnist; and Anne Poland Berg, Rich's public relations wizard.

My conscience won out though and I said, "Doris, a trip to the pet store for a new Music Shop animal is a must today—so it's sandwich-at-desk time. Please, please give me a rain check."

I'd have the sandwich Cora Lee had packed for my lunch. That would be no hardship as most Atlanta restaurants in the fifties qualified for a bout of indigestion rather than a Michelin Guide star for culinary excellence. Nevertheless, I regretted having to decline Doris's invitation. To my mind, the clannish newspaper crowd were a fascinating group—suitable subjects for movies and plays such as *The Front Page*—and more glamorous than the television people. Television was too new to have a history. Even lunch at the uncomfortable Luigi's was worth it to be with my writer heroines.

Back then, Luigi's overlooked train tracks, which had yet to be covered with today's parks and stores. Luigi's windows stayed open most of the time. As a result, regulars called Luigi's spaghetti carbonera, the Southern Pacific special. In fact, everything on the menu hinted of train smoke garnished with cinders.

Doris's company at Luigi's was worth a few cinders in the food, but Mr. Lummock's pet store had top priority today. If I'd worn a pair of dark glasses while walking over the train tracks, my eyes would have been protected from cinders, but the idea never occurred to me. Dark glasses were to be worn at the beach, or by Hollywood stars.

Last month, a tiny flying cinder had unerringly found my eye, and once again I sought help from a nearby doctor for the third time in a row. After he removed the offending grit from my eye, young Doctor Reese made such a point of showing me photos of his wife and twin baby boys, I suspected he thought my frequent visits were prompted less by a foreign object than a gleam in my eye.

Therefore, when I crossed the tracks on my way to the pet store just after the Dixie Flyer had chugged by, depositing the inevitable cinder in my right eye, I relinquished the pleasure of viewing more photos of Dr. Reese's family. Instead, I ducked into the nearest store, which turned out to be a tattoo parlor.

The Tattoo Parlor's business sign advertised *Tattooing While You Wait*—an intriguing statement for how else could one be tattooed? Could you leave your skin to be worked on while you spent the waiting period at the cake-decorating place next door? It seemed the juxtaposition of two such disparate establishments wouldn't produce much in the way of customer exchange.

The second I realized where I was, nothing but severe pain could have kept me in the parlor, which in my imagination conjured up visions of strange alleys in the orient, opium dens and white slavery. Such fears fled, however, before the immediate need to have that piece of coal out of my eye. The store owner removed the rock for me with far more deftness than the doctor, and we began to chat during the process.

"I've walked by here hundreds of times and I was always curious about Atlanta's only tattoo artist."

The tattoo artist, Dewey Meeks, said he was a Georgia boy, raised in Flowery Branch, a small town which hides behind a highway billboard. Joining the Navy in World War II, he was sent to the Pacific Theater. He confided he must have an artistic nature because the first time he saw the art of tattooing in Honolulu, he wanted to learn the technique.

Designs displayed on the walls of his shop included the routine battleship, and roses twining around the word "Mother"— interspersed with Dewey's original creations. He pointed to an exquisite butterfly which he said would look nice on me.

"Me?" I gasped. "A tattoo?"

"You'd be surprised at the number of lady customers I have ...I'd put it in a discreet place," he assured me.

I hastily said that I'd give the idea some thought...several years' worth.

"If I can't sell you an artistic butterfly, maybe you can use the wife's cake decorating business next door."

Aha! That explained a lot. But at this point my mind was centered on getting a live animal for the *Music Shop*. But who knows? Someday I thought I might go back for one of those beautiful butterflies.

Perhaps I did.

CHAPTER 9

AN UNPOPULAR CHOICE

The somewhat mysteriously named Peachtree Pet Store, since it was on Broad Street, had a depressing window display— a lackluster collection of three unkempt, unhappy-looking faded pink rabbits (no doubt left over from Easter), a parrot with a bad case of the molts, and two tan puppies of murky origin. I wanted to take them all home for tender loving care but that wasn't why I was there. I was a talent scout looking for star material.

A man whom I assumed to be Mr. Lummock was wrapping up a cat-scratching post for a woman when I came to the counter. He acknowledged my presence with a brief nod and then did a double take. "Why, it's Fran...look, lady, it's Fran."

Greetings of warm recognition from anyone except family and friends still came as a surprise. When Sheila and I had been on a recent shopping excursion, a troop of cub scouts kept me signing autographs for ten minutes. After they moved on, I apologetically said, "Sheila, the only reason I was the target is that schoolchildren don't see your morning show."

Although she remarked she had no desire to be bothered by a bunch of smelly little boys, I guessed that her nose was out of joint by their non-recognition. Fame is relative and recognition from strangers produces the same sensations no matter on what scale, large or small.

After Mr. Lummock's cat-post customer left, I described what I was searching for...something that was small, photogenic, lived in a cage, and needed food and water no more than twice a day.

Mr. Lummock ran his hands through the few remaining hairs on his head and pursed his lips in thought.

"Hum, how about a goldfish, Miss Fran? They don't take much care."

I considered goldfish for a minute...goodness knows the attention would be minimal.

"Oh, I don't know. I haven't been a fish person since I was eight and Daddy sent off for some imported fantail goldfish for our fish pond. As I recall, he told baby sister and me never to get soap in the pond, it would kill the fish."

Mr. Lummock, realizing I was vetoing goldfish, lost interest in my childhood story, but I finished it anyway. "We couldn't wait to dump a box of laundry soap in the pond to see if Daddy was right. He was! And mad...I still remember how mad he was. So no goldfish. Besides, too much light would reflect off the glass bowl."

"I know," Mr. Lummock snapped his fingers, "just the thing...a cute baby turtle. They don't take much care."

"Aunt Ethel sent me a pink one from Florida once. When it disappeared, the smell finally led us to its body behind a radiator. Nope, no turtles."

Mr. Lummock's rabbit suggestion also met with a black ball. At age ten when our house at Crape Myrtle Farm burned and we moved back to Atlanta, I never asked what happened to the chinchilla rabbits I'd raised. I found out when they reappeared in the form of a coat for my fourteenth birthday. After my tears had dried on the pelts, I overcame my grief and wore the coat until the fur came off in patches.

Snakes were out, hamsters weren't photogenic, dogs and cats needed too much care. By then, Mr. Lummock had exhausted his casting suggestions for *Music Shop* stardom.

"Oh, one last suggestion," said the remarkably patient man, the only outer indication of his wish to kill me—an enlarged vein on his forehead, "...and you probably won't like it either...how do you feel about white mice, the kind that pulled Cinderella's coach?"

Mr. Lummock led me over to a cage. "See, isn't he pretty?" The mouse came up to the bars and gave me an inquisitive look. "Little boys love them...and sometimes even little girls do...and they almost take care of themselves."

Before I knew it, I was out on the sidewalk with a new prodigy to groom for TV stardom. In the warm April sunshine, I headed back toward the station. Was Atlanta ready for a large white male talking mouse?

Both the mouse and cage were courtesy of Mr. Lummock in exchange for the relief he must have felt to finally find a pet for me which didn't bring forth a spate of negative childhood memories— that plus my assurance that we'd mention Mr. Mouse's previous home from time to time. Maybe Mr. Lummock would clean up the place if we sent him more customers.

When I walked off the elevator with Mr. Mouse, Candy, the switchboard operator, was occupied with her favorite pastime, eavesdropping on the switchboard. Candy, a former Turpentine Queen from Waycross, Georgia, had recently been hired by the station on the basis of looks and personality, but not switchboard expertise.

As yet, she hadn't mastered the awkward-looking machine with its octopus-like wires and heavy earphones. On days when the wires became hopelessly entangled, Candy's solution was simplicity itself—pull out all connections and begin again. The angry screams from the disconnected personnel were as loud as the ones Candy gave out now when she saw Mr. Mouse in his cage. Fortunately, before she split the eardrums of an unsuspecting victim, she lost her headpiece while ducking beneath the reception desk. In spite of my assurance that the mouse couldn't escape his cage, she cowered beneath the desk until I disappeared into our office.

Before I'd put the cage down on my desk, Dick followed Candy's act by yelling and jumping up on his desk chair. I stayed off balance with Dick half the time as I was never quite sure where or when he crossed the line that separated his serious side from his superb comic mind, a facet of his personality which eventually became entrenched in his gift as an actor.

I knew he was serious though when he looked at the rodent with obvious distaste and said in a near-stammer, "Whose going to take it out of its cage when its time to talk with it? Algernon was okay, but a mouse running around the studio is above and beyond...."

"I'll do it. It's a HE and he's tame. Look at those little red eyes and that nice white fur...he's sort of like a baby rabbit—once I get used to his tail." I touched his fur through the cage. "Besides, he's a wonderful excuse for a contest."

We ran contests as often as possible because they were popular, easy to run, and companies were generous about supplying us with prizes in exchange for free advertising.

"Fran, sometimes I wonder about you...nobody wants to win a white mouse...half the mothers in town are probably trying to get rid of one."

"Not to give away, Dum-dum, to name. A 'Name Mr. Mouse' contest...winner christens him on the air and wins a Schwinn bicycle."

Picking up the cage, I went next door to show Sheila the result of her suggestion. After she stopped shrieking, she said she'd climb down off the top of her desk if I'd take *that thing* away. Sheila said her fear of mice came from growing up in a 17th century Charleston, South Carolina, house that had housed generations of mice. I said I felt the same way about snakes and cockroaches—the latter a hardy breed destined to take over the earth someday.

With the reactions of Candy, Dick, and now Sheila, I began to question if our audience would feel the same, and to doubt the wisdom of my talent choice.

CHAPTER 10

"YOU NEVER KNOW"

Our Name Mr. Mouse contest drew 7,600 entries the first week. Even Dick began to feel more kindly toward our newest cast member—but not kindly enough to have anything to do with it. The mouse department was all mine and I kept the creature out of sight until show time.

The mail pull for the two-week contest broke a previous record of 6,800 in one week for a 'Draw Bozo the Clown" contest. We couldn't open all the letters and evaluate all those names. Perhaps it wasn't fair but we chose fifty a *day* at random. When we announced the winner, we were prepared to duplicate the prize if a double was in that mountain of unopened mail. The three finalists were Mr. McDoogle, Papa Longtail, and Sir Cedric. Sir Cedric won.

The 'Name Mr. Mouse' mail completely submerged the regular mail, but after Sir Cedric's christening on the air, the mail shrank back to normal. I had almost forgotten the hurtful birthday letter still resting in my top desk drawer, until another 'ugly' arrived. Typewritten on the same expensive-looking stationery, again with the address written in longhand. Then another came the day after that...three in one week, each as venomous as the last.

I wanted to talk to someone about them, but pride kept me from confiding in anyone at the station, and I didn't want to worry my mother; so I tried to shrug them off. Because no one knew about the letters, I hadn't realized that they were effecting my outward facade until the day our station manager, Carter Sever, called me into his office.

Carter, a native of Orlando, Florida, was well liked by the staff. His father had intended for Carter, an only son, to join the family's citrus grove business. Grapefruit trees lost their appeal, however, once Carter had worked at the University of Florida's radio station. From radio to television was a natural transition, although Carter's oft repeated lament: "Why, oh why, did I ever leave the peace and tranquillity of radio?" seemed to indicate he found television neither natural or normal.

He had blonde hair and a cherubic blue-eyed face, and he could have blended into his alma mater's current young student body with ease. I don't think anyone at our station was over forty. We were the equivalent of the present computer-age young Turks. Carter was our manager though and I restrained my impulse to first-name him when he was acting in that capacity, as of now.

"Fran, sit down a minute," he said, indicating a chair by his desk. "This isn't meant as criticism...I know how hard you work, and we all have off-days, but lately it shows on the air that something's bothering you...the old sparkle's missing."

I didn't know what to say.

"Is it personal or something here at work? You've just had a raise so it couldn't be that."

Should I tell him about the letters?

Carter continued, "You know how much we think of your contribution to the show, but maybe you and Dick aren't getting along—that can happen when people have to work so closely together."

"No, no," I protested, "everything's fine with the cast—as far as I know, that is."

Carter picked up a letter from his desk. "Bill Colvin brings in some of the fan mail...for example, this one from Mrs. Banner in Hapeville writes what a sweet, pretty, talented and down-to-earth entertainer you are...with an ability to manage all the joking on the show in a lady-like way. We—management—agree. You have a knack for reeling the cast in when they get too carried away."

It was almost worth whatever was coming next to hear Carter's kind words. Our former short-term manager believed a cat-o-nine-tails worked better than compliments.

"But, honey," Carter threw the letter back on his desk, "for the past couple of weeks, you've been way off in another country."

He was so understanding that I did what every woman in business dreads—I started to cry. Carter took that in stride; talent was supposed to be a touch emotional.

"It's those damned letters...they keep coming," I said between sobs. "Whoever writes them hits on my most vulnerable spots...when I make an ad-lib comeback to the teasing that makes our show, I think of those spiteful words...and freeze."

Carter reached into his desk drawer and pulled out the now familiar expensive-looking envelope. "You mean one of these?"

"You get them, too?" I asked in bewilderment.

"No, no, not personal attacks, just reasons why you should be replaced. I suspected they had something to do with your unhappy face."

He walked me to the door with a reminder that 98 percent of our mail was favorable and the station was behind me 100 percent.

I dried my tears and felt better

"Fran, grow a thicker skin, or I'll put you out of sight in the accounting department."

We both smiled at that because my arithmetic vagueness was no secret.

Back at my desk, I had a call from John Whitney, my fellow parakeet judge, asking if I remembered our dinner date for that evening. John suggested meeting me at the television station since it was only a short walk from there to Emile's French restaurant. In the forties, Emile's, Atlanta's oldest French restaurant, was located in a hole-in-the wall by the railroad tracks, but its immediate popularity caused it to be moved to a larger space.

Emile's menu was considerately printed both in English and French. I chose the calves liver and told John that as a child, my birthday dinner request was always the unlikely combination of calves liver and chocolate bread pudding. When I gave the calves liver order in its French translation of *foie de veau*, John said, "Well, I'm learning something new about you...you speak French."

"Menu French...in school we did mainly reading and grammar. My mother's major at Vassar was French, but she only gets to practice with the maple syrup salesman from Quebec...we've got enough maple syrup at home for pancakes every day for ten years."

John smiled. "My home town school didn't think we needed French...and when I got to the University, well, too much catching up in other subjects."

"What town, John, you mentioned it but I've forgotten."

"Madison, Georgia."

My face lit up. "Oh, I love that town, and I'm so glad Sherman didn't get near enough to burn all those wonderful antebellums."

We stayed on general topics and our conversation flowed easily. Not being fellow employees, we could speak freely of our many mutual acquaintances in the media. The unpleasant letters I'd received were very much on my mind and I was relaxed enough with him to confide the story. As a high-profile disc jockey, he'd been in the public eye far longer than I, so perhaps he'd have some advice on how to deal with the kooks who crawl out at full-moon time. In a few minutes, he had me laughing at one of his own experiences of that type.

"At least you're dealing with a semi-sane kook. Once when I was with WMRL in Milledgeville, one of the patients at the nearby mental hospital decided he wanted to be an announcer ... and that I was the boy to teach him. I had one long hairy night 'till they finally caught up with the poor fellow."

After that story, my letters paled in comparison. John advised me to read one on the air. The more I opened up about them, the less their ability to wound...like hobgoblins in the light of day. "Nothing like a damsel in distress...I predict an avalanche of favorable defense mail."

"Thanks, John, I'll try. I certainly haven't had any ideas of my own."

"I may not have taken French, but I did have a couple of psychology courses."

After we left Emile's, John walked me to the station to pick up Sir Cedric. I noticed how careful John was to stay on the curb side of the street. Many other similar gestures during the evening from the six-foot-four man made me think French may not have been required in Madison, but an old-fashion, no-elbows-on-the-table southern mother had seen to it that good manners were.

"John, you're a success in radio, everyone agrees Big John Whitney is Atlanta's number one disc jockey....Say! You said you were named for your father...surely they don't call him Little John?"

"No, I was Little John. But when I grew so much taller than my father, it made no sense. Now I'm Big John and he's still Dr. John. Maybe that's why I became a disc jockey; not room for two Dr. Johns in one small town."

"Hum, with your looks, you'd be a natural for television. Blue-eyed people with dark hair usually photograph well."

"No thanks. My hours are crazy sometimes but with a good contract and my own shows, I know when I'm well off. Besides, who knows if TV will last? Almost everyone can buy a radio, but how many people can afford an expensive TV set?"

"Shades of my Aunt Sue...she says it's a passing fad and not a very appealing one at that. Also it's an uphill battle for our salesmen to lure advertisers away from radio and newspapers."

By then, we'd reached the station lobby. I went upstairs and left John chatting with the security guard.

Candy's relief operator, Keith, a Georgia Tech student, glanced up from his books to give me an absentminded nod as I went by. The dark, empty offices contrasted eerily with the usual cheerful daytime bustle. The only light in the long hall came from the office of Jesse Hatch, the film editor.

A late night movie flickered on the lobby set as I passed it. Few top flight films trickled down to television in those days. The Hollywood studios were fighting the new medium with everything in their power, including such petty contract stipulations as forbidding some stars to be photographed with a television set, much less to be seen on the small screen itself.

The Charlie Chan movie now on the TV monitor was Grade A compared with our usual offerings—such Academy Award fodder as "The Shark God" with Ron Randall and Devera Burton, and "Crime Expert" with Manning Whiley and Barbara Everett. If you've never heard of them, neither had we.

Nevertheless, the novelty of seeing a free movie in the home attracted a sizable audience. A one-time viewing of the third rate films was torture enough, but Jesse was forced to view them over and over for timing the commercial cuts. No wonder his disposition curdled more by the day. Whenever Dick or I made the necessary visits to his office to collect our weekly supply of short musical films, Jesse doled them out as begrudgingly as if they were rare books.

After I'd switched on the office lights, Sir Cedric woke up and scrambled to the front of his cage. "Come on, old boy, Al's waiting for you at home...he's one person who loves you for yourself alone."

John escorted me to the parking garage. As he was putting the mouse cage on the car seat beside me, he leaned over to give me a good-night kiss and said, "All I can think of is Cinderella's white mice...do you suppose I'll be your Prince Charming?"

"In honor of our French evening, I can only say *on ne sais jamais.*"

"That sounds pretty, what does it mean?"

"One never knows, does one?"

CHAPTER 11

THE MASQUERADER

The following Monday, cameraman Red O'Brien was watching me feed Sir Cedric some of Mr. Lummock's special grain mixture, as a reward for a good performance.

"Fran, how much do you feed that creature? He's gained at least a pound since you got him."

"I only feed him what the pet store man recommended, but Al probably gives him tidbits at home."

Red frowned. "If that mouse gains any more, you'll need help to lift him out of his cage." Sir Cedric ignored that remark, having lost interest in anything but his grain dish.

Sir's popularity was growing daily and our audience apparently hadn't noticed that our *talking* mouse spoke with the identical south Georgia accent as our *talking* bird. The day Sir received more fan mail than either Dick or I, Dick complained, "Wasn't it W. C. Fields who said never work with children or animals.?"

"Why Dick, I do believe you're jealous of a mouse."

"There're other things I'd rather be upstaged by...listen to this," and he grabbed one of the letters. "From Frankie Lee Payne in Smyrna—'Dear Fran and Dick: The best part of the show is when Fran talks to Sir Cedric.' Next thing you know Disney will sign him and we'll be left high and dry."

Dick was only half teasing so I came to Sir's defense. "I gave you a choice of animals...you could have had a turtle, goldfish, hamster...."

"You know I didn't want anything." I must have looked dashed as he softened the rest of his speech. "I'll admit you've kept your word though, and taken the responsibility...but don't you think he's too fat?"

"Red agrees. Maybe Sir needs an exercise wheel and a stricter diet."

The first part of the week passed uneventfully with the high point being the arrival of a long-awaited shipment from the Snader sound-film, library. The package contained film which allowed us time to catch our breath during the show. Those three-minute musical shorts were the equivalent of today's MTV-cable musical shorts. Only what a difference. Instead of Madonna's "Like a Virgin" or Prince's "Love Sexy", we featured Tex Ritter (John Ritter's father) and the Westerners singing "Froggy Went A-Courting", or Les Brown and his Band of Renown playing "Blue Tango".

It was that Wednesday that I followed John's advice to read an edited version of one of my 'uglies' on the air. A last minute decision on my part, it took Dick by surprise. After I finished it, he looked so startled and uncomfortable, an unbidden thought crossed my mind. Perhaps our cast wasn't as harmonious as I believed. Nonsense. The letters were making me paranoid.

By Friday morning, as John had predicted, the responses in my defense began to arrive and I was in a lighter mood during our Friday hour.

After Dick finished his pantomime of Andy Griffith's "What It Was, It Was Football" (which first brought Andy to national attention), my interview with our newest star, Sir Cedric, was next.

Junebug and I usually began with a germ of an idea and winged it. We'd already given Sir some free-loading country cousins, George and Louie, who bombarded Sir with letters imploring their newly rich relative to share his palatial home in the big city with them.

Sir Cedric already appeared to recognize his new name and whenever I approached his cage, he came forward to put his paws up on the side, eagerly expecting food. But today, he stayed huddled up in the back of the cage, and I couldn't coax him forward. Finally, I reached in for him and was in the process of lifting him out of the cage when what I saw made me drop him in horror.

"My God, he's falling apart...his insides are coming out. Help! He needs a doctor."

I was so unnerved I forgot to watch my language. Television was so straitlaced then that a "My God" from Fran would have lit up the switchboard with shocked calls demanding I be thrown off the air. Fortunately, my neck mike clanking against the cage during my reaching efforts blocked out the sound of my voice. Red heard me though and quickly panned the camera back to Dick, who smoothed things over.

"Ah me, Fran says Sir Cedric has a bad case of ah...Coca-Cola...there's a lot of it going around now. Seriously, he only has a bad cold. Send him a get-well card, but no chicken soup... it'll leak out of the envelope. And now the Swingbillies will accompany Paul in his next song, which he dedicates to his girlfriend—'I've Been so Miserable Without You, It's Almost Like Having You Here'."

Whatever Sir's problem was, it had to wait until the show was over, but as soon as we gave our good-by waves, I rushed to see what was wrong with him. He was twitching strangely and even more of his insides seemed to be coming out. I was frantic.

By then Dick and the Swingbillies—Paul, Randy, Harry, Ruel and Junebug—had gathered around. I turned to Junebug next to me. "Junebug, hurry and ask Candy to call the nearest vet."

Junebug, a 200 pound good old south Georgia country boy, never hurried about anything except his lightning-fast wizardry with the guitar, so I wasn't surprised when he continued to peer into the cage.

"Junebug," I pleaded, "please hurry."

He shook his head and drawled, "Fra-yan, I know a lot about animals...Sir Cedric doesn't need no vet." A big smile spread over his face. "A midwife's more like it."

Dick heard Junebug and began clowning around with an imitation of Prissy and her immortal *Gone With The Wind* lines about not knowing anything about birthing babies. He finished with "...and I sholy don't know nothin' 'bout birthin' mice."

I ran to our cartooning easel, tore off a sheet of newsprint, and draped it over the cage. "At least, let's give *Lady* Cedric some privacy....I peeked under the paper. "Dear Gussie! Three down and heaven knows how many more to go."?

Later, back in the office, Dick was still laughing. "You certainly got a bargain with that mouse...you'll probably end up with at least seven of those little white worms. Ugh...aren't they the most repulsive looking things you ever saw?"

"That lummox of a Mr. Lummock. I can't believe that he didn't know a pregnant female from a male. I was too choosy and he just wanted to get rid of me." Dick was still chortling when I wheeled around, "And I don't want to hear any 'I told you so' from you either."

Dick studied the ceiling and murmured, "I didn't say a word."

CHAPTER 12

"ANOTHER MASQUERADER"

I couldn't wait to tell my friend Sheila about our impostor. She was in her office preparing to leave for Charleston and her brother's wedding this weekend.

"Sheila, guess what? Sir Cedric is really *Lady* Cedric."

After she heard the story, she said, "You certainly do have all the fun around here on your show. I'm so bored with dreary recipes and how many ways to take out grass stains, I may stay in Charleston permanently."

"Don't you dare...we'd all miss you terribly...and as for fun, I've had all I can handle today. Lady Cedric needs her rest so I'll come back for her tomorrow. Want to walk to the garage with me?"

"No, lots of letters to finish for the mail tonight."

"Well, at least I can take the ready ones for you." I scooped up the small stack in her out-going box. "I'm going right by the post office."

"Thanks, but that's too much trouble," she protested.

"Not at all." I gave a good-by wave. "They'll get picked up sooner. Happy wedding...you'll be such a gorgeous bridesmaid, you'll steal the show from the bride."

My car was parked in the Hunter Street garage as my usual next-door garage had been full of Rich's shoppers this morning. The garage was an easy walk and the post office only a block out of the way. I was delighted for the unusual opportunity to do my friend even a small favor. She was such a self-sufficient person with her own apartment and circle of friends that I seldom had a chance to be of service.

Although I wasn't exactly little Miss Milkmaid, I felt Sheila was far more sophisticated than I. For a brief period, I tried to copy her clothes, speech and mannerisms until Peace told me that she was tired of hearing Sheila quotes. She pointed out that what suited a five-foot-nine brunette from Charleston—whose natives feel superior to other southern cities—didn't translate well to a five-foot-six Atlantan. In other words, knock it off.

When I reached the post office, the windows were closed, but I was in time for the evening pick-up in the lobby. Sheila's pile was too large to push through the slot all at once so I slipped half the letters in. As I was about to drop the other half in, the top letter caught my eye. The stationery seemed familiar and although I'd never seen Sheila's handwriting as she always typed her memos, the writing on the destination Nashville envelope also seemed familiar.

Holding the letters in my hand, I stood there until an impatient male voice behind me said, "Lady, are you through?"

I jumped aside. "Excuse me, I'm sorry, yes...no."

I hastily pushed the rest of the letters in the mail slot, but I held onto that top letter.

So many thoughts were going through my mind. My 'uglies' came in the same type heavy, cream envelopes, but then the Crane Company sells a great deal of stationery. Although the handwriting seemed similar, like a snowflake or a fingerprint, no two people's handwriting is exactly alike. It can be enough alike though to need an expert to distinguish the difference.

Maybe I'd go to jail for tampering with the U.S. mail but this was one letter that wasn't going out tonight. Not until I compared it with those squirreled away in my desk drawer. I hoped my suspicions were unfounded...what possible reason could there be behind such hostility?

That night my sleep was disturbed. I wondered if Sir/Lady Cedric was suffering from post-partum depression, all alone with his/her babies in the silent, dark office. Several times during the night, I turned on the light to study Sheila's letter. Yes, it was the same. No, there were differences. Yes. No. I couldn't decide. Tomorrow I'd go to the office early, open my top drawer and compare the letters. Then I'd see the differences and feel guilty that I'd ever thought my friend Sheila was capable of such duplicity.

The next morning, I arrived at the station at 8 a.m. to pick up Lady Cedric and look at those letters. Our Monday through Friday people weren't in as the Saturday programming of mainly cartoons, westerns and wrestling used different staffing.

Alone in the office, my first action was to find Professor Watley's handwriting analysis book which he'd given me while a guest on the show. I spent a long while comparing the writing on the envelope I'd saved from Sheila's mail yesterday and the ones in my desk drawer. In a way, I was relieved that I couldn't fool myself any longer. Miss Anonymous *was* Sheila.

The rest of the weekend I was in mental turmoil, endlessly discussing my problem with patient Peace. Should I let Sheila know—or keep the pretense of friendship? Peace suggested I taper off gradually and let it cool of its own accord.

"Peace, how long do you suppose I could keep that up?"

She laughed. "I wasn't thinking. You'd last about a day before you blurted it all out."

The following Monday, I decided to leave Lady Cedric and her brood of six at home. For the moment, she was in no condition to star in anything but the role of motherhood.

How to handle Sheila was another question. I'd recovered from the first shock wave but the bruised feelings would take longer. When I reviewed our friendship, I realized that I'd been the aggressor. She'd tolerated my admiration but obviously, it was a one-way street. As for her letters...well, criticism can make us feel hurt and angry if we fear it holds a germ of truth. I'd have to work through that later.

Sheila wasn't due back until Tuesday. Her time slot was filled by an American history documentary—the story of traitor Aaron Burr, which in my frame of mind seemed an apt substitution for Sheila. When in doubt, do nothing. That was to be my course of inaction. The mystery was solved. Even though I'd miss the camaraderie I thought we'd had, I was consoled by the knowledge that the letter writer wasn't someone even closer to home.

Tuesday, when Sheila returned to her morning show, I was determined to stick to my course of calculated coolness. I'd spent the morning covering various sized cardboard stars with silver foil in preparation for my scheduled song, "Don't Let the Stars Get in Your Eyes". Studio A was empty at 11:30 so it was a good time for me to hang the stars from the ceiling. In that way, the camera could weave in and out of them, giving some illusion of space. Although our special effects were crude, sometimes they were effective.

I piled the thirty or so stars into a basket and left for the studio. Sheila's office was on my way and heretofore, I would have popped in filled with eagerness for the wedding details. Instead, I planned to give a dignified nod and sail regally past her door, showing as much of Aunt Sue's heritage as I could muster.

When I was well past her office, my feet jerked me around in a 180 degree turn so suddenly the stars almost bounced out of the basket. Instead of finding myself in Studio A, I found myself standing in front of Sheila's desk.

She looked up. "Oh Fran, I guess you want to hear about the wedding...it was a real Charlestonian bash, horse-drawn carriages...."

"Sheila," I interrupted, "Sheila, I mailed your letters Friday."

"Yes, not necessary," she hesitated, "but thanks anyway."

My immobile stance and steady gaze brought forth no reaction from that beautiful, impassive face other than an impatient and quizzical look.

"Well, dear, I've a lot of catching up to do so we'll talk about the wedding later."

I tried to follow Peace's suggestion and let it go, but I couldn't. Clearing my choked up throat, I continued, "I mailed them all...except the Nashville one. I saved it—to compare handwriting...to be sure."

A tear began to roll down my cheek, whether from anger or sadness I didn't know. "Sheila, why?"

Her long silence wasn't broken by a denial. At last she seemed to come to a decision and shrugged her shoulders. "Because I'm sick unto death of this stupid, stupid woman's show. It bores me silly, and besides...I wanted to work with Dick." She gave me a scornful look. "I'd be a hundred times better than you...you're a complete amateur."

I was frozen to the spot, speechless. What a revelation. Here I'd envied her training as a Shakespearean actress, when all along she'd yearned to be a song-and-dance girl like me. But why had she revealed it in such a spiteful, clumsy way?

Later, when I returned to our office from my star-hanging, Dick was concentrating on the real estate section of the morning paper. For the past couple of weeks, it took a butterfly net to catch him for rehearsals because he and Marge had decided to buy a house. Instead of ideas for show features, all I heard were descriptions of the latest house tour.

"Hey, listen to this," he said, circling an ad with a red pencil. "Outstanding value, new ranch home near Garden Hills and E. Rivers school...3 bedrooms and two baths. Youngstown kitchen ...(now why would we want a kitchen in Youngstown if we live in Atlanta?)...only $19,250." "What do they mean," I said, "only $19,250?"

"Yeah, real estate is out of sight now. Maybe we ought to wait," he sighed. "But we'd rather be paying off a mortgage than rent."

He went back to his circling. "No, too far out...ixnay, not enough bedrooms...."

I waited a few minutes and then interrupted his mumbles. "Dick can I ask you something sort of personal?"

"That depends, ask and I'll tell you."

"Would you rather have Sheila LeClaire for a partner?"

"Partner for what? Tennis, bridge, square dancing...?"

"No, you know what I mean, on the *Music Shop*."

He didn't answer for so long I thought he hadn't heard me, but he'd just found another 'possible.' "Lord, no! She's pestered me for months to use her on the show when you take your vacation." He began tearing out all the 'possibles' he'd marked in the paper. "Can't you see that block of glacial dignity putting on a red nose to sing 'Be a Clown?'"

"No," and I giggled at the thought.

"Anyway, she doesn't have your giggle. Also, there's the fact that you originated the show before I came on the scene...does that answer your question?"

"Yes, thank you."

"But the most important reason...," he stopped to scratch his nose reflectively.

"Yes, what?" I looked at him, eager for more kind words.

"The *most* important reason is that when Sheila wears those four-inch heels she's so crazy about, she's taller than I am."

My eraser caught him on the ear before he had time to duck out of the office.

Late that afternoon, I fed Lady Cedric before going home. She was eating for six now so I poured some extra grain in her dish."

"Oh, well, little mother," I said philosophically, "I've lost a friend, but then she never was a friend, only in my own mind." Lady's tail slipped out between the cage bars but I left it alone. I'd never become used to that tail. "But thanks to you, I've gained a family."

I stood there looking at those six hairless squirmies. Yuck, Dick was right, they did look like fat little white worms. Whatever was I going to do with them?

CHAPTER 13

THE BUSINESS PARTNERS

My preoccupation at the office with Sheila and Lady (nee Sir) Cedric hadn't blinded me to the realization that something was in the air on the home front. Each evening when I returned to 33 Fifteenth Street, my mother and our cook, Cora Lee, were seated at the kitchen table engrossed in earnest conversation. It wouldn't take a Charlie Chan to notice the abrupt silence when I entered the room.

Back at the office, after the poison pen letters' mystery had been solved, Sheila and I retreated to formal politeness whenever our paths crossed. The situation was further eased by the relocation of her office to the other side of the building—perhaps at her request. And Lady Cedric was back on the show. Her babies had quickly shed their worm-like appearance and turned into cuties. They were so appealing that Randy Jones, the Swingbillies piano man, took two home for his four-year-old. Randy said his son's only complaint was that the two babies couldn't talk like their mother. Another pair of the mice mysteriously disappeared overnight, and I often wondered if Dick had taken them home for his two boys. After his anti-mouse stance, he'd never admit it and I never asked.

The remaining two mice had joined Lady Cedric in her cage in the role of the aforementioned free-loading cousins, George and Louie. I crossed my fingers and fervently hoped that they were sisters. I wasn't up to any more on-the-air mice population explosions. Luck was with me. The two sisters and their mother became male impersonators as their true relationship was entirely too complicated to explain.

At home, however, the secretive conversations continued and I became more and more curious as to what Peace and Cora Lee could be up to that required such long conferences. A surprise birthday party? No, my April birthday had passed, and plans for Al's June party would include me.

One morning before I left the house, I cornered Peace in the library. She had her head stuck in a book entitled "Domestic Science and Home Management". That in itself was suspicious since she'd never before shown any interest in improving her skills in either field.

"Peace, I'd have to be deaf, dumb and blind not to know something's going on. What are you and Cora Lee plotting?"

When she told me what she and Cora Lee had in mind, the project was of a far more serious nature than a surprise birthday party, and I was appalled.

"Boarders? You mean strange people living here with us twenty four hours a day. Peace, that's a terrible idea...what made you think of such a crazy thing?"

"A five letter word, *money*, that's what," Peace said.

Since my fourteenth year when a less than scrupulous stockbroker, operating a high class bucket shop, swindled my widowed mother out of a considerable fortune, our finances stayed on pecarious ground. The broker, Benjamin Bradley, and his American Bond and Share Corporation had presented a gilt-edged front by occupying an entire floor of the William Oliver building in downtown Atlanta.

After moving his wife and family from New York into an imposing mansion on Habersham Road, Mr. Bradley had then set about entering Atlanta society—and their pocketbooks. A handsome charming man, this magician soon had would-be investors clamoring to turn over their portfolios to him. His uncanny expertise in choosing stocks which yielded high cash dividends became the talk of the town.

The bursting of the bubble also became the talk of the town. Bradley's ability to satisfy his customers was based on the Ponzi pyramid scheme of paying large dividends out of incoming capital. As long as he had a steady supply of new buyers, all was well; but the well dried up sooner than he anticipated.

His subsequent indictment and trial was front page news. The lawyers absorbed what money was left and the victims never recovered a penny. Mr. Bradley began serving time in a government boarding house, the Atlanta Federal Penitentiary, where he was guaranteed his food and lodging—which was more than his ex-clients could claim.

Up to this moment, I'd thought we Fifteenth Street ex-clients were holding our own, until Peace's bombshell.

She still owned the Ansley Park house. That, with the income from a small trust fund and my help, kept us off the relief roll.

"Mother, I can squeak out a little more help."

"That wouldn't do it, Fanny." Peace explained that taxes on the house had gone up to $150 a year. And according to Cora Lee's husband, Will, who stoked our coal furnace each dawn through the winter months, ours wouldn't last another winter. Our water heater was threatening to explode any minute; and hamburger had spiraled up to 33 cents a pound. Unless drastic steps were taken, she'd have to tap into her meager emergency fund.

"But, Peace," I objected, "a boarding house...that's so, well, so beneath your capabilities. Why don't you teach Latin at NAPS again.

The headmistress at the North Avenue Presbyterian School for girls was a former Vassar classmate of Mother's. When one of her instructors, the Latin teacher, eloped one fall, Miss Baker had pleaded for Peace to fill in for a few weeks. The few weeks stretched out to two years until she married my father.

Now she vetoed the idea of teaching. "These days I'd need a teaching certificate. Nope, I can read Latin and French, but that won't buy a new furnace...and actually Cora Lee and I are getting excited about our idea."

Peace's description of her partner in this venture, Cora Lee, draws a far better picture of that remarkable woman than I can. The following is from an essay Peace wrote for her Wednesday Morning Study Club. As my mother was born in 1884 and the essay was written in the fifties, it must be read in relation to the time and place.

HELPMATES

During all those years, when the slings and arrows of misfortune were working overtime on me and the heavens apparently decreed that like the manna of the Israelites, only enough legal tender for the mere subsistence of the day should fall upon me, the best and truest friends have been my ones of color. Their patient hands, willing dispositions, and kindly hearts have truly borne me along, and cushioned the rough road. Their names have been many, but whether collectively in thought or individually, I shall ever be grateful to them as they helped 'temper the wind to shorn lamb.'

It was Cora Lee who helped me begin the adventure of the paying guest. She was sent by Heaven to me when Frances, my older girl, was a baby. Both Frances and her younger sister, Peggy, loved her. In appearance she was a short round woman with the snubbiest of noses and flashing white teeth. She considered us her 'white folks' which was indeed a compliment.

She had the most hearty, infectious laugh I've ever heard—it lifted one's spirit. She was a past master at appeasing the appetites of hungry ones and could make a potent cornbread and a luscious lemon pie. People will find a good cook on a desert island. Not only was her cooking remarkable, but so was her management; meals on time, all pots and pans washed and put away and hot food ready for the dining room.

The children loved to repeat her many names. She'd had several husbands, and when acquiring a new one, she kept the names of the former ones, which must have shown her generous spirit and goodwill toward them. The result was a delightful litany of names—Cora Izzy Lizzie Lee Walker Williams Downing-which sounded like a royal title from the book of heraldry. And in our eyes, she was royalty.

Cora Lee always aided and abetted the children in their projects. One particular example comes to mind. After our house burned in the country, we spent the summer at the beach, St. Simons Island, before relocating in Atlanta. One day, on the way home from the Island village, the children and their father saw a small, white goat tethered in a yard.

For several days, all I heard from the three of them was how nice it would be to have that adorable creature. As we were not settled then, and had few belongings left, a *goat* was the last thing in the world I wanted. I looked to Cora Lee for moral support for my objections. Unfortunately, I found one more voice raised against me. The woman had a special place in her heart for goats and said she'd help take care of it. My only feeble victory was a promise that the goat would live on the farm until we were settled. That's one of the things I like about myself—I'm so firm with my family.

They piled into the car to find the goat's house and negotiate for the purchase. I resigned myself to the inevitable and was already wondering how we were going to fit a goat into the car on the trip home when four crestfallen faces came back into the cottage.

The goat lady refused to sell. It takes all kinds and on that day I was in the minority in my lukewarm admiration for nanny or billy goats.

The children's long disappointed faces brightened when Cora Lee said, "Fetch the crab baskets...if you hurries, we can catch enough for deviled crabs for supper ...that's more fun than an old goat anyways." Of course it was.

By the time I was advised of their plan, Peace and Cora Lee had already chosen the three most suitable of the six upstairs bedrooms to be used, plus they could convert the downstairs library with its adjoining bath into another bedroom. Four rooms to let; and already Peace had the perfect supply source to fill them.

Mr. Tharpe, principal of the High Museum of Art, located on the nearby corner of Fifteenth and Peachtree Streets, was chatting with Peace after church service one Sunday when he mentioned his difficulty in locating rooms for his female students. The school attracted young people from Georgia and even neighboring states and Mr. Tharpe said it was a headache to find good places for them.

I remained unconvinced. "What about Aunt Sue? Me on the hated television, and you running a boarding house! She'll have a conniption."

Peace touched the tip of my wrinkled-up nose. "Aunt Sue has a harder head than you, my dear. She'd rather have me solve my own problems than have a passle of indigent relatives on her hands."

"Well," I sniffed, "apparently I'm the only person in town you haven't told all about this." It seemed to be my month for hurt feelings.

Peace took my hand. "Fanny, I knew you'd be upset but with Al in school and you away all day, it'll be wonderful to have some young women around the house.

She paused and glanced across the room at a pastel portrait of my sister Peggy as a child. "Sometimes I miss Peggy so that I don't feel life's worth living."

I must have looked stricken by that remark because she hastily amended, "I didn't mean it literally, but our boarders' venture would ease the money crunch, plus give me a sense of purpose, which church, bridge and study clubs don't."

Of course, thinking of it only from my viewpoint, I hated the idea. No more privacy, and God knows what we'd draw in the way of roomers. As my Sagittarian mother often read my mind, she answered my unspoken thought. "Mr. Tharpe assured me that he'd hand-pick only nice, quiet girls for me."

With one last stab at dissuading her, I said, "Mother, have you considered that you know nothing about running a boarding house?"

She stopped me with her rebuttal. "As for that, Missy, you didn't know anything about television. At least I'm on familiar ground...it's the same as keeping house for a family. I know I can make a success of it."

I wasn't too sure of that. Peace had a 'give me the luxuries and to hell with the necessities' approach to practical matters. It might work, however, as long as Cora Lee stayed with us—she was the sensible one.

Peace turned off my cold water shower with a parting twist. "Besides, I grew used to a house full of girls at boarding school and college."

That brought my first smile since she'd confided her unwelcome idea. "I doubt that many New Orleans Storyville madams can make that statement."

My remark brought only a look of non-comprehension from Mother...New Orleans madams weren't in her vocabulary.

For the next couple of weeks, the two women turned the house upside down with painting, furniture rearranging, and stocking up on supplies. Cora Lee's current husband, Will, helped with the heavy work. I knew when I was licked and stayed out of the way.

Long before the four 'hand-picked, nice, quiet' art students were due in September, Peace and Cora Lee were ready for business, and they grew impatient to see some concrete results of their work. I didn't know it, but Peace began slipping a small "Room for Let" sign in the front window after I'd left for work—on the off chance she might net a walk-in to experiment on before fall.

Al, who couldn't keep a secret any better than any other six-year-old, tattled on her, but not before the sign brought in a fish—and what a fish.

Janice Butler was a soft-spoken, conservatively dressed brunette from Rome, Georgia, a fair-size city in the north Georgia. Obviously well-bred, she volunteered the information that she'd recently left her husband because of his brutal cruelty toward her.

Peace's marshmallow heart was touched, and she immediately settled the woman in the converted library. I came home that evening to find Peace and Cora celebrating their auspicious beginning by raising a glass of sherry.

Peace proposed a toast, "Here's to Janice, our first boarder. Long may she stay." And the two business partners clinked glasses.

CHAPTER 14

SOUTHERN COMFORT

The subject of Janice, our new boarder, receded to the back of my mind during the following week. I was fully occupied with working on much needed new material for the *Music Shop's* insatiable appetite.

Dick and I waited a decent interval before repeating our repertoire of popular record pantomimes, so constant additions were necessary. Memorizing the words with precise timing, appropriate gestures and dance steps took lengthy rehearsals. After legendary Paul Whiteman, the King of Jazz, had commented on a recent visit to our station that we were the best pantomimists he'd seen, we concentrated even more on that particular feature.

As a consequence of all that rehearsing, it was Friday evening before I managed to join the family dinner table and catch up on the home news.

"Mother, how's Janice? I haven't seen her since she moved in."

Son Al started to say something but Peace quickly shushed him, so I continued. "I'll say this for her, she's quiet. If the September students are like Janice, I'll have to eat my words."

"Frances, this is my first chance to tell you this." Peace gave me a look of discomfort. "When I hadn't seen Janice in a couple of days, I began to worry."

"Don't tell me your first boarder has skipped already?"

"No, would that she had. On Wednesday, I decided to peek in her room to be sure she was all right. When I saw her lying across the bed, I thought she was ill—until I saw the pile of Southern Comfort bottles by the bed."

Southern Comfort is a sickly-sweet peach brandy. To my mind, it makes cough syrup taste like ambrosia. I know my eyes widened with horror. "I can imagine nothing worse than getting drunk on that stuff."

"When Janice sobered up," Peace said, "she told me that Alcoholics Anonymous was helping her, so I called them. The woman on the phone said although AA never gives up, she personally felt Janice might be a hopeless case." Peace looked as if she were about to cry. "Janice is from Rome all right, but that's about all she told me that tallies."

Apparently it was the sad tale of a popular young matron active in a community with a great deal of social drinking going on, which, in her case, had finally become compulsive. Her husband, a well-to-do business man, had seen her through many failed cures. At last, for the sake of their two young children, he'd sent Janice home to her mother without them.

The AA informant said that Janice had been in Atlanta for some time and so far, their efforts had failed. However, she'd apparently added that if Peace was interested in helping, they'd cooperate.

Inwardly I groaned at that last statement. Mother had a Florence Nightingale streak in her, and Alcoholics Anonymous was one of her allies. Peace might dissipate with a glass of sherry upon occasion, but she'd been seated in the front row of AA meetings with her latest to-be-rehabilitated charge so often, I'm certain the town thought she was one of their core members.

She'd discovered that excellent organization when all else had failed with her beloved younger brother, who not only recovered due to their program, but became head of the Atlanta chapter, a post he filled until his death.

So here was a worthy challenge—an evidently hopeless case involving an intelligent young woman, a long-suffering husband, and young children. Bells rang, trumpets blared, and Peace rolled up her sleeves for an all-out campaign.

She enlisted more kindred spirits. She had two friends from her church circle, plus Cora Lee; she worked them up into the proper fervor for the crusade of Janice versus the demon rum, or in this case, Southern Comfort. I agreed to lend a hand when possible and my long-time friend and temporary house-guest, Kitty Wiley, said she'd do the same. Kitty, a singer with Sleepy Slocum and his Rhythm Kings, was staying with us until the band went back on the road.

The battle plan cry was "Never leave Janice alone." Her tearful assurance of wanting nothing in life but to be restored to her husband and children made us feel that our support and belief in her could do the job.

For two weeks, we kept to our schedule, which was damned inconvenient and boring for everyone. During that period, I reached the conclusion that when someone makes a mess of their life, no matter what the cause, the people around them suffer as much. But then, Peace claimed I was inclined to be more of a cynic than she.

At the end of two weeks, the result of our amateur regeneration program was promising. Janice had been attending AA meetings faithfully with nary a slip. We all began to feel the glow of satisfaction that comes from teamwork for a good cause.

On a hot, humid Wednesday evening, our girl scout troop was well into its third week of triumph. Al was in my room watching me rehearse a pantomime of Eartha Kitt's singing of "C'est Si Bon." He liked to imitate his mother throwing herself around in front of the mirror and making funny faces. One silly backward hopping step always made Al laugh. He begged me to do it some more so I was backward hopping out of the door when I backed into Janice. I apologized for bowling her over with my act and invited her in to join the fun. After a few minutes of conversation, she explained the reason for her visit.

"Fran, I'm supposed to give a short speech at the AA meeting tonight and I'm terrified." Lifting up a strand of her brown hair, she gave me a distressed look. "Peace said you'd know how to help me with this birds nest."

She'd said the flattering magic words. My experience in the fashion world made me consider myself somewhat of an authority on grooming, so I promptly accepted the role of Pygmalion. Janice was still a young woman with natural good looks which her self-abuse had not marred. When I finished with the make-over, she looked like an Ava Gardener clone.

Unfortunately, the next morning when we saw her weaving up the front steps, we knew my Galatea's resolutions had dissolved like cotton candy the night before. Peace laid the failure of *Operation Janice* on my doorstep. She maintained that if I hadn't made the woman look so good, perhaps things would have worked out for the better. Sadly, Mother put Janice to bed and pondered her next move.

That evening following Janice's return at dawn, the door bell rang and I opened it to find a respectable looking middle-aged gentlemen standing on the porch. He announced he was Mr. Collins, sent by the AA to help Janice. We knew AA does send people at all hours to rescue its stray sheep, so we invited him in with relief and hastened to comply with his request to see her.

Peace and I went into Janice's room and tackled the job of getting her into the living room. It was equivalent to carrying a 130-pound sack of molasses but between us, we poured her onto the couch. She slumped there underneath Grandfather Brooks's austere portrait, while we eagerly awaited Mr. Collins's instructions. Expecting him to perhaps suggest hot coffee for her, I prepared to drape Janice around Mother while I went to get the coffee when Mr. Collins said, "Maybe she'd like some music."

To my mind, music was not high on the list of Janice's present needs, but not being a professional, I decided it was a form of therapy. Baudelaire said music fathoms the sky—so maybe it could reach Janice. Mr. Collins sat down at our baby grand piano and flexed his fingers.

"Oh dear," Peace whispered to me, "if I'd known someone from the outside was going to play, I'd have had Mr. Latimore tune it."

"It would still be out of tune," I whispered back.

Mr. Latimore, who made his bi-annual tuning visits accompanied by Mozart, his seeing-eye dog, admitted once he hated piano tuning—which is probably why our piano stayed more or less off-key; but added that a sightless person is limited in employment options.

Peace suffered more from the discords than the rest of us since she had the best ear. When sister Peggy or I, and now Al, hit the same sour note three times in a row, she'd wince, then in her exasperation would ask us why we continued striking the wrong note while searching for the right one. Nonetheless, she'd cut off her ears rather than change to a tuner with perfect pitch.

After Mr. Collins ran a few practice scales on the instrument without comment, Peace relaxed. Our surprise visitor paused, stared at the ceiling for a few moments and then began furiously pounding out the Venusburg theme from Wagner's *Tannhauser*. Peace and I were mesmerized by the performance, while our patient swayed gently to and fro between us—but *not* in time to the music. Janice's two book-ends carefully looked anywhere in the room except at each other, as we both knew we'd have difficulty controlling hysterical giggles.

After a half-hour of the unexpected concert, Mr. Collins rose from the piano bench, gave a jerky bow, asked us to call him if there was anything else he could do, and departed out of the front door.

For a few more days, the situation dragged on, but our rescue squad failed all attempts to coax Janice back into her former state of sobriety. No matter how hard we tried to cut off the supply, she outwitted us. Peace's recruits lost heart and suggested she do the same.

At the end of her forbearance, she once more called the AA and explained the problem to the same woman she'd spoken to before about Janice's case. Peace asked, "Do you suppose it might help to have that nice Mr. Collins from AA give us a hand out here again?"

There was a pause, then, "Mrs. Peace, we don't have a Mr. Collins here, not as a member or on the staff. I don't know *where* he came from, but he wasn't from AA."

While Peace was digesting this mystifying piece of news, the woman continued, "Furthermore, in my own opinion, you're wasting your time with Janice; she comes to AA to find men—period."

Peace was so deflated after she hung up the phone that her only solution was to wire Janice's mother to meet her daughter at the Rome bus station the following day; a solution which Janice resisted every step of the way.

From start to finish, *Operation Janice* had taken over a month and I for one was heartily sick of maudlin self-pity, AA meetings and empty Southern Comfort bottles. All our time, energy, and loving care had been for naught. Peace was so exhausted that she feebly agreed to count to ten before she threw her personal life into such high gear again with her salvaging efforts.

A few weeks later at the breakfast table, Peace found a letter from Janice in the morning mail. After she'd read it in silence, Cora Lee and I asked simultaneously, "What'd she say?"

Peace replied, "I'm so relieved to hear from her, with such good news, too; she's only had iced tea since she left us. In fact, she's doing so well, er, well, she would like to return to Atlanta and stay with us again." Peace folded the letter back into its envelope. "How do you think I should answer?"

Cora Lee rolled her eyes up in her head. "Miz Peace, so help us, you mean after all we's been through, you don't know?"

"Oh, Cora Lee, she *was* a sweet thing, and if she's improving so much," Peace looked down at Janice's letter, "well, I don't see why...."

"Lord luv a duck, Peace," I interrupted, "if she's doing so well, she's better off where she is. Write and tell her we're full, which we soon will be."

Cora Lee's eyes came back down out of her head with relief. "Don't worry, Miz Peace, you'll find another lost lamb, you always do."

Come September, the art students had moved in—Claudine, Betty Sue, Gretchen, and Sarah. Sarah Dent from Eufala in Alabama and I are still friends many decades later in spite of her insistence that we got off to a bad start.

She was the first to arrive and remembers that I greeted her with this cryptic remark, "I hope you're not one of those nice, quiet girls who like Southern Comfort."

Sarah, who wasn't familiar with the peach brandy, said, "Indeed I am. I'm used to a lot of southern comfort in Alabama ...and I expect to have just as much here in Georgia."

For a long while she was to remain puzzled by my chilly reception.

CHAPTER 15

ANYTHING FOR A GOOD CAUSE

"What's a telethon?" I asked.

Bill Colvin had invited Dick and me to his office to discuss a matter of paramount importance. With Bill's gift for turning a pea into a watermelon, we seldom agreed with him on the importance of a subject. We could count on one unchanging element in Bill's ideas however—more work for the *Music Shop* gang.

The 'thons are commonplace now. But in April of 1953, when Bill told us that WLWA-TV was producing Atlanta's first local telethon, my question, "What's a telethon?" was one of genuine curiosity.

"What it sounds like," Bill answered. "A television marathon. On June 7th, Dick and you are going to be on the air all night for the Atlanta Muscular Dystrophy Association. You'll keep going 'till the pledge phones stop ringing."

Dick and I looked at each other in disbelief. Whenever we thought management had exhausted every possible way to increase our work load, we were impressed anew with their ingenuity. Dick groaned. "No way...we're already pulling out miracles instead of rabbits for that hour a day. Why not fire us?—easier than killing us."

Bill said, "You two have been under those studio lights so long your brains have frizzled. You won't be alone...it's going to be the biggest TV show Atlanta's ever had, with lots of local talent, and thanks to yours truly," Bill hooked his thumbs under his suspenders, "some nationally-known stars."

"Clark Gable?" I asked, perking up. Dick looked more interested also and asked, "Ingrid Bergman? Sophia Loren?"

"Nope, but we have Robert Alda (Alan Alda's father and best known for his long-running role as Sky Masterson in the Broadway musical *Guys and Dolls*) and—for the kids—Captain Video and his Video Rangers."

Captain Video, played by former radio actor Al Hodge, was the star of his popular children's show of the fifties. It was *so* popular that New York's Mayor Impelliteri changed his fireside chats to another time after learning he was up against the Captain.

The space ship Captain was much handsomer than his space ship, which looked as if your Uncle Willie had knocked together a few cardboard boxes and trimmed them with bicycle handles and tin pie plates. Oblivious to its questionable construction, a large loyal following regularly climbed aboard the flimsy vehicle along with the gallant Captain for supersonic space adventures.

"Okay, Bill, " Dick made a brushing gesture with his hands, "that takes care of Fran and the under-ten population. Now how about me?...Ingrid or Sophia, or both."

"I know you're kidding, but you're not too far off, we've got a beautiful foreign star who can sing...Ilona Massey."

"What's an Ilona Massey...sounds like one of those South American Andes animals."

"Dick, "I protested, "she's been in lots of pictures...several with Nelson Eddy...I remember *Balalaika* and *Rosalie*."?

Dick took aim at Bill with the paper airplane he'd just finished. "That explains why I've never seen her."

Contrary to Dick's opinion, Ilona Massey was not that obscure. She was a star of operettas in her native Hungary until the mid-thirties when MGM brought her to Hollywood. It was the custom of the big studios to always have a quick replacement for any well-known star in case said star became too temperamental. In Ilona's case, she was earmarked as a substitute for Jeanette MacDonald. The Nelson Eddy-Jeanette MacDonald pairing was a great success at the box office but less successful in real life. Not only could Ilona replace Miss MacDonald should she become too obstreperous, but she had great potential to be a star in her own right.

"Bill," I asked, "my ignorance knows no bounds today. What's muscular dystrophy and why are *we* doing a telethon for it?"

"That last question is a good one," Dick nodded in agreement. "Fran and I learned the hard way, from some of the free benefits we've done, that many of these professional 'charity show' producers leave town with the cream. The local charity gets peanuts."

"Yeah," I added, "'member that slick New York bunch who staged the Metropolitan Orphanage show? They skipped town with everything but the orphans."

Bill said WLWA-TV was actually producing the show and every cent beyond the basics, such as renting the Tower Theater, would go to the M.D. Association.

As for the disease itself, I learned that muscular dystrophy is a slow wasting of the body's voluntary muscles and that most of its victims were male children.

Bill continued with his lecture. "A wonderful woman, Wenonah Chambers, one of the chapter's founders, has been a big help."

I gave Bill a dubious look. "What's this wonderful woman's salary for her interest in such an obscure disease?"

"Nothing," he said, and gave a wicked smile before going on. "No, Wenonah's only motivation is that three of her six children have muscular dystrophy."

Bill enjoyed my embarrassment over harboring suspicions about his prize helper. Yet, as Dick mentioned earlier, some of our previous experiences with the rampant greed of fund-raisers had made us wary.

Still in the future were the Jerry Lewis annual Labor Day M.D. telethons featuring hosts of celebrities. He's raised millions through his efforts and our goal in 1953 of $50,000 seems paltry by comparison. Ours was notable for several reasons, nevertheless—we had two months instead of the usual year to prepare; it was Atlanta's *first* such effort; we familiarized our public with the disease plus fund-raising in the same telethon; and we went over our goal by $20,000.

Two weeks before June 7th, the *Music Shop* began featuring guests involved in the project, either as volunteer talent or M. D. representatives. Dick was the designated master-of-ceremonies and my role was to relieve him when he needed a break and to cue the different acts upon occasion. We were also prepared to perform. At least that's what we *thought* until a Wednesday, three days before the telethon.

The question Dick's Atlanta following often asked me as his *Music Shop* cohort was, "Is Dick as cheerful and good-humored as he appears on TV?" I could honestly answer in the affirmative. This Wednesday, however, was an exception. Dick came into the office like a sudden thunderstorm and slammed the morning paper down on my desk.

"Did you see this?" he asked, opening the paper and pointing to the article. I shook my head. "Marge caught it this morning...read it and prepare to join me in a posse."

I read the headlines of the article. *Muscular Dystrophy Aid ...Television's Tony Mann Leads Telethon Saturday.*

If I turned my head back and forth as if watching a tennis match, I could keep up with Dick's pacing. "Keep reading," he commanded.

"'Tony Mann, TV star who won fame as *The Black Spider* on a spine-tingling series, was in Atlanta Tuesday from New York for the all-night television marathon to be put on by WLW-A....' Jeez, the paper can't even get our call letters right! But I don't see what's wrong...this Tony fellow is just another of Bill's 'stars'."

Dick motioned for me to continue. "'A motorcade, including the telethon stars and many of Atlanta's most beautiful girls will parade down Peachtree at 11 a.m. Saturday'...Dick, I still don't see...."

Continuing to read down the page, I saw the reason for Dick's summer storm. "Ah, here it is... 'Mann, a professional in helping cities collect funds for muscular dystrophy research, will be the telethon's master-of-ceremonies.' " I stopped reading.

"Remember?" Dick shouted, "Remember? Bill swore on his honorary Confederate Colonel badge—no professional fund-raisers—no hotshots from New York."

At that moment the phone rang and Bill, Dick's posse quarry, was on the line asking if he could bring Tony Mann by our office for an introduction. Bill added he hoped the morning paper's misleading article wasn't upsetting to us.

"Some of us are," I admitted. "I never was anything but spackle in the cracks, but you'd better be ready for some explaining to Mr. Van Dyke."

Bill stuttered and said Dick was still the official emcee but, uh, Tony Mann was a skilled fund-raiser gifted in milking audiences for phone pledges. "Before this show is over, you two will be on your knees to thank anyone who'll fill time." Well, admittedly we were on new ground, and after the two men left our office, I said, "Tony seems nice enough...a bit smarmy but the curly blonde hair and cleft chin help. I never saw *The Black Spider*...hope it wasn't typecasting. Dick, what'd you think of him?"

I looked up to discover I was talking to an empty office. Dick had taken his small squall elsewhere.

CHAPTER 16

THE BIG PARADE

The telethon activities began early that hot Saturday morning with a press breakfast for the visiting stars. It was held at the Henry Grady Hotel; and afterward the parade would begin.

The night before I'd been up past midnight, washing my hair and collecting costume changes for the next 48 hours. To keep my page-boy-length hair presentable for daily public appearances was a chore but not as big a one as the agonizing decision of what to wear for such a complicated day. At last, I hoped my choice of a cotton floral print sun-dress with pink and lavender poppies on it wouldn't look too country-come-to-town next to our Hollywood star, Miss Massey. At such a time, I longed to kiss my elbow in order to turn into a man with a crew-cut and one suit.

Before the breakfast, Tony Mann, Dick and I were invited to join Miss Massey in her hotel suite. When we arrived, her husband, Charles Walker, greeted us at the door. While waiting for Ilona to appear, we learned that Charles, a jewelry designer, had his own West 58th Street store in which to display his elegant wares.

Ilona came into the room. A beautiful blonde whose heavy tan made *me* look as if I needed a blood transfusion. I burn before I can acquire that fashionable shade of tan—so coveted before the medical profession discovered too much sun was harmful.

"Miss Massey, I'm envying your gorgeous tan...do you tan easily?"

"Heavens, no, Charles and I spent a month in Portugal—most of it on the beaches."

Her yellow dress was becoming with her tan but no more elaborate than my floral print. Due to her warmth and friendliness, we were chatting like sorority sisters when we left to meet the press downstairs.

We ate breakfast in one of those interchangeable commercial hotel rooms where the food matched—rubbery eggs, sawdust sausage, and red-eye gravy for that southern staple, grits. Ilona had never tasted grits and didn't ask for a second helping.

Ilona and Charles had been introduced to each of the thirty people in the room before we sat down at the long table. After the meal, Miss Massey rose from her seat, answered a few questions from the reporters, and prepared to depart. She stopped to shake hands with Paul Jones of the *Atlanta Constitution.* "Thank you for coming this morning, Mr. Jones...I hope we'll meet again this evening." Next she paused behind the chair of radio station WQST's manager, Walter Fleming. "Mr. Fleming, I hope to see you at the telethon also."

I thought she must have had a previous conversation with those two gentleman, but when she thanked each person there by name, I realized that was not the case. I turned to Charles who was seated next to me and said with astonishment, "That's incredible...no name tags or place cards...and she doesn't know any of these people. How does she do that?"

Charles smiled. "The telethon will be a long night, Fran, so you can ask her the secret then."

Fifteen minutes before the 11 a.m. parade, we gathered at the motorcade's starting point, the intersection of Peachtree and West Peachtree. Bill Colvin, hidden behind two bulky florist boxes, was waiting by one of the cars. With a deep bow, he presented Ilona with one of the boxes, and then hurriedly thrust the other one on me.

Ilona opened her box first and lifted out a corsage of four gigantic virulent-purple orchids surrounded by imitation silver leaves. It would have been worthy of Al Capone's funeral. She said in a faint voice, "My, how, er, how lovely. And so *large*, I'll look as if I'd won something."

Dick, who was standing nearby, mumbled under his breath, "The first Derby race."

By then I'd opened *my* box and lifted out a corsage identical to Ilona's with one slight improvement, three orchids instead of four. "Bill, such a surprise...and very thoughtful of you."

"Yes, the Garden Gate Florist gave them to me free for a mention on the telethon," Bill boasted in his booming voice.

At times I wondered at "Big-Foot-In-Mouth" Bill's choice of a public relations career. He talked so much and so fast, no switchboard screened the messages from brain to tongue.

The parade starter blew his whistle, indicating it was time to get into our designated cars. Georgia's Lt. Governor Marvin Griffin and Atlanta's Mayor Hartsfield were in the leading convertible; next came Robert Alda and Ilona; and behind them, Dick and I were assigned to a cardinal-red Oldsmobile with Colvin as our driver. Following us, Miss Georgia and Miss Atlanta had drawn a white Olds. The rest of the cars were filled with various officials and pretty girls.

Our red chariot bad been sitting in the broiling Georgia sun all morning and when I sat down on the leather seat, I immediately shot back up. "Dick, don't sit, you'll be electrocuted...we'll have to walk."

Up and down the line, people were popping out of the cars like toast from an electric toaster. The parade was sabotaged before it began.

Bill Colvin may have had scant tact and no taste in corsages but his quick thinking showed me why he was effective in his job. He spied a news-stand across the street, dashed over, and came back with an armful of magazines for us to sit on. other drivers followed suit—much to the delight of the news-stand owner. Bill garnered a round of applause from the parade participants and my issue of *Popular Mechanics* saved me from a second-degree burn.

Twelve motorcycle policemen led the motorcade in the slow journey down Peachtree Street toward our destination, the WLWA-TV studios. It wasn't as good as a New York ticker tape parade, but it was impressive enough to attract a respectable line-up of Saturday shoppers along the sidewalks.

Our long-time Mayor Hartsfield drew many cheers and shouts of "Hi, Mayor", from the crowd, and the stars, Ilona and Robert, received friendly stares of non-recognition from the natives. Some scattered but warm 'hello's' greeted Dick and me, but judging from the whistles and waves from the crowd, we should have ridden in the car with Miss Atlanta and Miss Georgia. Wearing white bathing suits with blue ribbons across their contest winning chests, and riding in the white convertible, they were the real stars of the parade.

Our motorcade continued to creep along Peachtree Street in the glaring sun until it suddenly came to a dead halt.

We were in front of the Loew's Grand Theater (scene of the 1939 premiere of *Gone With The Wind*). The Mayor's car had stalled.

I looked with longing at a sign outside the theater that read "Air conditioning Inside." In 1953 air conditioning was the exception, not the rule. I hadn't thought to bring either a sun hat or suntan lotion with me, and I was uncomfortably hot. And I felt silly—seated in a motionless red convertible on Peachtree Street and covered with enough orchids to keep a DAR convention happy. One parade from this viewpoint was enough. I'd rather be watching it.

The sight of any parade reminds me of a special New York City one in the forties. It might have changed my life if I'd been able to run faster. Sitting there in the blazing sun, waiting for our motorcade to move again, I found my thoughts running backward.

I was recalling one stunning autumn day while I was working for the John Robert Powers model agency. I was standing on the corner of 54th and Fifth, holding a black patent leather Cavanaugh hatbox—the trademark of a Powers model until the call girls appropriated it. Attempts to cross the street were thwarted by a parade celebrating the rodeo opening at Madison Square Garden.

The parade came to a temporary halt on Fifth Avenue and I started to weave my way to the other side. I put one foot off the curb at the same time a gray horse reared near me. The rider, dressed in full cowboy regalia, quickly calmed him.

He was beautiful—not the horse, the cowboy. If life were an MGM movie, this was boy-meets-girl time. He tipped his ten-gallon white Stetson, leaned over the saddle and smiled. "Miss, and I do hope it's Miss, ole Henry didn't scare you, did he?"

I smiled back and said, "*Yes* to the first and *no* to the second, I've lived on a farm."

"Are you coming to the rodeo tonight?"

I shook my head.

"Listen," and he began searching in his shirt pocket, "if I give you a pass to my box, will you come to the show? I'll meet you there."

Quickly deciding nothing terrible could happen to me in Madison Square Garden, I nodded an okay. He was still searching for the ticket when the parade suddenly resumed. He called for me to follow along until be could find the pass.

The crowd closed in on me and when he saw my predicament, he shouted instructions all the way into the next block. I couldn't hear him so I blew him a good-by kiss and went on my way.

Who knows? If I'd been able to run through the crowd, I might have spent my life raising Arabian horses on a ranch with a Gary Cooper look-alike. On the other hand, it's probably just as well. I'm not all that fond of horses anyway.

The movement of our convertible lurching forward once again, pulled me back from the forties to our '53 motorcade. We continued on until Colvin skidded to a stop in front of the studio building.

"Okay, kids, parade's over...everybody out...unless you need a ride back uptown."

I un-stuck myself from the sweltering car and clambered out. "Bill, can you wait a minute, I have to run upstairs for more records."

"Okay, Junior, but make it snappy."

In the office, I grabbed the records and came back to the sidewalk just in time to see the red convertible disappearing around the corner with that rat Colvin at the wheel.

Slowly, I unpinned the wilted orchids from my equally wilted floral dress and threw them in the gutter.

Imagining the corsage was Bill Colvin's head, I was about to stomp on it when I remembered Cora Lee's choir practice that evening. An hour in the refrigerator would revive the flowers and she'd be the envy of her congregation.

I picked up the orchids, trudged across Forsyth Street to the bus stop, and climbed aboard the Atlanta transit system, jammed with Saturday shoppers.

On the ride back up Peachtree, nobody waved.

CHAPTER 17

"THE GREAT ATLANTA TELETHON"

The telethon itself went by in a blur. Peace and Al came to the theater for a short while that evening and were introduced on the show. Ilona autographed her photograph for Al and he thanked her politely—but he preferred the one from Captain Video.

One hundred-and-fifty telephones were available for people to call in contributions. In return for a pledge, Atlantans could request to talk with the stars or ask them to perform. Ilona agreed to sing a Hungarian song for anyone who'd pledge $100 and Robert Alda agreed to have his hair cut on camera.

Tony Mann reminded the audience several times an hour of the serious purpose behind the telethon and introduced some of the muscular dystrophy children.

As for Dick and I, we performed many pantomimes, both together and separately. My most requested number was "Diamonds are a Girl's Best Friend" and each time a viewer called for it, I wished they'd chosen something requiring an easier clothing change. It was a struggle to get into my homemade costume consisting of a white bathing suit trimmed with fringe, black net stockings and an armful of Woolworth's finest rhinestone bracelets.

The dawn hours were the nadir. Calls slowed to a trickle and we scraped the bottom with the acts we presented. One was a little girl who shouldn't have been up that late, or early, who tap danced standing on her head while hooked into a cut-out packing case. The Loutrelle Ukulele Club's performance rivaled our program director, Roger Van Duzer, in their ability to make each musical offering sound alike. Through it all, Dick kept a steady pace at the microphone and only relinquished his emcee role while fulfilling pantomime requests.

After eight o'clock on Sunday morning, we found the calls were beginning to pick up. Reinforcements arrived with fresh acts. We were getting our second wind.

At noon, Tony Mann mentioned that he longed for a drink of something stronger than Coca-Cola or coffee. Tony, Dick and I were the only three performers who'd stayed with the telethon since the beginning and were in agreement that Tony's idea might keep us going into the afternoon stretch. The hitch was where to get such a drink. Georgia liquor laws varied from month to month and county to county, but there was one never changing rule—no spirits could be sold on a Sunday.

When I told the men that I thought I could find a bottle, they were impressed. "If I'm lucky though, you'll have to drink whatever I bring back."

Tony assured me that if my St. Bernard mercy mission yielded nothing but 'white lightning', he'd be grateful.

When I came out the stage door into the theater's parking lot, the bright sunshine blinded me after my 14 hours spent under artificial lights. Before I had adjusted to the world outside the theater, the five-mile drive to the Ansley Park Golf Club was over. Sunday church-goers I passed on the street, or the slow-moving golfers on the club's course, seemed far removed from my recent environment.

When I entered the club, I wasn't as confident of my boast to the two men as I had been. My membership was a recent one—but a bit of a fluke. In an enlightened and advanced gesture, the Ansley Park Golf Club Board had lately voted three business women's honorary memberships—making their club the only one in Atlanta to allow a single woman to belong—without being the widow of a deceased member.

When I confided the purpose of my errand to Worley, the head bartender, I was pleased to find him handing me a bottle of Scotch on the house. He'd been watching the telethon on the bar TV set and said, "Miss Fran, if a wee drap can keep you all going 'til afternoon, well, consider it my contribution."

Back at the theater with the precious bottle in my hand, I opened the stage door, raced up the stairs to the first landing, and had made a sharp 180 degree turn for the second flight of stairs when the bottle hit the railing and crashed to the floor. With no sleep for me for many hours, my mental state was so brittle I sat down on the concrete steps and cried as if I'd consumed the whole bottle of Scotch by myself.

In later years, after Dick admitted to a drinking problem, I've wondered if that broken bottle was symbolic. During *Music Shop* days, there was no portent of such.

When I returned to the stage and told my sad story, Tony Mann said, "Fran, are you sure it's all gone? Here, let's take a straw and a paper cup...maybe we can rescue a swallow."

Tony turned out to be a good sport and fun. Each regular performer had his own phone and mine was next to Tony's so we spent time talking with each other between calls. I felt I knew him well at the end of the 19-hour show, an illusion brought on by the extended-time capsule atmosphere. He said he'd be in Atlanta again in a couple of weeks, after a New Orleans assignment, and asked if we could have dinner together. I was so groggy by then I forgot to find out if he was married.

The telethon had gone on the air at 9 p.m. Saturday night and we finally signed off at 4 p.m. Sunday afternoon. We had no idea any of our audience would be masochistic enough to stay with us throughout the whole show until we received many letters similar to this one from the Simmons family in Morrow, Georgia:

Dear Fran and Dick,

We want to congratulate you two on the wonderful work you did Saturday night and Sunday. You both showed what troupers you were by sticking it out through the complete program.

and Sandra Strickland of Dallas, Georgia, wrote:

Dear Mr. Van Dyke,

You did a grand job on the MD Marathon. I admire you greatly. And please tell Fran Adams she looked beautifully ravishing and that Miss Ilona Massey couldn't hold a candle to her, even if you did say she was a dumb blonde (Fran, not Ilona).

Atlanta's first telethon had been a big success. The pledges came to $70,000, a very large amount for that time. The long night and day had been worth all our efforts. The muscular dystrophy children, with their inspiring smiles and courageous air, despite most of them being in wheelchairs, had such a good time being on the show, we were able to discard our initial fear of exploiting them.

When it was all over, everyone was on a euphoric high and didn't want to go home immediately, so Tony Mann invited the cast to celebrate at the local Variety Club. Ilona and Charles stayed only a few minutes since they had a night train to catch for New York, but we vowed to keep in touch.

"Ilona, after the press breakfast, you said good-by by name to a number of people you'd just met. Charles said you'd tell me your secret of how you can do that."

"I'll do better than that, Fran. When I get home, I'll *send* you my secret."

We'd been like shipboard acquaintances, fun while it lasted, but I thought I'd never hear from Ilona again—or Tony Mann either for that matter. I was wrong on both counts.

CHAPTER 18

DECISIONS, DECISIONS

The following week, true to her word, Ilona's secret arrived in a brown paper parcel with note inside:

"Dear Fran,

I hope you get as much from this as I did. Perhaps if I'd found the secret earlier, MGM and I might not have parted company. My Hungarian English couldn't compete with the Gabor sisters. Charles may come to Atlanta on business soon, in which case, we'll look forward to seeing you and our other new friends. A wonderful experience. Affectionately, Ilona."

I couldn't wait to open the package. I don't know what I expected—a magic elixir to inhale, or an Alice-in-Wonderland 'DRINK ME' bottle, either of which would enable me to gain instant memory for names to connect with faces. I was already dreaming of to what heady heights such an ability might carry me.

No more peering nearsightedly at scraps of paper with hastily-written illegible names. No more fixed stares directed at someone's chest area instead of the face in order to read name badges at civic gatherings. No more sneaking into dining rooms for a glimpse of place cards. No more southern-sugar dear, darling, or sir to cover up my lack of name knowledge.

I fantasized on the benefits from such knowledge—my expertise might even dazzle management into making me the first local woman newscaster.

Eagerly, I cut the twine on Ilona's package, tore off the brown paper and said, "Damn." I was glad Ilona wasn't around to see the disappointed look on my face. A *book* wasn't *instant magic*; my hectic schedule didn't leave me that much time for study.

The book title, *Memory by Association*, was self-explanatory. Its jacket blurb guaranteed that if the reader mastered the techniques within, he or she would be happy, successful and rich. Another 'How To' book—the kind that made only its happy author rich and successful.

Quickly I leafed through it, noting some of the instructions: Be certain you hear the correct name. Repeat it as often as you can during the conversation without sounding like a parrot. Associate the person's name with something else, no matter how ridiculous. When introduced to Mr. Ashcraft, you might think of an ash can. Or with Mr. Bowman, an archer. Mrs. Bray, a donkey. A substitute word can make the name come alive for you. Or so the book claimed.

Memory by Association was about to be consigned to my desk drawer when the picture of Ilona confidently bidding farewell to each of the thirty people at the telethon breakfast came to mind. If a Hungarian could learn the trick from a book, so could this Georgian.

My phone rang and John Whitney said, "Fran...."

"Well, hello Mr. Cotton-Gin."

"What's that all about?"

I told him Ilona's memory secret had arrived in the form of a book which recommended associating a name with a key reminder—and Eli Whitney invented the cotton gin.

"Honey chile...I don't want to discourage you before you start, but if it's all the same, I'll stick to Big John."

"I wasn't planning on a permanent 'Cotton-Gin'...I was practicing on you."

"Okay, you can practice on me all weekend 'cause Elaine's expecting us."

Uh-oh! I gave an unseen grimace into the telephone. John's sister, Elaine, and her husband lived on Lookout Mountain near Chattanooga, Tennessee, a few hours drive from Atlanta. I'd met them when they were in Atlanta recently and Elaine had urged me to visit when John and I could find a mutually agreeable weekend. She and husband Tom had a guest house on their property which she suggested John and I could share.

My grimace was caused by my uncertainty in deciding whether I wanted to *share*. In a way, I liked the *status quo*, but realized that the situation must either evolve or dwindle. When two consenting adults see as much of each other as John and I had since spring, and one is consenting and the other isn't, something has to give. Although Doris Day managed to leap-frog to the last reel with nothing but a good night kiss in her fifties movies, real life doesn't work that way no matter what the decade.

My mind churning with indecision, I decided to hedge. "John, I look forward to seeing Elaine and Tom again but I'll have to get back to you after I check with Peace."

"You know your mother'll be home, but...hold on air time coming up."

Having a conversation with John while he was on the air was like talking to a mynah bird with the hiccups. I was left holding the phone for long stretches while he gave his between-record patter.

"Okay, I'm back...but let me know soonest so I can call Elaine."

Our relationship had begun in an easy, friendly low-key way (if you could call low-key having John hold me by my heels outside the Kimball House window while I rescued a wayward parakeet). It was like a warm, comforting fire on a rainy night, and I didn't think I wanted it to blaze up into anything more right now.

Grand passions take a great deal of time and energy. I'd had one *coup de foudre* and one of those bolts of lightning in a lifetime is enough, thank you very much. Particularly if the aftermath leaves you feeling like a windswept prairie or the Mojave desert far longer than anyone should have to walk around in such a condition.

Perhaps I could say Peace was busy this weekend, and postpone my decision until the next weekend, and then the next— no, that wouldn't be fair. Sooner or later, I'd be left with nothing but this uncomfortable picket fence I was sitting on.

I asked Candy at the switchboard to give me an outside line so I could phone home. Cora Lee answered and said she was glad I called as she needed some things at the Tenth Street Market. Peace had forgotten half her list this afternoon, and if we wanted dinner tonight, I'd best not forget.

"Where's Peace now?"

"She's gone to Miz Alma at the Tenth Street Beauty Palace, and I'm pressin' her dark blue now...the one with the diamond buttons."

"Must be big doings at the church tonight."

"No ma'am, Miss Fanny, Miz Peace got a date with a man." Cora Lee gave one of her infectious laughs. "I tole her that 'cording to my 'sperience, all good men is dead or married, but she's goin' anyways."

"For heavens sake, who is it?"

Cora Lee told me she'd said too much already, she'd let Peace tell me, and I wasn't to forget her list.

I hung up the phone and racked my brain to think of who my mother's dinner date could be. A long-lost cousin? I don't know *now* why children of any age think their parents lose interest in the opposite sex the minute they become a Mother or a Father. But, back then, I couldn't imagine my mother out for an evening with a gentleman, although tales of several broken engagements before marrying my father indicated a high degree of popularity in her youth.

She was still in her forties when my father died and always seemed younger than her chronological age, and I was surprised she didn't have more attention. A clue may be found in a dim memory of a Sunday afternoon drive with Peace and a visiting acquaintance from her Vassar college days, Mr. Kendall Muzzy. Baby sister Peggy and I went with them and spent the afternoon squealing with laughter over our clever—to us—whispered rhyme of "Mr. Muzzy is so fuzzy and fuzzy is as fuzzy duzzy." Since Peace persisted in taking Peggy and me as chaperons on her outings, that might explain her lack of male companionship.

By the time I left the office, I still hadn't figured out who Peace's gentleman caller might be.

CHAPTER 19

OF OLIVES, MAPLE SYRUP AND THE POWER OF ASSOCIATION

On my way home, I stopped at Mr. Randall's Tenth Street Market for Cora Lee's requests. While waiting in one line at the check-out counter, I decided to change to a shorter line. In the process of changing lanes, I swung my juggernaut of a cart around and made a clean sweep of an intricate pyramid of ripe olives in glass jars.

Twenty-five or so glass olive jars had crashed to the floor. And those olives rolled and rolled. People would be skidding on olives into next week at Randall's Market. Although Mr. Randall seemed as ready to cry as I was, he allowed as how the display shouldn't have been in between two lines. I silently agreed with him and said that I'd mention his fine store on our show. He didn't look as if he thought that was much of a bargain for a case of olives, but thanked me anyway.

I drove my hard-won sack of groceries home from the market without further incident and found a spot for the sack on the back porch table.

"Cora Lee," I hollered, "I'm home, and this is as far as I can carry this bag." I noticed the rest of the table was covered with bottles labeled 'Trois Rivieres Maple Syrup, Quebec's Finest.' "Good Lord," I said under my breath, "that dratted maple-syrup man's been back...I wish Peace would quit feeling sorry for him."

Only the hardiest, most optimistic door-to-door salesman would be willing to gamble on the climb up the many steps and terraces necessary to reach the houses built along the crest of our Fifteenth Street hill. Quebec natives must be a hardy breed as the maple-syrup man had climbed our steps for years—and had been rewarded for his persistence.

"Look at that," I said to Cora Lee, who was collecting the grocery bag. "We're still working on last year's batch. It'd be cheaper for Peace to practice her French with a teacher."

Cora Lee glanced at the array of syrup bottles and grumbled that she didn't have any more storage room, and we already had enough syrup for a trunk full of pancakes and a barrel of waffles. Then she added, "And that furrin' fellow's been pouring that sweet syrup in moah places than just them bottles."

I didn't know what she meant by that enigmatic remark until I went inside the house and met Peace coming down the stairs, looking elegant in the dark blue, so becoming with her hazel eyes and chestnut hair. Peace's hair had silver streaks long before the beauty specialists made them fashionable.

"Mother, you look beautiful. And now the shoe is on the other foot. I'm dying to know where you're going and with whom."

Peace looked as if she wished she'd made it out of the house before I came home, a feeling with which I was all too familiar.

"I'm having a lovely treat...an international evening...dinner at the Chinese Camellia Gardens and then 'The Baker's Wife', that French film at the art theater...with Mr. Duval."

"Who's Mr. Duval?"

"Oh Frances, you know him. He's been coming to the house for years...brings that wonderful maple syrup...and let's me practice my French."

The maple-syrup man. I'd paid so little attention to him that I didn't remember his name. A fleeting impression of a pleasant enough fellow, with a mustache too sparse to balance out a mouthful of poker-chip teeth. He was about the same height as my five-foot-five mother. Years of carrying syrup cases, however, had given him a stoop which made him seem shorter.

"May I be so bold as to ask why, after all these years, the syrup man suddenly feels the need of companionship for an evening... that's a long wait for even the most cautious of fellows."

Peace, somewhat huffed, told me sarcasm didn't become me and that since his last year's visit, Mr. Duval was a widower.

Just then the doorbell sounded, and I went to the door to welcome Mr. Duval with as much forced civility as I could muster without cracking my face.

"You are surprised, no?" Mr. Duval shook my hand and smiled at Mother.

"I'm surprised, yes," I answered. I was about to tell them to have a good time and be home early but they were already out of the door, chattering French all the way down the front steps.

Disconsolate, I stood in the doorway, watching them until they reached the sidewalk and wondering at the host of childish emotions which surfaced in me—a supposedly grown woman. All right, since I was feeling like a child, I'd do what I did in my childhood, I'd have a talk with Cora Lee.

"Cora Lee, what'll we do if she marries that fellow?"

In my imagination, I had Peace married and living in the snows of Quebec. I'd often worried about leaving Peace alone if I married again, but the other way around was a new thought.

"Pshaw, Miss Fanny, you always was the worrienest chile...always asking what's for dessert before you even has dinner. Jus' be happy yore mama's having a nice evenin' out."

The comfort I took from Cora Lee's words lasted until the next morning when I at last broached the subject of John's invitation to me to visit his sister sometime soon. Peace said that for her later would be better, as she and Mr. Duval had plans for every evening until he left town the following Monday.

Still brooding over Peace's announcement, I drove to the office where my first action was to ask Candy to put in a call for John Whitney. With a certain amount of inner relief, I had decided I was going to tell him our weekend would have to be postponed— because my mother had a date every night with the maple-syrup man. He'd have a hard time swallowing that one even though it was the truth.

John was surprisingly sympathetic and said he realized that even my agile brain couldn't conjure up an excuse like a maple-syrup man for my mother. He'd tell Elaine we'd be there the next weekend after this.

It was later that day when the station manager, Carter Sever, came into our office to say a few key personnel, including the Van Dykes and me, had been invited to a small reception Friday at the Capital City Club. WLWA's Board of Directors was honoring Mr. Harold (Dry Hole) Tully, who, with five of his oil company executives, was flying to Atlanta via Lear jet from Galveston, Texas. Carter added he would appreciate it if we'd make the effort to be there.

When Dick asked who Mr. Tully was that he rated such a warm welcome, Carter looked unhappy and said, "Mr. Tully is considering buying the station."

Television stations in the early fifties were not immediate get-rich-quick fountains. Advertisers stick to the tried and true, and television was not yet in that category. Our station had changed hands more than once since its inception, but, as in Washington politics, civil servants keep thing going no matter who's in power at the top. The various owners so far never influenced our day-by-day efforts to fill time, so the performers paid scant attention to a changing of the guard. That was Carter's department.

The prospect of a takeover by a wealthy Texan, however, had Carter disturbed. "It's one thing to be owned by a corporation. The Board walks through a few times a year, and we never hear anything from them unless the red ink gets too deep," said Carter, voicing his apprehension that the transfer of ownership to one man would result in more personal supervision.

"Maybe Mr. Dry Hole won't be so bad, and anyway, he hasn't bought it yet. Don't worry about dessert before you've had your dinner, "I said, quoting Cora Lee's admonition.

I asked Carter how Mr. Tully had acquired his colorful nickname. He explained that Tully had hit a succession of dry holes while drilling for oil. Soon after marrying a wealthy woman whose family owned large chunks of downtown Dallas, he had finally hit a gusher. The adage of 'them what has, gets' certainly applies to Dry Hole Tully.

"And Fran," Carter added, "I'd prefer that none of us call him 'Mr. Dry Hole' on such short acquaintance. I think we'd better be safe and stick with *Mr.* Tully."

"Carter," Dick teased, "with Fran's new memory-by-association theory, you'll be lucky if she can stick to Dry Hole. So far this week she's called Mr. Millican of the Atlanta Boys club, Mr. Pelican—and Mrs. Potts, the Humane Society representative, Mrs. Chambers."

Carter just shook his head and left, and after he'd gone, I defended Ilona's book. I told Dick it took practice to get the hang of it, and if Ilona, who grew up speaking Hungarian, could master the theory, then certainly I should be able to do so in my own language.

Dick, who had been raised in Illinois, said he thought Southern was another language, which might explain my difficulty with the instructions. He also felt there was such a thing as being too creative with the association idea and that surreptitious peeking at a written name might be preferable to calling Mrs. Potts, Mrs. Chambers. "And, Fran, what you did to Mrs. Tucker...well, I'm surprised the poor woman didn't walk off the show."

I blushed, and said, "Never mind, I know I can make it work.

Dick merely threw me a skeptical look and walked out of the office.

CHAPTER 20

DRY GULCHED AT THE RECEPTION

The week ground on during which we added a new feature to the *Music Shop* audience-participation—charades. The postcards our audience sent in with their charade suggestions were put in a hat and we drew one each day to act out. If no one guessed the answer, the sender received a prize.

Management allowed us to try almost anything as long as it didn't cost money and didn't offend anyone. In those days, however, the sensibilities of our audience were strewn with unlikely minefields. One day I said, "Oh, fudge" on the air and couldn't believe it when a Mrs. Fudge wrote a letter of complaint.

Dear Fran,
You used our name in vain by saying "Oh, fudge". Please say, "Oh, divinity or peanut brittle" before you give us a complex.
Sincerely, Mrs. G. D. Fudge, Macon, GA.

After reading it twice, I realized that Mrs. Fudge was having fun with me, but we received so many odd complaints, one could never be sure.

It was Friday morning at breakfast, the day of Mr. Tully's reception, when Peace announced she and Mr. Duval had decided to stay home with Kitty Wiley, my singer friend, who was still waiting for her band leader, Sleepy Slocum, to come through with a road tour.

Explaining the change of plans, Peace said, "Kitty's beau, Max, is going to give a hypnosis demonstration here at the house tonight, and also tomorrow night. I didn't think anyone would be interested except Maurice and me, but guess what?"

I was intrigued at the idea myself, and said, "Well, what?"

"Yesterday, I told my neighborhood bridge group about Max, and Bless Pat, they *all* want to try it—that's bound to be worth staying home for; maybe I can find out why Marie Liede always overbids."

Max Hornbuckle, Kitty's current flame, was an interesting man. He'd tried various means of livelihood, the type of occupations often found in movie stars, and writers' biographies—prize fighter, encyclopedia salesman, artist, and student of the famed hypnotist, Franz Polgar. The last item on the list was of great interest to Peace and she queried Max at length on his experience in that field.

Peace's knowledge of esoteric subjects often astonished me. Until Max's appearance, I'd never heard her discuss Franz Polgar. Or Dr. Friedrich Mesmer, who in 1760 was the first physician to place his patients in a trance like state in an attempt to draw out diseases from them.

Unlike Peace, then most Atlantans thought hypnotism was only a stage act or parlor trick, not to be taken seriously. It wasn't until 1956, with the publication of a bestseller, The *Search for Bridey Murphy*, by Morey Bernstein, an amateur hypnotist, that hypnotism and past-life regression became household words. As usual, Peace was ahead of her peers.

And, as we continued to sit there over breakfast, she was fast getting ahead of me. "So," she added, "Maurice and I will be here with Al watching Max's demonstration...if you still want to visit John's sister."

Hum, now it was *Maurice* instead of *Mr. Duval*! "Thanks, Mother, but I've already canceled on that, and your plans work well for me...a command appearance at a reception tonight."

It was then that Peace requested I remember Maurice's correct name." You've called him Mr. Quebec, Mr. Molasses, everything in the world but his right name, and I'm tired of it."

In reply to my lame excuse of attempting to master Ilona's memory association book, Peace said it was a poor alibi. "You've been taught all your life that southern gentlewomen aren't rude and unkind, which you certainly have been to Maurice. In the past, I haven't cared for some of your friends, but I've never been rude to them."

Mother was right. I didn't want to remember Mr. Duval's name and I *had* been rude about it."

Still a bit ruffled by Peace's reprimand, I drove off to the office. The change of dress I'd brought for the reception I stored in the ladies room closet, and then I settled down to work. The day went swiftly, with no more surprises until shortly before airtime. Candy buzzed me and said I had a long-distance call from New Orleans.

"Candy, are you sure?...I don't know anyone in New Orleans."

Tony Mann, my telethon buddy, came on the line to say he'd be in Atlanta tomorrow evening to collect on my dinner-date promise. Every time I thought I had this weekend under control, it galloped away in another direction like the horse with two heads when its rider yells, "Charge."

I had no recollection of making any firm date with Tony, but those telethon hours now seemed another world, so perhaps I had. "I need to think a minute, Tony...because this weekend has unraveled several times."

Mentally I quickly reviewed my situation. I had no worry about Al as he had a plethora of sitters. No question about the whereabouts of John as he'd agreed to work this Saturday night in order to be free next weekend. I hadn't lied to John when we changed dates because my reason was valid at the time. On the other hand, I'd prefer not to run into him.

Memories of Tony's dimpled chin and the fun we'd had at the June telethon tipped the scales. I answered, "Why not. Call me after you've checked into your hotel tomorrow."

Later, on this frantic Friday, I pulled under the porte-cochere of the Capital City Club a few minutes before six. The Club owned a handsome late 1800's yellow-brick mansion downtown, and while I rode the elevator to the second floor, and the private party room behind the Mirador Room, I reviewed Carter's fears of a Texas takeover—and found I didn't agree with him.

The present station owners had no interest in anything but the annual financial report. Maybe a bigger-than-life generous Texan would give our *Music Shop* enough money to put on a decent show, and I wouldn't need Fifteenth Street as a prop department. Peace was weary of having her sheets used as togas and her ivy bed torn up for laurel wreaths on our show's drama days.

On my way through the Mirador Room, I paused to admire the exquisite Menaboni bird paintings on the mirrored walls of the room. Athos Menaboni is one of Atlanta's most famous artists and his bird paintings are comparable to Audubon's.

I couldn't stand there forever delaying the most difficult part of going to a party solo—those few moments after first entering a crowded room. Then it occurred to me that this was an opportunity to try out Ilona's memory book on a larger scale. Facility in glibly reeling off the Texas contingent's names correctly on first introduction would surely impress management with my poise—and my potential to graduate to a more serious role than that of the wide-eyed, naive, tap-dancing blonde.

The party had already formed into small groups so I headed for Carter who was talking with four strangers whom I assumed were the out-of-towners. Carter introduced me to the Texans as the female half of the station's most popular show, "Fran and Dick's *Music Shop*." I heard all the names, and had no trouble following Ilona's book's instructions. Mr. Redwine looked like a porcupine, and Mr. Ralph Virgin from Lubbock, Texas needed no memory key. Mr. Hart Watters was easy for he talked about his boat in Galveston and his love of the water. And, after Carter's morning discourse on Mr. Tully, I needed no key for him.

Ilona's book had a point. If you concentrated, it was a piece of cake. I would write Ilona a heartfelt thank-you note tomorrow, telling her I hadn't worked up to a roomful of thirty unknowns, but thought I'd made a good start.

After chatting with several guests, I felt I'd spent ample time at the reception and decided to leave. With Ilona's impressive example in mind, I returned to the original group to make my courtesies. I successfully said good-by to Mr. Redwine, Mr. Virgin and Mr. Watters. Visions of candy canes and all the equipment we could buy with a larger budget were already floating through my mind when I came to Mr. Tully. I turned my full reservoir of southern charm on him.

"I can't tell you how much I've enjoyed meeting you, Mr. Gulch...uh...Gully...er, I mean Tully."

The memory book's instructions had worked eventually but in the meantime, I'd insulted my target while waiting for my brain's computer to kick in. At least I'd heeded Carter's admonition not to call him by his nickname. Mr. Tully was not a good ole Texas 'just call me Dry Hole' boys. His frosty glance, from eyes cold enough for a guillotine operator, made me lose my optimistic hope of a Daddy Warbucks for our Little Orphan Annie of a television show. The men with him seemed to have similar ledger books for hearts.

After a few minutes of good-by chit chat, Mr. Tully shook my hand and said, "Pleased to make your acquaintance, Miss Pam...that's right, isn't it?" I nodded my head in agreement. Either he hadn't heard my name correctly or he, too, was studying Ilona's book. Under the circumstances, I thought it a blessing. If Mr. Tully's first decision upon acquiring the station was to fire that girl, Pam, he'd have difficulty finding the name on the employees' roster.

CHAPTER 21

TOO MANY MEN

The next morning, Saturday, Tony called to say that he had checked in at the Henry Grady Hotel. Since he had a car, he suggested meeting me at the house at eight. That evening I dressed early in order to catch the beginning of Max's hypnosis session. When I went downstairs, the seven women in Mother's bridge club were all seated in the den off the living room listening to Max's preparatory talk before his demonstration.

Kitty Wiley had seen Max's act enough to be blasé and was rehearsing her version of "Doggie in the Window" at the piano with Al seated beside her on the bench—one of the few times I'd ever seen him there voluntarily.

Then the doorbell rang, and rushing to open the door, I wondered why Tony was so early. On the porch, a broad smile on his face and a book under his arm, stood Big John Whitney.

Fortunately, the light in the entrance hall was so dim, the shadows concealed what must have been a dismayed look on my face.

"Hi, honey, I had a few minutes to spare on the way to work so thought I'd fit in some reading time with Al. I promised him some more *Treasure Island*." John had begun reading aloud to Al one evening while waiting for me and discovered they both enjoyed the experience.

Now what was I going to do when Tony Mann came whistling up the front steps? I hadn't planned this but I felt as guilty as I had in high school when I made late dates. By the time we'd walked into the living room, I'd arranged my features back to normalcy. Al joyfully exchanged "Doggie in the Window" for *Treasure Island* and he and John settled on the sofa for some serious reading.

Hoping against hope that Tony hadn't left his hotel, I raced upstairs to call and was relieved when he answered. "Tony, we'd have to drive right back downtown for dinner, so I'll make it simpler by meeting you in the lobby there in half an hour...'bye." I hung up before he could say anything. A better idea anyway since it would take all evening to explain that loony-tune group downstairs.

I threw my summer wrap and purse out of an upstairs window onto the lawn below, walked quietly down the stairs, slipped out of the kitchen door, and drove my car into town.

After Tony and I had dinner at the hotel's Paradise Room, we watched a floor show of puppeteers from Leslie Caron's movie, *Lili*. I was *not* having a good time. I fretted over my abrupt departure at home and hoped John hadn't noticed. Moreover, Tony didn't seem half as attractive as I remembered him from the telethon. My first impression of a too-smooth smarminess returned and a faint band of lighter skin on his left ring finger made me suspicious of a wife in New York, although no mention was made of one.

After we danced a couple of times to Parker Lund's orchestra, I decided I'd stayed long enough for politeness sake. My suggestion for Tony to ride down on the elevator with me to the parking garage was met with an invitation for a nightcap in his room before I left for home.

I laughed and said that a house detective would knock on his door within five minutes if I went upstairs with him.

"Not if I'm registered as Mr. and Mrs. Mann—which I am."

Oh, no, not another one of those! Tony had seemed so different during the telethon, showing such compassion for the muscular dystrophy children and being a wonderful sport throughout. Maybe I'd have to develop muscular dystrophy to bring out the best instead of the beast in him.

"Thanks, but no thanks, Tony." He was still arguing with me all the way across the lobby to the elevators. After I'd punched the 'Down' button, he grabbed my arm and said, "Oh come off it. Don't pull that Atlanta belle routine on me. For Chris-sake, you modeled in New York, you've been around."

I turned and shrugged off his hand. "In New York, I lived at the Barbizon Hotel for Women—no men allowed above the mezzanine ...and the John Robert Powers agency wasn't exactly Madam Polly Adler's." By that time a couple of passers-by began to stare at the scene. Tony reddened and backed up a step. I couldn't resist adding, "Furthermore, I left New York because it was full of creeps like you."

Doris Day didn't have a corner on the fifties indignant-exit market because, just then, with exquisite timing, the elevator doors opened. I leaped into the elevator and watched with relief as the doors gently closed in Tony's surprised face.

The next Monday when I said good-morning to Candy, I looked at her with more sympathy. Since Candy's first day on the reception desk when I offered to take over the switchboard while she went on an errand, she'd chosen me as her favorite among the female personnel. After that incident, Candy asked my advice on various subjects, including men. She followed some of it on the 'various', but paid little heed to my warnings on the latter.

Candy, dressed in one of her un-businesslike outfits: frilly sheer blouse, tightly cinched wide belt, six crinoline petticoats, and both her arms heavy with charm bracelets, was the first person to greet the steady flow of business representatives who called on the station. She was as friendly as a little red wagon and as a result seldom languished at home of an evening. My concern stemmed from her lack of radar in detecting unsuitable men from the suitables. But after my Saturday evening tangle with Tony Mann, no wonder Candy paid no attention to my advice on men. Her maiden Aunt Myrtle in Waycross, Georgia, could have given better counsel.

Certainly I was relieved that the past week was over. Mr. Duval left town with promises to return soon, and I'd carefully addressed him by that name on Saturday evening. Carter didn't announce that the station had been bought by Mr. Dry Hole Gulch over the weekend, and apparently I would hear no repercussions from Big John Whitney.

That last delusion was soon shattered, however, by a call from Big John, whose first words were, "Oh what a tangled web we weave when first we practice to deceive."

"John, let me explain. Truly, when I last talked with you, I didn't know Peace and Mr. Maple Syrup planned to stay home." Silence at the other end. "And that Tony Mann was going to turn up to remind me I promised him a dinner." More silence. "You're as bad as Aunt Sue...how'd you know where I was?"

"Fran, your face is becoming well-known in Atlanta, and Parker Lund, the Paradise Room's band leader is a good friend of mine...if you'd told me the problem, I would have understood."

"Honest now, would you really?"

"No, I'd have been mad as hell...and still am."

The phone went dead. I signaled the switchboard.

"Candy, you cut me off."

"No, I didn't, he hung up."

I sat there for a minute before tackling the day's *Music Shop* format. My personal life was getting out of hand but working was a good diversion. The sight of Sheila LeClaire's half-hearted wave as she waltzed by my office reminded me she still had eyes for my job, so I reasoned I'd better get on with it.

I pushed aside some of the debris on my desk and the back cover of Ilona's *Memory by Association* book caught my eye. On it, a list of twenty-six similar 'How To' titles was advertised, among them such tempting ones as *How to Increase Your Money Making Power*, *How to Manage Yourself*, *How to Motivate Men*, and *How to*

Pick Men. But having had so little success with how to have an instant memory for names, I wanted no more 'How To' books.

I sighed. Peace wasn't happy with me, Carter Sever wasn't considering me for the position of Atlanta's first anchor woman, Dick's comments on my name-mangling still rankled, and John Whitney wasn't going to call back any time soon. I picked up *How to Become Rich, Famous and Successful* with *Memory by Association* and deep-sixed it into my wastebasket with some regret. I hated to admit it but some Hungarians were smarter than some Georgians.

A few minutes before show time, I reviewed Monday's format with Dick and said, "Instead of me, I wish you'd interview Mrs. Wingbate from the Humane Society today. She spells danger until I kick the word-association habit."

"Sure thing, but I can't see anything dangerous about a respectable matron from the Humane Society."

"Dick, you haven't had the benefit of my memory-training course. Take my word for it...if Mrs. Wingbate heard me call her 'Mrs. Dingbat' for the fourth time during the show, she'd be dangerous."

CHAPTER 22

TENDER EGOS

I recall in particular one Monday morning in September of 1953 that got off to a really rocky start. When I looked at the thermometer outside my window at seven in the morning, it already read 85 degrees, and that promised a scorcher of a day.

After I turned on my bedroom's four-leaf-clover ceiling fan, I struggled into a girdle and stockings. As soon as I had them on, I elected to take them off. The air-conditioned ladies room at the office would be a more comfortable place to finish my dressing on such a hot day. I dismissed the temptation to go girdle-less. At that time, no part of a woman's anatomy was supposed to jiggle so we did our best to solidify the back end as much as possible.

I'd finished dressing and was ready to join the others downstairs for breakfast when I heard a loud crash in the living room. Before I could investigate, Al came running up the stairs.

"Mother, come quick, the piano's gone through the floor."

A morning that begins with a piano failing through the floor does not augur well for the rest of the day, but I thought he was teasing. "Oh, so that's all...I thought we'd had a Georgia earthquake."

Seeing that I didn't believe him, Al grabbed my hand and pulled me downstairs, and sure enough, half of our piano had disappeared through the floor.

Once Cora Lee's and Peace's laughing spells subsided, Peace explained that they'd decided the baby-grand would look better in another corner of the room. They'd forgotten about the large air vent in that corner, however, and the back leg of the piano plummeted through the grating, leaving the two front legs sticking up in the air like some large overturned black beetle.

Al saw the accident as a stroke of good fortune and raced for the phone. "Mother, I'm going to call Aunt Georgia to tell her I can't practice."

"Oh, no, you don't...she'll be happy to let you use her piano 'til ours gets back on its feet."

His face fell. He hated to practice and I wondered why I insisted he keep up his lessons his Aunt Georgia Adams so generously gave him. In spite of his lack of enthusiasm, I knew he'd appreciate some musical knowledge later on in life.

Between the fallen piano and an, "Oh, I forgot, teacher gave you this note to sign," from Al, I didn't get a good running start on the week. Management didn't care if we prepared for the show in the middle of Peachtree Street as long as we presented one at 4 p.m. each Monday through Friday. Time was precious though, and I did like to get to the office early on Mondays.

As I walked into the lobby, I was late, hot and cross. Lady Cedric's cage plus a shopping bag of things from home to use on the show, felt heavier with each step I took.

Peace had often complained that whenever she missed household items such as an egg beater or a hammer, she could find it by tuning in to the *Music Shop*. It was after I convinced our director, Martin Magnus, to list "Margaret Peace, Prop Master' in the credits at the end of the program that she stopped complaining about the missing items and actually began giving me ideas for the show. Now, if we didn't use them, her feelings were hurt.

Candy, with a big smile on her pretty face, waved a handful of pink message slips at me before I could get past the reception desk. "Fra-yan, guess what?"

"Candy, I don't have time for guessing games this morning, save it for later."

"No, no, wait a minute, I know something you'll like...you're going to have a TV Digest write-up."

After the unnerving start of my morning, Candy's words made me think there was hope for the day after all. The Atlanta TV Digest was a new and welcomed publication. The public wanted to know more about the programs and performers than the local papers could print. Heretofore, we'd depended on the morning and evening papers, which were owned by the same company, which in turned owned WSB-TV, Atlanta's most powerful television station.

The papers tried to be fair in their coverage, but our management was delighted to have another source and enthusiastically cooperated with the new magazine. The prospect of some *Music Shop* publicity was pleasing.

"Well, well, Candy, that *is* good news. How'd you find out, are you psychic?"

"No, I'm not sick." Candy shook her red curls. "Anyway, I heard Bob Jensen from the Digest tell Mr. Sever."

Our house had furniture moving around in it this morning, but at times, I wondered if much was moving around in Candy's upper story. But her sweet disposition, with its calming effect on all the high-strung characters around her, made her a good receptionist.

Now she was glancing up at me apologetically. "I'm sorry I didn't get all they said," she continued, "but the article's supposed to be about what your own favorite TV shows are."

"Candy, Candy," I said in a disapproving tone. "One of these days somebody's going to cut a willow wand and whale the tar out of you if you don't quit leaving those switchboard keys open...accidentally on purpose."

She turned raspberry pink. "Aw, Fra-yan, you know that's not true," and then grinned. "Say, when are you going to have another date with Big John Whitney?"

It was my turn to redden, and not from the 95 degree heat outside. I didn't want my personal life held up for speculation by the station personnel.

"Don't take on...I'm teasing...besides, a lot of times I tell you things you *want* to hear."

Candy's tip was confirmed later on in the day when Bob Jensen's call came through. He was the TV Digest editor, and like most editors, searched ceaselessly for article-hanging hooks. His hook for Helen Parris of WAGA-TV and me was "Have you ever wondered which television stars other TV performers watch?" I doubt that many people sat up nights thinking about the subject, but the Digest managed to fill a two-page spread with the title "Fran and Helen Can Pick 'Em", accompanied by photos of us and our choices, Jack Webb of *Dragnet* fame and Edward R. Murrow, the newsman.

Bob sent me an advanced copy a few days before the Digest hit the news-stands but I hadn't thought to show the piece of fluff to Dick. Several articles had been written about us as a team, but Dick had received far more publicity as a performer. He and his former partner, Phil Erickson, had been a featured pantomime act on a national level in New York's Blue Angel, Chicago's Chez Paree and Martha Raye's Five O'Clock Club in Miami. And they had been on Ed Sullivan's *Toast of the Town*.

As Dick was always the first to correct an out-of-town visitor or guest celebrity if they assumed I was his secretarial assistant, his reaction to the Digest article was quite unexpected.

On the Thursday morning the article came out, I picked up a few extras, for Mother and for my files, from the stack of Digests on Candy's reception desk. She told me Dick and our director, Martin Magnus, were already in our office.

When I reached the door, I realized that Dick was in the midst of acting out a comedy skit. I quietly backtracked into the hall so I wouldn't interrupt. Wearing a yellow mop wig and a green flowered apron from our costume supply, Dick was reading aloud from the latest TV Digest in a falsetto voice and with much fluttering of eyelids. His audience of Bill Colvin, cameraman Red O'Brien, and Martin, were showing their appreciation with loud guffaws.

"Fran, a loathsome blonde...no, no, that word is 'lissome'... lissome, what does *that* mean?...anyway Fran picks for Number One, the tall, dark and handsome hero of *Dragnet* and *Badge 714* series, Jack Webb. Fran says, 'Why he's so dreamy to me I can't tell you...but he is. He has the most individual and persuasive voice on TV today, beautiful brown eyes and a wonderful way of handling himself. When you see the painstaking detail of those shows and realize that Webb is greatly responsible for most of it...you can't but admire the man."

A very funny imitation—sarcastic, but funny. If I hadn't been the target, I probably would have laughed as hard as the three men. Dick's back was to me and he resumed still in the falsetto voice and with even more fluttering of eyelids, "Fran adds that...", but by that time Red had spied me in the hall and was making frantic pointing motions. Dick whirled around and without missing a beat continued, "Fran adds that she's a traitor and should have said that Van Dyke is her favorite television performer."

No matter how kind, good-natured, professional or well-intentioned an actor is, ego and top billing is all-important. Scratch a performer, and perhaps anyone in a creative endeavor, and you'll find an insecurity far beyond what you'll see in those who follow more mundane pursuits. An efficient CPA can usually find work, but a performer depends on public acceptance and sometimes a six-months-old baby has a longer attention span than the public's. The 'What Ever Happened To?' question haunts even the most gifted performer upon occasion. The thought that this adulation can't last turns many of them into monsters with a 'gather ye rosebuds (and dollars) while ye may' philosophy.

Though still somewhat ill at ease, I entered our office determined to hide my hurt feelings. "Gad, why do things sound so much worse in print...I don't remember making such sappy teenage groupie remarks." I put on a good face and laughed along with the men. "And Dick, you are my favorite performer, but Bob had specified someone on network...which you surely will be someday."

Dick fumbled with taking off the apron and wig, and the other three men remembered pressing duties elsewhere.

"At least Jack Webb will never hear all that southern gush," I said, putting a period to the incident. "If I'd gone on about *you* that way, Marge would have had my scalp for sure...consider yourself Lucky Pierre."

Dick looked as if he hadn't considered that angle. But his impromptu show was over, and we went on from there with our efforts to fill another daily hour with something amusing and sometimes thoughtful—and with as much community service as we could shoehorn in without losing our audience."

CHAPTER 23

AUNT SUE
AND THE CAT HOUSE

A day or so later, while going through a fresh snowfall of paper, I came across one of Colvin's invariably-marked 'Urgent' memos. "I wish with all my heart that Bill would give us more warning on the guests he books," I said to Dick who was hovering nearby. "Have you seen this?" I began to read aloud. "'Either of the following will guest on the *Music Shop* today, Wednesday September 9. Two stunt men—or a dog act. If the dog act shows, there will be several dogs involved.' I swan...there's a big difference between stunt men and a dog act!"

"Maybe not as much as you'd think," Dick commented. "I hope it's dogs 'cause I've got some good dog jokes. Have you heard the one about the dog that visited the flea circus and stole the show?"

I held my nose. "I think what you meant was you have some jokes that are dogs. Suppose it's the stunt men, got any for them?"

Dick said that offhand the nearest one that came to mind was an accident joke—about the man who was so unlucky he ran into accidents that started out happening to somebody else—but he wasn't sure that was a good one for stunt men.

I was still grumbling about Bill's thoughtless scheduling. "He knows we have the Humane Society on Wednesdays...if it's dogs instead of stunts, we'll be up to our kazoo in canines."

The Humane Society was one of our favorite community service projects. We both loved animals (with some notable exceptions), so not only were we giving time to something we believed in, we also benefited from the hard-to-beat audience pull of a basket full of newborn kittens or puppies.

My personal interest had been augmented by Aunt Sue's election to the Society's board, another addition to her list of causes. Peace said Aunt Sue might never tell me herself but she'd softened her hard line on my television career. When the Society's President, Mr. Yarborough, said he was delighted to meet television Fran's aunt, that was a new experience for her.

To further open her eyes, he showed her a copy of a letter of gratitude he'd recently sent to me.

Dear Fran,
During the last year, adoptions of dogs and cats from the Atlanta Humane Society reached a new high. The turnover in animals in our over-crowded Shelter has averaged five to six hundred a month, double from last year. Much of this stepped up placement is due to the appearance of the animals on your popular program....

Each week, the conscientious Mr. Yarborough sent me the name of the official spokesman who would arrive with the animals. Today in his letter, I noted the name, Mrs. Bowden, and hurriedly added it to our format. Getting ready for the show always made me think of Uncle Tom's Liza frantically crossing the ice floes. She had the hounds baying behind her, we had time nipping at our heels.

A half an hour before show time, Candy buzzed me from the reception desk to say our guests from the Humane Society were in the lobby as well as two men from the Kit Carson Wild West Show. Relieved to know we were to have stunt men, I turned their welcome over to Dick while I went to greet Mrs. Bowden.

Two minutes later, I went flying into the office, unstrung and babbling, "Oh my God...it's Aunt Sue...she's the Humane Society today. I can't stand it!"

Dick couldn't understand my attack of nerves. "Slow down there, you weren't in this bad a state when we had Helen Hayes."

"There's no time to explain. If I try to interview 'Mrs. Archibald Davis', I'll make a botch of it...my stutter'll come back. Dick, do it for me...pul-eez. I'll even throw in an extra Saturday."

"No can do...Martin already has me scheduled as part of the stunt men's act. You and Aunt What's-her-face will have to slug it out...why does an old aunt bother you anyway?"

Why indeed? Reverting to childhood, that's why. Now, mumbling to myself that I was a grown professional woman, I marched back out to explain procedure to Aunt What's-her-face. There she sat, hatted and gloved, with her ever-present chauffeur, Grant, standing beside her. He was holding a basket with five orange-and-white kittens.

Aunt Sue's hat-pulley-system had dropped an awe-inspiring creation onto her head this morning. It was one of Mrs. Frobisher's, the Lullwater Road milliner—a wide-brimmed beige felt covered with iridescent pheasant feathers. All those dead birds it took to make her hat didn't seem apt for a humane society interview, but, a minor point.

After I recovered my equilibrium and heard Aunt Sue's explanation for the substitution (Mrs. Bowden left town unexpectedly), I was delighted with the Board's choice. I knew she'd be an effective guest with her lifetime of club work and public speaking behind her—an opinion reinforced by the professional way she produced a list of topics to be discussed.

Candy said she'd escort Mrs. Davis to Studio A when the time came, and I left them chatting cozily. Candy could warm an igloo.

When the show finally began, everything was going smoothly. I unhooked the microphone from around my neck, in order to hold it up to Aunt Sue when it was her turn to speak, and I began her introduction. "Once again we have a representative from the Atlanta Humane Society, that wonderful organization that devotes so much time, money and compassion to the animals who can't speak for themselves. But one look at what Mrs. Davis has brought today, and I think you'll agree, they *can* speak...in their own way." The camera panned to the kittens at Aunt Sue's feet.

I continued my introduction. "Mrs. Davis is a newly-elected Board member and well-known for her civic work...I know our audience will want to hear why she decided to devote her time and energy to the Humane Society. Mrs. Davis....?"

I leaned over to hold the mike in front of her. Her mouth was working but no sound came out. The only expression on her face was terror, and the pheasant feathers on her hat were quivering so, I thought they might take off for a flight around the studio. As I'd never known Aunt Sue to be at a loss for several thousand words on any subject, I thought for one scary moment that she'd suffered a slight stroke.

Then, I realized the problem. This Waterloo of many an Atlanta corporate head was paralyzed with camera-fright. She'd never appeared on television before. As her symptoms cropped up often in our other guests, Dick and I knew how to recognize them. Even I had occasional minor attacks, no matter how accustomed I was becoming to having my every word and facial expression exposed to thousands of people whom I'd never met.

Diversion was the answer, so I said to the cameraman, "Red, the kittens are so lively now, maybe we'd better get another picture of them."

Good old alert Red quickly aimed his camera at the kittens while I shook Aunt Sue gently on the shoulder. "Listen, Aunt Sue, Dick's doing a commercial now, so you aren't on the air. Let's go over the questions again."

She relaxed, and when Red's camera back to us, she didn't realize it. After a minute, she'd forgotten her fears. She hadn't spent years wheedling and blackmailing the Atlanta patriarchy for charitable contributions for naught. Once she accepted the camera as yet another source of potential donors, she came through like a trouper.

I wound up the interview with this question. "Now, Aunt...er ...Mrs. Davis, let's talk about the Humane Society's future plans... any immediate goals in mind?"

She scooped up one of the calico kittens from the basket, held it toward the camera and announced with enthusiasm, "I'm so happy you asked that question. Our main goal this year is fundraising for a desperately needed new cat house."

After we concluded the interview, Aunt Sue stayed in the studio and watched the rest of the show. I was conscious of her critical eye until I noticed the pheasant feathers on her hat quivering again, this time from laughter at the foolishness during our program.

As soon as the cameras' red lights were off, Dick grabbed a hat from our costume pile and passed it around to the Swingbillies and the crew. "Okay, everybody, ante up...here's your chance. We all know the main thing Atlanta needs is a new cat house."

Dick collected forty-two dollars in the hat, and Aunt Sue received it with gracious thanks on behalf of the Society. On the way to the elevators, she patted me on the arm and said, "Fanny, that nice young man with you made a very generous gesture."

She stopped for a moment to ask Candy for an envelope to hold the cast's contribution and then she, and Grant with the kitten basket, walked onto the elevator.

Suddenly Aunt Sue put her hand on the elevator door to keep it from closing, and with a puzzled look on her face, said, "I've always prided myself on a good sense of humor, but for the life of me, Fran, I don't understand why everyone in the studio was laughing about such a serious subject."

We'd covered many subjects with much laughter, so I didn't understand what she meant. "What serious subject?"

"I don't see anything funny about all those poor little kitties needing a new cat house."

Grant's sudden coughing fit almost caused him to drop the kittens—and saved me from further discussion.

CHAPTER 24

OF MIMEOGRAPHS AND MOVIE STARS

The following morning I had a session with my *bete noire*, the mimeograph machine, a.k.a. the Purple People Eater. It was our Dramatic Players skits that forced me into an acquaintance with that forbidding piece of machinery, and we disliked each other intensely. On drama days, I had to use the darn thing because my typewriter couldn't handle the seven script copies we needed.

Memorizing a script was out of the question, but our forgiving audience didn't expect perfection from our informal, laid-back show. Furthermore, our lenient viewers didn't think it strange to hear excerpts from plays such as Noel Coward's *Blithe Spirit* or Shakespeare's *Julius Caesar* done in cornpone southern.

But back to the mimeograph machine. My prayer for our obsolete stencil duplicator to behave was unanswered that morning. The creature went berserk, wildly spraying me with purple ink and spewing paper all over the room. Now, when I visit a copy shop and insert a page of copy into a machine, press a button, and a clear, crisp copy comes out, I marvel. No more whirling rollers, no more messy passionate-purple ink pads, and no more stencils to prepare.

But this September morning in '53, I wrestled my *bete noire* to the floor and somehow gouged out seven copies of our script. We were doing an Old West skit in honor of our afternoon guest, western actor Bill Williams. (Bill was the husband of Barbara Hale, Perry Mason's Della Street, and later in the fifties, he starred in the *Zorro* series).

After my frustrating time spent in the copy room, I was riled enough to tackle our program director, Roger Van Duzer, on the subject of some secretarial help. On my way to his office, I bumped into him in the hall. "Roger, look at me...just look at me."

"You look okay...except what's that purple stuff all over your face?"

"Don't act as if you don't know...everybody who comes out of that copy room looks like they belong to some Hindu caste."

Roger said he'd never seen Melba, his secretary, look like that, and from now on, he'd ask her to run off my stencils.

"Oh, Roger, you're an angel...I'm so grateful."

"Anytime, Fran, anytime." He patted me reassuringly on the arm and continued down the hall, saying over his shoulder, "Only one condition, give Melba your stuff a couple of days ahead of time."

The bastard. That was the catch. He knew we never had anything ready until the last minute. Standing there with my purple face and black thoughts, I was steamed up enough to ask General Manager Carter's secretary, Louise, if I could see Carter about an important matter. It seemed I could.

"Fran, good to see you." Carter got up from behind his desk and shook my hand. "Great minds...as I was going to drop by your office later to tell you the good news...."

"Mr. Sever," I began, "the only good news I want today is that help is on its way."

Carter didn't seem to hear me and went right on to tell me his good news—Jack Webb, of *Dragnet* fame, was coming to Atlanta next week for a law-enforcement convention. Carter, a police buff, had heard it from Atlanta's Chief Jenkins.

"Jenkins says his friend at the Los Angeles Police Department reports Jack is available for a short interview on behalf of the Law Enforcement Association."

I was impressed. Atlanta in the fifties was not on the circuit for big-time celebrities' publicity jaunts. We usually snagged the ones in the middle, on the way up or down. Therefore, a star of Jack Webb's stature appearing on our show was a major coup. The original *Dragnet* series was the most innovative and successful police series in television history...and they did it with a minimum of car chases and violence. The program was given credit for helping to destroy the myth that policemen are dull-witted comedy foils for wise-cracking private eyes. The documentary-style narration of Joe Friday (Jack Webb) and the famous catch-phrases "My name's Friday—I'm a cop" or "just the facts, ma'am" became a part of the language of the day.

"You can show him that favorite-performer TV Digest article of yours," Carter teased.

I colored up and said, "I'll never hear the last of that lapse into school-girl syrup."

Carter assured me he admired Webb also, and his regard had risen even more after his recent tour of the Los Angeles Police Academy on a trip to the West Coast.

"The LAPD guys think he hung the moon—they have a regular shrine at the Academy...a glass case with a real Badge 714 in it...

photos, history of the show, the works. And he's donated a swimming pool and gym to the Academy."

The excitement of Jack Webb's proposed visit made me forget the original purpose of my visit to Carter—to plead for much-needed secretarial help. One thing about live television, everything moves so fast that by the time you have a handle on something, another something pushes it aside.

In spite of my attempt to appear unimpressed, I was star-struck. I grew up during the period before television, before "everyone is famous for fifteen minutes," Andy Warhol's quote. Movies and radio and theater shows were our entertainment, and to me, the movie and stage stars had a mystique lacking in the later television stars, who came into our living room gratis. Television made them seem more accessible, more familiar. But Jack Webb was in a class by himself.

I hurried back to our office, wanting to share the good news with Dick, and thinking it was too bad we didn't have more time to give Jack Webb's visit an impressive build up. We hadn't had anything this big since our male talking rat, Sir Cedric, birthed sextuplets on the show.

Before I could say anything, Dick waved one of Colvin's memos over his head. "Guess who we've got on the show next week?"

I made a quick decision not to one-ups-manship him and swallowed my reply that Carter had already told me.

"What's all that purple stuff on your face?" Dick didn't wait for an answer and began giving me hints. "Dum-de-Dum-Dum...this is the city, Los Angeles...I work here, I'm a...."

"Jack Webb," I squealed, and we both began to discuss plans.

Dick decided that for such an important occasion we shouldn't depend on our usual ad-libbing, but write a real script. We'd do a *Dragnet* take-off.

"What if he doesn't take kindly to funning about his show?" He looks like a serious fellow...oh, dear, I do hope his feet aren't made of Mississippi mud...the veneer has been pretty thin on some of those Hollywood types."

Dick grinned, "Yeah, remember Yvonne de Carlo?"

Yvonne de Carlo first starred in a Technicolor musical, *Salome Where She Danced* in 1945. During 1953 she starred in seven films and was in Atlanta on a promotion tour of *Sea Devils*, co-starring Rock Hudson. And the local RKO representative had booked her for a *Music Shop* appearance.

The dark haired, gray-blue-eyed Miss de Carlo, wearing an exquisitely cut white linen suit, looked every inch the glamorous star when her escorts, five RKO men, ushered her into our Studio

A. She cordially acknowledged all introductions and then asked when the interview was to begin. When she discovered that the minions had brought her to the station forty-five minutes early, she demonstrated that her 'spitfire' roles came somewhat naturally to her. She picked up the nearest projectile, a bowl of salad greens Sheila LeClaire intended to use on her cooking show, and saved Sheila the trouble of tossing it.

The RKO men solemnly picked iceberg lettuce leaves out of their hair and off of their suits while trailing behind Miss de Carlo as she stormed out the door. We had no idea if we would see the star and her retinue again. Much to our relief, she returned in time for the interview—and charmed us all. She made no reference to her previous appearance. Neither did we.

Even though that happened some weeks before, Dick didn't have to remind me of the incident.

On the following Thursday, Jack Webb arrived, accompanied by so many Atlanta policemen I hoped that major crimes in the city were on hold for the day. During the time Mr. Webb spent in Studio A, all station personnel found an excuse to peek in the door.

Dick and Randy of the Swingbillies, read the skit we'd worked up and I only had one line—the last one. But it was a *very* important line. Here, in its entirety, is the script we used..

SCRIPT: Fran gives the introduction: "In honor of our visiting star today, the Music Shop presents our version of a Dragnet episode—'Hairnet—the Mystery of Goldilocks and the Three Bears.' Dum-de-Dum-Dum."

Dick: My name's Friday, I'm a cop.

Randy: My name's Thursday, I'm a cop, too

Dick: My partner Thursday and I were working the night watch out of homicide. We'd just received a call that Papa Bear had been murdered. Thursday, do you know who the killer is?

Randy: No, but I brought in our chief suspect, Goldilocks. I talked with her for over an hour.

Dick: Does she know anything?

Randy: She does now.

Dick: I just found a body out in the street.

Randy: Good, you may keep it for your honesty.

Dick: But it was Goldilocks.

Randy: Goldilocks?

Dick: Yes, she was found wearing a derby and slacks.

Randy: At least, she died like a man.

Dick: Here's a hospital report on Father Bear. They performed an autopsy.

Randy: What'd he die from?

Dick:The autopsy.

(Telephone rings)

Dick: Hello, Homicide, Friday speaking. Oh, hi, Wednesday. Okay. (hangs up phone)...Mama Bear's been murdered too. She was pushed into the freezing vat at the popsicle factory...Let's go to the Bear's house and investigate.

Randy: So we climbed into the car and I got behind the wheel. I knew we were headed for trouble ... I can't drive. It was so foggy that I followed the white line on the road for ten miles before I found out I wasn't following a white line—it was a Good Humor truck with its vanilla leaking.

Dick: In here, Thursday, this is where the Bears live.

Randy: How do you know?

Dick: Look what's on the floor, a people-skin rug...and there's Baby Bear, he's been murdered.

Randy: The killer must still be here...the body's warm.

Dick: It oughtta be...it's on the stove. You'd better examine it for bullets and then check with ballistics.

Randy: What's ballistics?

Dick: I don't know, but they *always* say that on Dragnet.

Randy: No more clues here, let's search the barn...It's so dark in this barn, I can't see a thing.

Dick: Well, Thursday, hold my hand.

Randy: Okay, Friday...Hey Friday, Friday, where are you?

Dick: I'm over here.

Randy: Then whose fingers am I holding now?

Fran: Moo-o-o-o-o-o.

If Jack had any clay on his feet, he didn't expose it that day. One of the best interviews we ever had. Dick handled most of it and my only bad moment came when he mentioned that his blonde sidekick, Fran, in a recent TV Digest article, had chosen Jack as her favorite television performer. I was afraid he'd quote some of that slush, but nothing more was said.

At the close of the interview, Mr. Webb turned to me and asked if I had any unanswered questions. I restrained myself from asking him to give me a call should he ever leave his wife, and instead asked what was the primary advantage and disadvantage of doing a show based on actual police files.

He said, "The main advantage is that no matter how efficient the cops are, our writers will never run out of cases to dramatize because the crooks keep giving us new ones. The disadvantage is that it's a challenge to re-create a case in twenty-six minutes which the police have been working on for six months—or longer."

Jack also mentioned a movie, *Pete Kelly's Blues* due to begin production February. In it he would play a coronet player in a 1920's Dixieland band. Then he had to leave, and regretfully, I watched him go out the studio doors.

CHAPTER 25

MY BRIEF AFFAIR WITH JACK WEBB

That evening at the dinner table, I thought the subject of our celebrity guest, Jack Webb, would be interesting to everyone, including Claudine, Betty Sue, Gretchen and Sarah, our recently-acquired boarders. Peace enjoyed hearing about the adventures of my day and the people who visited the station so I began to describe the interview.

"Peace, Jack (I felt Jack and I were on a first-name buddy basis after today) has a gift of making you feel you're the one person in the world he wanted to meet...he's not tall...or conventionally good-looking but...."

"Peace," Claudine interrupted my tribute to Jack, "can you show me how to cut the pattern for my new blue material?"

Claudine Suggs was my least favorite of the four girls—a short chunky redhead with a face like a soup plate' and hands that looked more suited for holding a ball team's bat than an artist's brush. She came from Plains, a southwest Georgia wide space in the road nobody had ever heard of, but to hear her brag, Paris was a backwater village in comparison to Plains. The baby sister of three brothers, she was bossy and spoiled.

"I wouldn't have bought such expensive material if you hadn't promised to help," she scolded, ignoring my Arctic glance. "Can we start tonight...oh, Fran, were you saying something?"

"Well, Jack Webb...."

"Mother," Al said, "who's Jack Webb? Hey, look, Peace taught me to wiggle my ears today."

Al demonstrated his newly discovered talent for ear wiggling. Then the four girls asked Peace to teach them. Gretchen laughed so hard, she had to leave the table. I made a mental note on the possibility of an ear-wiggling contest on the *Music Shop*.

"Al," I said, giving him a hug, "you're a fast learner...it took Peace ages to teach me the right ear alone."

By then, I realized no one was particularly interested in my day with Jack Webb. His *Dragnet* series came on after Al's bedtime, and as far as Al and his second grade friends were concerned, all television came from the same black box. Dick and I were just as famous to them as Uncle Miltie Berle or Roy Rogers.

Gretchen recovered from her laughing fit and came back to the table. "Peace, after you do Claudine's dress, can you help me with my art history test?"

I gave up, and went into an old fashioned sulk. Our house was no longer ours. I detested sharing meals, bathrooms and living space with these interlopers...and more to the point, I resented sharing *my* mother. These twits were acting as if she were their mother.

Then, glancing over at Peace presiding over the long dining-room table, I began to notice a few things. Before the students had arrived, the three of us seldom ate in the main dining-room; instead we used either the breakfast nook off the kitchen or our big round kitchen table.

Until now, Peace had lost the habit of setting the table with nice things, but tonight the chandelier was again sparkling and the polished silver was placed on a starched white damask tablecloth, along with the flowered Limoges napkin rings, and a bouquet of yellow mums in Peace's treasured cut-glass bowl.

I grudgingly admitted to myself that meal time was more festive these days—and Peace had an animation to her which had been lacking for a long while. She said she'd always longed for a large family but people persisted in inconsiderately dying on her. I realized that this past September was the first time since Peggy's death that our mother hadn't lapsed into a blue funk around sister's September birthday time.

On the following morning, my office phone rang and John Whitney was on the line. He hadn't stayed mad with me over that absurd Tony Mann episode for long and I was happy about that. We chatted for a few minutes before I heard a suspicious click. I asked John to hold and I'd be back in a minute with some hot gossip. I quietly put the phone down, tiptoed out to the reception desk and stood behind Candy's chair.

Candy was so intent on listening in, she didn't see me until I leaned over and hissed in her ear. "Candy Higgins, if you ever eavesdrop on my calls again, I'm going to go up the side of your head with this whole switchboard...now cut it out, you hear?"

Candy heard.

John howled when I told him why I'd left and then said, "I've just learned I'm not working Saturday night, so let's do something special. How about dinner and the floor show at the Biltmore?"

"I accept with pleasure...Laurette and Clymas, the dancer team in the floor show, gave us a sample on our show this week and they are great."

Our destination for Saturday night, the Biltmore Hotel was for many years the largest and most elegant in town. it stood at the corner of West Peachtree and Sixth Streets, and boasted of its Empire Room which overlooked a garden filled with magnolias, azaleas, camellias and boxwood. There was even a terrace for dancing during the summer months.

That Saturday evening, my escort walked up the front steps of our house at exactly 7:30. Radio announcers tend to be prompt, an occupational trait.

Earlier in the evening Peace had gone to a friend's house for a bridge supper so she wasn't available to stay with Al. Neither was Cora Lee. Although she and husband Will lived close by in our garage apartment, her regular Saturday night choir practice was an engagement not to be broken for anything less than a death in the family...and we'd have to negotiate that one.

My sitter problem was finally solved by Betty Sue Darby, one of our boarders. A genuine "nice, quiet girl" from Savannah, Georgia, she volunteered to tuck Al in bed. Al had all four of our boarders under his thumb, and I hoped a recent article I'd read, that said a child couldn't have too much love, was true. I didn't want his new subjects to turn him into a rotten little despot.

On our short ride to the Biltmore, I warned John to be prepared to have me order a big dinner as the mere act of walking into the Empire Room gave me a ravenous appetite.

"Hum, I think the food's okay, but hardly good enough to send anyone's taste buds into rapturous abandon."

"No, it's not that, it's all those years of starving to death when I was modeling in fashion shows there."

We found that a balcony table had been reserved for us near the steps down to the dance floor. John asked me to dance and the discovery that he moved with an easy, natural grace and led with firmness pleased me. Fred Astaire and Ginger Rogers were my generation's dancing idols, and many a woman of my era fell in love with a man because he could dance well—not always the best of reasons.

As we began our dinner, the roast-beef special, I decided to give John a review of the Jack Webb interview. I was filling him in on the details when the maitre d' ushered four men to a table on the main floor just below our table on the balcony tier.

I leaned over to John and whispered, "Speak of the devil, John...look! I can't believe it...there he is. That's Jack Webb."

John looked down at the men. "Not such a surprise, this *is* the only decent hotel in town. Why don't you say hello to your good buddy Jack?"

"You know I wouldn't be that pushy...and I'm proud of the other diners...see, nobody's bothering him."

"Maybe everybody isn't as gooney about him as you are."

I shook my head. "I'm *not* gooney about him, but he really was so nice. He told Dick and me if either of us got to the West Coast to be sure to call his office."

John gave me a skeptical look. "Honey, I've been around entertainers a lot longer than you have, and one thing I've learned... don't take what they say too seriously."

I was listening with half an ear, wondering if it would be too gauche to give Jack a friendly wave if he happened to look up our way, when I saw him get up from his chair. My eyes followed him as he walked along the edge of the dance floor and up the balcony steps. He was heading directly for our table.

Reaching over, I grabbed John's hand. "John, he's coming over to speak...now I can introduce you."

"Thrill, thrill," muttered John, looking anything but thrilled.

By then, Jack Webb had reached our table. I was stretching out my hand with a big welcoming smile on my face when the familiar voice said, "Miss, don't scream...just get up slowly and turn around." Mystified, I followed his instructions.

The voice continued. "I think the back of your dress is on fire."

Jack and John sprang into action, both of them frantically flapping napkins on my smoldering fanny. As soon as Jack was satisfied they'd succeeded in saving me from becoming a Fran flambé, he explained how it happened.

"It was a piece of luck...I looked up at the same time a waiter was emptying ashtrays there." He pointed to a service trolley behind me. "He wasn't paying attention and a still-smoldering cigarette flipped into the back of your chair."

I craned my neck around to see a burnt hole the size of a silver dollar in my beautiful first-time-worn blue silk. I breathed a sign of relief that I wasn't wearing borrowed finery. Sheila had selected the dress especially for me at a Rich's sale. She may have been a false friend but she had a good eye for clothes.

"Oh, dear," I said, "no more dancing tonight."

"Okay, young lady, glad you're not hurt...it's a good thing that material wasn't as flammable as some."

My rescuer turned to leave but I put my hand on his elbow. "Jack, I can't thank you enough, you're a true life detective...and again, I want to tell you how much we enjoyed having you on our show."

Jack Webb's famous face showed no comprehension.

"You know, the *Music Shop*...day before yesterday...you were on our show." I pointed to myself. "I'm the blonde."

A flicker, but no great light turned on. "Oh yes, er, Anne wasn't it...well, glad you're all right."

Dum-de-Dum-Dum...just the facts, ma'am...and off he went.

The silence at our table was finally broken when I said, "You'll have to admit he's a good detective...nobody else noticed my dress was sending up smoke signals."

"He missed his calling," John said, "he should have been a fireman. And if he can't remember *you* from one day to the next, he's no detective."

I gave him a grateful glance. "My mother is the Cliché Queen of the South and right now is where she'd pull out the 'pride goeth before a fall' one."

John covered my hand and said the reason he didn't notice my dress was that he was having a small brush fire of his own that evening.

"Uh-oh," I said, "I think I'll wait until it's at least a barn burner...besides, didn't you just tell me not to take entertainers too seriously?"

John gave a good-natured shrug. "That's what I get for earning my living with words...never know when to shut up."

It was the Monday following my date with Big John that Aunt Sue made her habitual morning call to Peace. Mother was so busy these days, she'd managed to limit Aunt Sue's monologues to a mere ten minutes rather than the former half hour, and after she told me what they'd discussed, I wished she'd made it even shorter.

Topic number one had been Aunt Sue's debut on the *Music Shop*. It had caused such favorable comments from friends and strangers alike that the Humane Society suggested she be their regular spokesperson on a weekly basis.

A cold shudder went through me at the idea. A disembodied, disapproving Aunt Sue on a telephone line was far preferable to a live Aunt Sue at the studio each Wednesday. Dog acts and stunt men were easy, but an elderly strong-willed relative, who'd discovered she was a frustrated actress, was more than I could bear.

Roger, our program director, would have to explain to Mr. Yarborough of the Humane Society that having the same person on the show each week wasn't as effective as having different people. My mind was so occupied with composing an elaborate plea to Roger, I almost missed Topic Number Two.

"Oh, yes, and Aunt Sue wanted to know more about this radio fellow beau of yours and is it serious?" Peace had a questioning look of her own.

For a moment, I wondered if Aunt Sue had added clairvoyance to her other talents. Atlanta, a small town in many ways, was not *that* small. Peace swore she'd never mentioned him to her, so how had the old biddy learned of my evenings with John Whitney? I could have introduced Jack Webb to Aunt Sue as one great detective to another.

I might as well be living in Claudine's Plains, Georgia, where they probably had only one telephone operator—who would know every secret in town...except how to keep her mouth shut.

Telephone operator...only one operator...aha!. A vision flashed through my mind—Aunt Sue sitting in the station lobby last week cozily chatting with Candy. Candy, who's no better than my seven-year-old Al at keeping a confidence. I had warned her that someday somebody was going to whale the tar out of her.

Wait until I get my hands on that girl....

CHAPTER 26

A VARIETY OF PICKLES

"No, no, Mrs. Wynelle. I'm sorry but we have not found your watermelon pickles."

I held the phone away from my ear and let Mrs. Perry Wynelle (Gladys to her friends) of the Good Hope Homemakers' Club let off steam. Good Hope was a hundred miles from Atlanta but the long distance charges hadn't discouraged Mrs. Wynelle from calling me almost daily since her *Music Shop* appearance a week ago.

Our first *Music Shop* guest on behalf of the fair had been Ivan Allen, chairman of the Fair. During the interview, he stressed that this year's fair was the best ever and urged his fellow Atlantans to support it. A decade later, Ivan Allen was to become nationally known when he served as Atlanta's Mayor during the turbulent Sixties. Due to the farsightedness of both black and white community leaders, Atlanta was spared the violence which plagued many southern cities during the integration years.

In addition to Ivan, we'd interviewed the 4-H Livestock Scholarship winner; two contestants for Queen of the fair; and the holder of last year's blue-ribbon for flower arranging.

When Bill Colvin came into our office to tell us he'd scheduled another event, a pickle-making demonstration, I balked.

"Bill, flower arranging is one thing, but we don't do cooking demos on the *Music Shop*—that's Sheila's shopping show turf."

"You don't know what a bonanza I'm giving you...the pickle competition is the biggest fight since Tunney knocked out Dempsey."

"What do they do, throw pickles at each other? Hm-m-m... maybe it'll fit into our show after all."

"Be serious, Fran, this is the tie-breaking year and there's a lot of money involved." Bill went on to explain that for the past four years, representatives from two Georgia Homemakers Clubs, Mrs. Wynelle of Good Hope, and Mrs. Perlis of Valorette, batted the blue ribbon and a considerable cash prize back and forth and that both were bent on breaking the tie this year.

"At first they were dead set against the idea—but I syruped them up enough to turn their sour pickles sweet."

I gave a yawn. "Bill, I still don't get it, what's the point?"

"Don't you see," Bill said, with exasperation at my lack of appreciation, "they'll make the *actual* pickles they're entering in the contest right here on camera...it's great publicity—for them and the fair."

Dick didn't share Bill's pickle enthusiasm any more than I did. "Fran, the pickle-pussies are all yours...the only pickles I care about come with a ham on rye, hold the mayo."

On the day of the demonstration, Good Hope's delegate, Mrs. Wynelle, a billowy pudding of a woman wearing a raisin-purple felt hat, arrived first. I installed her at one end of the spacious studio kitchen usually used by Sheila. When Mrs. Perlis of Valorette appeared a few minutes later, I settled her at another counter as far away from Mrs. Wynelle as possible.

No introductions were necessary as the two women knew each other well from the pickle, jelly and preserve arena of previous fairs. They exchanged polite but cool greetings. If it had been a wrestling match, my money would be on Mrs. Perlis, a banjo-eyed woman who looked as if she could toss several watermelons over her shoulder with ease.

After the women unpacked their baskets, I explained that I'd talk with each of them intermittently throughout the program to check on their step-by-step progress. In this way, the homemakers in our audience could follow the recipes of the competing champions.

At this suggestion, the mulish looks on both the women's faces made me realize things were not going to go smoothly. Prize-winning pickle making has more secrets than the CIA and neither Mrs. Wynelle nor Mrs. Perlis had the slightest intention of sharing the touch that made hers different from her neighbor's.

Like so many times on the *Music Shop*, I slid around the problem instead of meeting it head on. Rather than dwelling solely on the subject of pickle making, I said, "Mrs. Wynelle, I know the Homemakers' Clubs deal with a wide range of homemaking skills. While you're cutting up those watermelon rinds, perhaps you'll tell us about some of their other activities."

Mrs. Wynelle was happy to do so. "Last month we gave our bake sale which made enough to buy new outdoor furniture for the Good Hope Convalescent Hospital."

Next I was able to get her to repeat her sure-fire recipe for Fresh Mountain Apple Cake, but any poor soul who expected to learn how to make watermelon pickles that day was out of luck.

As another divisionary tactic, I asked our audience to send in their favorite pickle or preserve recipe. The winner we chose would receive the *Music Shop*'s Blue Ribbon, plus a Broil-King Broiler.

The show turned out to be even more confusing than usual that day. We had scheduled more guests than we could comfortably handle, plus we were doing a first-time-tried pantomime of the Johnny Mercer-Margaret Whiting recording of "Baby, It's Cold Outside."

Grateful when the show was finally over, I thanked the two pickle ladies for their appearance and some of the staff and I helped pack up their equipment and utensils. Walking with them to the elevator, I wished them both the best of luck, waved good-by, and promised to come to the fair.

I had absolutely no more thoughts of pickles until Mrs. Wynelle's first frantic call from Good Hope the next morning. Somewhere, somehow, during all the excitement, she'd lost her jar of prize pickles. The last time she remembered seeing the jar, it was sitting on the studio kitchen counter before some staff members and I began packing her basket.

"Hold the phone, Mrs. Wynelle," I told her, "I'll go check." I headed for Studio A, humming Ella Fitzgerald's "A-Tisket, A-Tasket, I Lost My Yellow Basket." Since the studio had been in constant use, I wasn't surprised when I couldn't find her jar of pickles. Lamar Gene Skiles, our prop man who had helped pack Mrs. Wynelle's basket after the show, had no recollection of what he'd put in it.

I went back to the phone. "Mrs. Wynelle, I'm sorry, no luck. If it turns up, I'll surely let you know. In the meantime, why don't you whip up another batch?"

Mrs. Wynelle told me she'd made a gentleman's agreement with Mrs. Perlis that the pickles prepared on the *Music Shop* would be the exact same ones entered in the fair. The Fair-A-Ganza was publicizing the competition with that understanding. "And besides," she wailed, "a new jar wouldn't be mature enough."

"Oh, yes," I agreed, trying to appear knowledgeable though I hadn't the slightest idea what she was talking about, "that, too, is to be considered."

That evening when I pulled into the driveway, Peace and Al were in the backyard. Peace was cutting the few zinnias still left in the garden for a centerpiece, and Al was helping her by picking off any mildewed foliage.

Mother enjoyed planning meals, arranging flowers, and creating a homelike atmosphere for her newly-adopted daughters, her boarders. She loved having the house full of young people. Her experiment with the art-student paying guests had brought back the welcome sight of her dimples, and for that reason, I was becoming more reconciled to the idea of strangers in our house.

While Peace snipped away, she asked, "How was your day?"

"A real pickle, I'll tell you about it at dinner."

Al gave me a hug, stuck a red zinnia behind my ear, and asked why leaves got yucky at the end of summer but flowers didn't. Peace said, "Ask your mother." I said, "Ask Peace."

Al looked at us in disgust. "I'll ask Cora Lee, she knows everythin'." Since I agreed with Al's statement, I followed him into the house to consult with our authority. Whatever explanation she gave him on the subject of mildewed zinnia leaves seemed to satisfy him, and I tackled her next on the pickle subject.

"Cora Lee, you used to make the best green-tomato pickles when we lived at Crape Myrtle Farm. Did you have a secret recipe?"

"No, Miss Fanny, Miz Peace reads a recipe from the cookbook and I follows...mebbe I puts a little something extra."

"There," I said triumphantly, "you did have a secret recipe."

"'Twarn't no secret...nobody ever asks me and now I disremembers."

But she did clear up my ignorance on what 'mature' meant in the pickle and relish world...same thing it means with anything else—aging. The longer pickles age, the better they taste, so no wonder Mrs. Wynelle didn't want to give Mrs. Perlis an edge by having to make a new batch.

At the dinner table, the adventures of the pickle ladies as a topic of conversation was far more successful with our art student boarders than Jack Webb had been.

Sarah Dent said, "My mother makes the best bread-and-butter pickles in Eufala...or the whole state of Alabama for that matter."

"Sometimes, you can make big money with recipes," Claudine claimed. "Back home, Mrs. Tuttle sold her apple chutney recipe to the Heinz Company for thousands of dollars." Her comment made the seriousness with which my two pickle ladies took the fair's competition much more understandable to me.

Peace held up her hand for silence, announcing she had a pickle story of her own. She was a born story teller which the art students had quickly discovered and always enjoyed.

"Once upon a time," she began, "when Al was about three-years-old, his mother and I took him to Daytona Beach. On Sunday we decided to change our bathing suits for something suitable for church and then lunch at the elegant Clarendon Hotel."

Al, who liked her stories best when his name was mentioned, now looked around the table and said importantly, "Oh, I 'member that."

Peace smiled and went on. "During lunch, a nice-looking young waiter came to our table carrying a large tray with several dishes of pickles and relishes on it. I pointed at some pickles and asked him what they were called. He stared down at the tray for a long while, then shook his head. 'I'm sorry ma'am, I don't know... you see, I'm just the substitute pickle passer.'"

Peace said she often wondered if he'd climbed the ladder of success to eventually become the head pickle passer. Also, the boy's answer had so tickled Peace that she taught Al to say "substootoot pickle passer' whenever well-meaning people asked the child what he wanted to be when he grew up.

CHAPTER 27

PHOTOGRAPHS AND PICKLE PROBLEMS

It was the same evening we heard Peace's pickle story that Betty Sue during a conversational lull, hesitantly said, "You'll all be glad to know I finally made a date to pose for a Pop Summers' photograph."

In spite of Betty Sue Darby's gift as an artist, her timidity and lack of self-confidence made us all try to bring her out of her shell. She was the only offspring of elderly parents, who'd lost hope for a child until her arrival surprised them. I doubt she'd ever been out of their sight before she arrived on our doorstep in the fall of '53.

The Darbys had reluctantly given in to Betty Sue's pleas to enroll in Atlanta's High Museum school. She attempted to comfort them with the fact that Atlanta was a scant 250 miles from the coastal city of Savannah. Another favorable factor was the school principal's assurance that he would place their precious child in the care of an eminently respectable widow nearby. The Darbys' capitulation was complete after Aunt Sue wrote them a testimonial to her niece's impeccable character on her 'President of the Georgia Federation of Women's Clubs' stationery.

For the first week or so after Betty Sue arrived, she spoke so seldom the other girls assumed she was a stuck-up snob from Savannah until the night a mouse in her bedroom frightened her into running to Claudine's room. By the time Cora Lee trapped the critter, Claudine and the other girls realized Betty Sue suffered from shyness, not snobbery.

Due to the combined good-humored teasing and camaraderie from the other students, and to Peace's warmth, Betty Sue began blossoming out, and the news that she'd overcome her bashfulness enough to pose for a Pop Summers' photographic session was proof of how far she'd come.

The other girls already had a handsome collection of free photographic portraits from Pop. It was Gretchen Rosser, our North Carolina boarder, who took credit for finding Pop Summers, and she kept a proprietary interest in him.

"Hooray for you," she congratulated Betty Sue. "Pop took a lot more of me last week. He says I'm his favorite model because I remind him of some old-time movie star he was crazy about...Colleen Moore."

Claudine asked, "Who's she?"

"I'll never forget her in *Lilac Time* with Gary Cooper," Peace said, "I cried buckets. She was one of the most popular stars in the '20s and '30s...she wore her hair in a Dutch bob with bangs like Gretchen's."

Claudine turned to Gretchen. "You cut your bangs so short last time, you looked more like Moe in the Three Stooges than any Colleen Moore...and I'll bet she didn't have to peroxide her mustache."

Gretchen's hand immediately flew to cover her mouth. She was a lively, talkative brunette, who did slightly resemble the famous silent-film star. Her only physical defect, if you could call it that, was an unusually hirsute upper lip.

Trust Claudine to zero in on the one thing a body was sensitive about. Maybe living with too many brothers had encouraged her mean streak. Before I could think of a zinger for Claudine, Peace said, "Gretchen, how'd you come up with such a treasure as Pop? Portraits are so expensive...you girls are lucky to get all those beauties for free."

"He's in my photography class...at first, I thought he was some old geezer trying to get fresh when he asked if I'd walk around to his apartment on Lombardy Way to pose for him."

Later, however, she had learned that Veasy Summers (he preferred to be called Pop) was a harmless, recently widowed, lonely old man who'd known Peace's Lombardy Street neighbor, Marie Liede, for many years. When he retired from the post office, he'd signed up for the Museum school's photography course.

Gretchen had decided there was no harm in posing for him, and when we saw her beautiful photographs, we all wanted to pose for Pop. He wasn't the equal of his heroes, Alfred Stieglitz and Edward Steichen, but he was so professional we wondered why he was taking the Museum course.

Gretchen asked Betty Sue what she planned to wear for the photographs. "Gee, I don't know, white's supposed to be good in pictures, but I didn't bring anything white with me."

It was my chance to help. "I know what, Betty Sue, I have a long, white, ruffled, off-the-shoulder bridesmaid's dress stuck in the back of my closet...you'd look like a Dresden shepherdess in it."

Betty Sue accepted my offer with gratitude and said she was beginning to look forward to her session with Pop.

The next morning I suffered through another of Mrs. Wynelle's increasingly unwelcome calls regarding her, so far, unsuccessful pickle hunt. I'd no sooner hung up when Candy buzzed to say that Peace was on the line. Peace so seldom called me at work that my first thought was of Al. At once she dispelled my fears by saying, "Frances, don't worry, both Al and I are all right...but I've had some terrible news...and I don't know what to do about it."

"What is it, Peace, did somebody die?"

"No, no, nothing like that. It's Betty Sue...oh dear."Peace began to cry over the phone.

"Betty Sue? Is she sick, an accident, or what?...Peace, quit crying." I tapped the mouthpiece of the phone with my knuckle. "I can't help if I don't know what's wrong."

"Betty Sue called me from the city jail," moaned Peace.

"Well, that's nothing to go to pieces over, her art classes go on location all over...probably doing some nitty-gritty Hogarth-type scenes."

"Frances, she's not *at* the jail...she's *in* the jail."

I told her that was ridiculous and there must be some mistake. Peace finally pulled herself together long enough to tell me what happened, or as much as she knew. Betty Sue, who had left the house at eight in the morning to go to Pop's photo session, had been wearing saddle shoes, a blue and white striped cotton dress, and a daisy-print scarf over her head to hide her hair curlers. Because of the drizzle, she feared her hair would lose its curl by photo time. Peace said she'd made Betty Sue go back upstairs for a raincoat.

A few minutes past eleven, when Peace answered the phone, it was Betty Sue calling from the Decatur Street jail. As Mother understood the story, in between the girl's sobs, it seemed that two policemen came to Pop's apartment while he was readying his camera and lighting equipment. They said they had a warrant for Pop's arrest, and when they saw Betty Sue coming out of the bedroom where she'd just changed into my white bridesmaid's dress, they said the little lady had better come along with them, too.

"And Frances, the police didn't even give her time to change back to her school clothes." Peace sounded more upset by that than the fact that Betty Sue was in jail. "Just told her to grab her coat and purse."

"Mother, that's the least of our worries...the main thing is to get a lawyer...you'd better call her parents."

"No, no, that's the first thing she told me...she doesn't want them to know. I don't either...they'll surely think I haven't taken good care of the child."

"Call Aunt Sue, Uncle Archie was a judge, she knows tons of lawyers."

Peace's silence clued me that she wasn't crazy about that suggestion. "That's a last resort, she already thinks we're unstable. How about that lawyer you used to date, Philip Raine?"

"Mother, he's a corporation lawyer, I doubt he even knows where the city jail is...don't worry, I'll find somebody."

I hung up the phone, but in spite of my confident assurance to Peace, I sat there a minute with no idea how to proceed. We'd had little experience with this type of thing. Where was Jack Webb when I needed him?

The thought of Jack Webb gave me an inspiration. Carter, our station manager, had friends on the Atlanta police force. He could find out the charge against Betty Sue and what to do to get her out. I hurried next door to ask his secretary if I could see him for a minute.

Louise said, "Gee, Fran, you just missed him. He went to Gainesville for a Georgia Poultry Association lunch."

After that disappointing news, I had to think of something else. Haunted by the vision of our nice quiet Betty Sue sitting in the Decatur Street jail, I grasped at straws. First I'd call John Whitney and if I couldn't reach him, I'd try Philip Raine. One of them might know of a lawyer who specialized in rescuing innocent Savannah maidens.

John was on the air but Suzanne at the WQST switchboard put me on hold until his first break. At the end of our disjointed conversation, interrupted by John's in-between-records chatter, he said, "Fran, the main message of your garbled story is that you need a lawyer pronto to get Miss Savannah out of the pokey."

"Right, then we'll go from there."

"Okay, I'll call my ex-wife's baby brother, Warren Daniels. He's fresh out of law school but can find his way into the jail...I'm not sure he'll find his way out, but he passed the bar exams so he must know *some* basics."

I hung up and decided John was looking more and more like my white knight. Shortly after that, he called to say Warren was on his way to the jail. When I relayed the message to Peace, she was relieved but still said, "I won't draw an easy breath 'til Betty Sue gets home."

Between my lost morning looking for lawyers, and Dick's absence filming a commercial in Buckhead, we had to run hard to get the show together by four o'clock. I called home, just before leaving the office around six, and asked Peace if Betty Sue had returned. Peace said. "No, but she and Warren are on their way."

No sooner than I came in our back door, Betty Sue and Warren came up Thirty Three's front steps. Our delicate-looking art student was one sad-looking white dove, still wearing the now wet and grimy bridesmaid's dress, its torn hem trailing below her raincoat. Shared feminine vanity made me pleased she'd at least been able to remove the hair curlers before her trip to jail.

Peace invited Warren to stay for dinner and the young lawyer accepted with alacrity. Betty Sue ran upstairs to change and when she returned, the now radiant girl didn't look anything like the same bedraggled creature we'd seen before.

At the dinner table, none of us could wait to hear Betty Sue's story. The most timorous of the four girls was now a heroine— Queen of the Big House. None of us had ever seen the inside of a jail. Even old mammoth-mouth Claudine interrupted with only an occasional "and then what happened?" during Betty Sue's recital. Warren corroborated her story from the time he entered the scene.

Today's episode actually had its beginning some months ago. Pop and his wife had been tenants of a Lombardy Way apartment for many years, and shortly before Mrs. Summers had died, the couple signed a five-year lease.

Mrs. Berenice Posey, their land lady, had been happy to have such decorous, prompt-paying tenants all those years so it came as a shock to Pop when Mrs. Posey asked him to vacate. She told him times had changed and she could get twice the amount he was paying, a sum beyond his means. He reminded her of his signed lease and thought the subject closed.

Listening to Betty Sue's story, the suspicion crossed my mind that the real reason behind the land lady's out-of-the-blue ultimatum stemmed from all those casseroles she'd probably made for the bereaved widower. Instead of looking to her for consolation, the old fool had signed up for a photography course at that den of orgies and artists, the High Museum of Art, resulting in a gaggle of giggling young girls running in and out of his apartment.

If Pop had liked macaroni and cheese better, probably none of this would have happened. He didn't, so his land lady had her idea on how to break his lease. She swore out a warrant for his arrest on the grounds that he was using her property for immoral purposes—taking pornographic photos.

Poor Betty Sue was just in the wrong place at the wrong time when the police knocked on Pop's door. Swept up in the dragnet, she spent the day, bewildered and disoriented, in the bull pen with a dozen other women, none of whom the Savannah Darbys would have considered suitable companions for their only child.

"Pop was somewhere else in the jail and I knew he wasn't in any better fix than I was," Betty Sue said. "The only person I could think of to call was Peace."

"And quite right you were, dear."

Warren was seated next to Mother at the dinner table, and when Betty Sue stopped for breath, he turned to Peace. "Mrs. Peace, after I sprung Ma Barker here from the slammer," and he looked at Betty Sue with an un-lawyer-like twinkle in his gray eyes, "guess what she said...said I'd have to get Pop released, too, before she'd leave. So as of today, I have two new clients."

Before the police would release his clients, they had to wait until the roll of film in Pop's camera came back from the darkroom. A search of the apartment had yielded nothing more titillating than a few movie-magazine-type cheesecake photos. So the police had confiscated the film to see if it substantiated Mrs. Posey's charge.

"When the photos came back," Warren said, "everybody was hanging around waiting to get a look at something juicy...if I hadn't been so danged mad, it would have been funny to see that roomful of embarrassed cops. Betty Sue, tell 'em what was on the film."

Betty Sue blushed and looked uncomfortable at being the center of so much attention. "Pop was working on a class experiment, the best lighting for dark objects...the whole role of film was one picture after another of a black telephone."

"Even Mrs. Posey couldn't make a vice ring out of a telephone ring," Peace joked.

Then Warren said, "Betty Sue, you and Pop have a good case against both the city and Mrs. Posey for false arrest...I'd be happy to take the case."

"Oh, no, Warren," Betty Sue blanched. "Then my parents would know... I'd be back in Savannah in a minute...and never get back to Atlanta."

Warren retracted the idea hastily. "Well, maybe not. Still, I think we ought to discuss the matter over dinner Saturday. What do you say?"

Betty Sue hesitated and glanced at Peace who was nodding her head in a 'yes' motion. "Okay, we can talk about it...but that's all."

During the conversation, Cora Lee had been in and out of the room and hadn't missed much. She'd made Betty Sue's favorite banana cream pudding for dessert and when she brought it in, she said, "I'm 'bout the onliest person here who knows what sufferin' Miss Betty Sue has today...that Decatur Street jail is the nearest thing to hell they is. I never been 'carcerated myself, but I leaves Mr. Williams, my second husband, 'cause he spent too much time there."

Al was right when he said that Cora Lee knew everything.

So Betty Sue survived her day as a guest of the Atlanta jail, and if the eager way she ran to the phone when someone hollered,

"Betty Sue, it's Warren again," was any indication, she must have thought the trip downtown was well worth it.

She may have been happy to get calls from Warren, but I was weary of long-distance calls from Good Hope. I'd long since renamed it Lost Hope, Georgia.

The day before the Fair-A-Ganza was to open, I groaned aloud when Candy told me she had Mrs. Wynelle on the line. I wanted to tell Candy I was out, but I took the call.

"Fran, I'm sorry to bother you again but I couldn't wait to tell you the good news...I found my jar of watermelon pickles."

For the first time since our conversations had begun, I could be sincere. "That's wonderful, Gladys...I'm happy for you...and glad we didn't lose the pickles here. Where were they?"

"Under the car seat. Can you imagine? I must have looked there a hundred times...they were wedged in so far back, I missed them." She chattered on and on.

Finally I said, "Gladys, our director just told me I'm needed in the studio...I've got to ring off."

She paid no attention and said, "I'm *so* relieved. Now I can enter the contest fair and square. Wish me luck, Fran, I just know...." I haven't any idea what she knew as I had gently put the phone back on its hook. Enough was enough.

I thought both the porno and pickle cases had come to a satisfactory conclusion until a day or so later a heading in the *Atlanta Constitution* caught my eye: "No Peace Preserved Between Pickle People."

According to the article, Mrs. Wynelle of Good Hope had broken the tie this year, walking off with the blue ribbon and a cash prize of five thousand dollars. Mrs. Perlis of Valorette was calling foul. "The whole thing is pretty upsetting and not up to the Homemakers' Clubs standards," Mrs. Perlis said yesterday. "Mrs. Wynelle and I agreed to use the pickles we made on the *Music Shop* television program—even though it gave them only five weeks maturation time. Our Valorette Homemaker's club could have also switched our entry for a more mature one, but we were honest."

The article went on to quote Mrs. Wynelle of Good Hope as saying both pickles entries were the same age and it sounded like sour grapes on the part of Mrs. Perlis.

Was there no end to be no end to the pickle puzzle?

The article struck me as funny, so I asked Dick, "Do you remember the pickle ladies from the fair a few weeks ago?"

"Sure, what about 'em?"

"One of them won the blue ribbon and the other accused her of cheating."

Dick wrinkled his nose in distaste. "All I can say is that the judges wouldn't have given the jar they left here anything but the raspberry."

It hadn't occurred to me to tell Dick about Mrs. Wynelle's pickle hunt. We had no time to tell each other of every detail of our shows. Fans constantly gave us such gifts as homemade cakes, cookies, jellies and even cross-stitched tea towels, so when Dick saw a jar of pickles on a counter after the studio cleared of people, he innocently assumed it was a token of appreciation. He took it home to his wife, Marge.

"How can you say those pickles wouldn't have won?" I asked him.

"'Cause when Marge opened them for Sunday dinner, they looked moldy. She threw them away."

"I wonder what went wrong with 'em?"

"I know from nothing about pickle making," Dick said. "Maybe the jar stayed too long in our hot germy studio."

"Or maybe it wasn't sealed tight. When I go home, I'll ask Cora Lee. She's my pickle authority."

The newspaper article reminded me of Peace's story about the waiter who was a substitute pickle passer. I examined my conscience for half a second and then decided it wasn't my duty to blow the whistle on Gladys Wynelle, *another* substitute pickle passer.

CHAPTER 28

COUNTERIRRITANTS

"Mother, why're you hitting your head on the 'figerator door? That looks silly." Al, seven at that time, was standing in the doorway of our kitchen.

On this October morning, the events of the previous month involving my two detectives, Jack Webb and Aunt Sue; the pickle puzzle; and then Betty Sue's day in jail, were all fartherest from my mind. Rhythmically and gently, I was thumping my head against the refrigerator door.

"Honey, it's a good counterirritant."

"What's a count...count...what you just said?"

"A counterirritant is something which bothers you as much or more than something that's already bothering you."

He still looked perplexed.

"For example, you're getting over the measles now, right? Well, when you were having the measles itch, if you'd broken your arm, God forbid, that would have taken your mind off the itch. Understand?"

"But Mother, you don't have the measles...so why're you hitting your head on the 'figerator?"

I sighed. "Al, it's too complicated...go practice that piano piece Aunt Georgia gave you, 'The Happy Farmer.' You can call it 'The Happy Counterirritant.'"

After asking me when his grandmother Peace was coming home, he finally left me alone. I decided to stop addling my brains and go back to my task of preparing breakfast trays for our two patients upstairs. Al was feeling so much better he didn't need to eat in bed this morning, and I was filling in for Cora Lee as she deserved a day of rest after a hard week of nursing.

When the doorbell rang three times, the mailman's signal that he had something important to deliver, I hurried to open the door. A smiling Mr. Barnes handed me a post card.

"Miss Fran, you finally heard from your ma...I knew you were anxious. They're having a grand time in spite of the Florida freeze and she wants to know why you haven't written."

"Thanks, Mr. B., but if I told her how things are going here, it would spoil her vacation."

Some time ago, Peace's good friend, Maude Elbert, had invited Peace to drive with her to Palm Beach and spend a couple of weeks at her cottage there. This was too good an offer for Peace to miss. She hadn't had a break in a long while, and Cora, the girls and I convinced her to accept.

On departure day, Maude arrived early in the morning. We all gathered, shivering, on the front porch for the send-off. Bare trees and hoarfrost on the grass inspired many wishes that we could tag along with Peace to the land of palm trees and warm weather. No sooner had she given the last wave, when our weather-beaten Noah's Ark sprung its first leak. A portent of things to come.

On the way back into the house, Cora Lee said, "Miss Fanny, Al didn't touch his breakfas' this mawnin'."

I dismissed her concern. "He's probably just upset about Peace leaving town." But when I came home that evening, Al greeted me with the news that he had poison ivy. He'd caught a bad case of it last summer at YMCA camp, but late October isn't poison ivy season.

I felt his forehead. "Al, you have a fever, I'd better call Dr. Cathcart."

What Al had was measles. Dr. Cathcart left, with instructions for me to keep Al quiet and in a darkened room in order to protect his eyes. That treatment hadn't changed since *my* childhood. Cora Lee and the art students combined efforts to keep Al amused, and I worked at home as much as possible.

Al had a light case and the crisis passed quickly. Things were simmering down to normal when Claudine remembered she'd never had measles, so she proceeded to have them—which meant trays for her breakfast, lunch and dinner.

At least she didn't have to be constantly amused. Sympathetic Betty Sue, having had the measles, spent a great deal of time in Claudine's room trying to alleviate the invalid's boredom. And when Claudine's mother sent curtains from Claudine's bedroom in Plains, Georgia, thinking to make her feel more at home in Atlanta, Betty Sue offered to hang them for her.

It was a thoughtful gesture but more thought on the proper modus operandi for hanging curtains would have saved everyone a lot of grief—especially Betty Sue. She learned a rickety chair plus two suitcases does not a ladder make, and ended up in the twin bed beside Claudine—her broken leg in a cast. The tray count went up to *three* for breakfast, lunch and dinner, but with Al on the mend, we very soon dropped back to two trays for our temporary infirmary.

So that's where matters stood this Saturday morning in October. Having fed the girls, I had a breather until lunch time and decided to work on my first "schlock" commercial. The dictionary says the word is derived from the Yiddish noun, *schlag*, meaning *blow*, and is slang for cheap, inferior merchandise. TV time salesmen used the term for a long fifteen minute or more carny-type commercial effective in selling such items as gimmicky kitchen gadgets, steak knives, and sure-fire hair restorers. Schlock is still on television, but now stations run several shorter ads together, rather than one long pitch covering the same items.

Male announcers handled those commercials, and until now, I considered fifteen minutes of non-stop fast patter beyond my capabilities. Martha Lord, the station's only sales woman, thought otherwise. Citing Betty Furness's outstanding on-the-air success since '49 pitching the merits of Westinghouse refrigerators, Martha had sold a food-freezer company on the idea of a woman doing their midway barker-type commercials.

My refusal to tackle such a challenge held until she said, "Have you any idea what the Glacier Freezer Company will pay you for a series of schlock's?"

After she named the figure, I said with astonishment, "You're kidding! No wonder the men fight over them." Mentally, I added to Al's college fund and put a down-payment on a new car.

Martha had handed me the company's brochure. "Here, take this home...write it up in your own words...more natural that way. We'll begin the first one next Wednesday before the six o'clock news."

After making myself comfortable at our kitchen table, I carefully read the brochure. I was relieved the offer didn't sound like a complete snake-oil scam and began to work up some enthusiasm for the product. The company offered to include, with each freezer sold, a full supply of frozen foods as well as fifty-two prime steaks, one for each week of the year.

I was writing down all the reasons why our family couldn't wait another minute to own a six-foot long, three-foot deep freezer chest when Al came back into the kitchen.

"Mother, I practiced, now can I go outdoors?"

"'May I,' but in this case, maybe 'can' is right because you've been sick."

He'd been cooped up so long I relented, helped him with his coat, and watched him scamper happily out the back door. Five minutes later, however, he was back. "Mother, I need my rubber boots."

"Al, whatever for? The sun's shining...and you don't like to wear them even in the rain."

"I need my boots to play in the lake...the one in the front yard."

Never having had a lake in the yard before, I thought it best to investigate. Cora Lee, coming in the door as I was going out, joined me.

Al was right. A well bubbling up in the middle of the yard had created a half-foot deep lake over our entire lawn. Floating in Ansley Park's newest scenic wonder were apple peelings, toilet paper, and various other unattractive articles which delicacy prompts me not to enumerate.

"Miss Fanny, "Cora Lee said, "where's that watah comin' from?"

I called Vern's Tenth Street Plumbers. Mr. Vern answered my call for help immediately. The short, wizened man, armed with a wrench, was soon standing beside me on our porch watching the steadily rising water.

After weighty consideration, head shaking, and the pulling of his nose, he reached a conclusion. "Little lady, you got a real problem here."

I was all too aware of that. I could see it and I could smell it. I stifled an observation to that effect and waited for Mr. Vern's solution.

"Yes-siree bobtail, little lady, this ain't no one-man operation...I'm gonna need helpers and equipment."

This little lady was feeling more like a Lilliputian by the minute, but the water was rising so fast I agreed with him. One puny man armed with a wrench was totally inadequate to tackle a lake far more worthy of the U. S. Army Corps of Engineers.

Mr. Vern left for reinforcements, and Cora Lee and I retreated to the kitchen. She began talking to herself and disappeared into the walk-in closet which held our canned goods. In times of stress, which were frequent at 33 Fifteenth Street, Cora Lee often used the canned goods' closet as her own personal praying chapel. I thought she had a better pipeline to the Lord than I did so I didn't disturb her. Presently she reappeared with her arms loaded with canned goods.

"Cora Lee, what are you doing?"

"Miss Fanny, that watah's rising so fast, it make me swimmy-headed. Mebbe we oughter take some food upstairs."

I laughed. "Cora Lee, we're not going to have a flood. At least I hope not, we'd never get Betty Sue out of the house with her cast."

Shouts coming from the front yard indicated Mr. Vern was back. We returned to our post on the front porch and watched as he and his army from Plumbers Union Local 404 sloshed around the yard. After circling the lawn a few times, the men met in the middle for a conference—then repeated the process. I was reminded of the "Pool of Tears" in *Alice in Wonderland* where the water kept rising higher and higher as the animals went round and round in circles.

At last Mr. Vern puffed up the front steps and got down to business. "Little lady," he began, (I winced at his use of that term again but refrained from pushing him off the porch), "you got a major problem...a busted main sewer, only we don't know where the bust is." Mr. Vern paused for dramatic effect. "So we got to dig around the whole pipe 'til we find it. Yes-siree," and Mr. Vern clapped his hands in what I hoped was preparation for the hard job ahead and not a gleefully sadistic gesture of anticipation over the bill, "It's a big job and we got two ways to handle it."

He went on to say that if his men did the digging, it was an all-day job. On the other hand, last week he'd bought a new piece of machinery called a Roto-Rooter. If I was willing to be his first customer to use it, the company claimed the gadget could do the job in an hour—or so.

"The Roto-Rooter costs $100 an hour...so what'll it be, little lady, the digging or the rooter?"

I clenched my teeth and scrunched up my face in an effort to figure in my head how much four men, all day, stacked up against and hour, or so, of Roto-Rootering. What if the contraption didn't live up to its advertising—and that "or so" haphazardly stuck on the end of the 'hour' quote made me uneasy.

A look at the water now running off the sloping lawn onto Fifteenth Street made my decision for me. I gambled and said, "The Rooter."

Mr. Vern did everything but give me a big black cigar in approval. "That's what I'da said meself."

I wondered if that remark meant he'd make more money. "Mr. Vern, if our tree roots and sewer pipes are guinea pigs for the new Roto-Rooter, how 'bout a discount?"

Mr. Vern slapped his thigh and laughed all the way down the front steps. "Miss Fran, no wonder yore TV show is so good. You're the funniest woman I've met in a coon's age."

While the plumbers were using the Rooter, one of the men noticed that our water meter was ticking crazily away. Unable to stop the meter, he took delight in keeping count and shouting out, "Boy howdy, look at that thang go...fifty bucks...whoopee, it's hit a hundred and still going."

The thought of what all this entertainment for the plumbers union was going to cost made me as swimmy-headed as Cora Lee. None of this mess was anyone's fault yet our promise to Peace— that all would be as smooth as tapioca pudding while she was away—haunted me.

The plumber was still counting when I went into the house to call the Atlanta Water Department. After the operator connected me with several dry creeks, she finally reached a sympathetic soul. "Uncle Billy here, what's the matter?"

I began talking at the same breakneck speed at which the water meter was ticking until 'Uncle Billy' made me slow down. He agreed it was an emergency and promised a man from the department would be out immediately.

True to his word, he sent an agent, who slowed the meter to its normal pace. Nevertheless, the agent said I must appear before the Atlanta Water Board in order to have the several-years-worth-of-water bill adjusted.

After the meter man, and Mr. Vern with his Roto-Rooter had left, Cora Lee and I collapsed on the front porch swing, too tired to go into the warmth of the house. Our recently acquired artesian well was capped, much to Al's disappointment. He'd rather have a lake than a lawn any day.

We sat there in silence, watching the water gradually recede. A dumpy gray pigeon pecked at an apple core left on what was once our beautiful lawn.

I broke the silence by putting my arm around Cora Lee and asking, "Okay, Cora Lee, where's Noah's white dove? That's the least we deserve for today."

Cora Lee knew her Bible from cover to cover so no explanations were necessary. "Miss Fanny, I thinks a pigeon is sort of a dove, so mebbe we got ourselves a dove after all."

"Yes, and I thinks Mr. Vern got himself a pigeon...I wish I hadn't flunked arithmetic."

CHAPTER 29

COMING IN FROM THE COLD

When Peace arrived home on Sunday, all was serene. Will had cleaned up the yard, Al and Claudine's spots were gone, and Betty Sue was hobbling around on crutches. After Mother listened to our tale of woe, she understood why no one had written.

"Peace," I asked, "did you happen to meet a retired plumber on one of those Florida beaches? We sure could use one in this old house."

"Plumbers!" Peace exclaimed, "I never met so many plumbers in my life. During the freeze they had down there, the pipes in the cottage burst. Maude and I were surrounded by plumbers of every size and shape...but we never thought to ask if any of them were bachelors."

The next morning, Monday, before I drove to work, I told Peace her vacation made us realize how she made a hard job look easy. Now if I could do the same with my first schlock commercial, I'd be in high cotton with a new avenue for making extra money.

Too unsure of myself to leave anything to chance, I'd written down my entire fifteen-minute spiel covering benefits of owning a Glacier deep-freeze chest.

A few minutes after leaving the house, I ran into a sudden frog-strangler of a shower. Unable to see well enough to drive, I parked along the street and used the time to rehearse my speech. Fifteen minutes of normal conversation seems a short while, but on the air, that length of time can seem like fifteen years.

The TelePrompTer had yet to be invented. That device, an enlarged line-by-line reproduction of a script on a moving roll of paper attached to the camera, is a life saver for a performer with memory blanks. These days, if the eyes of a person on your TV screen move ever so slightly back and forth, he isn't necessarily a shifty-eyed individual, he's reading a TelePrompTer.

When the rain finally let up a little, I drove on to the studio. I had a heavy week ahead as the Swingbillies and I were carrying the *Music Shop* without Dick. He and Marge and the children had gone back to Illinois for a visit. Program Roger Van Duzer came to the rescue by volunteering to play medleys of musical comedy hits and to help me with the commercials.

By lunch time, I was congratulating myself that I had the afternoon's show organized. As I unwrapped one of Cora Lee's super chicken-salad sandwiches, Martha Lord came dithering into the office. "Fran, I've just this minute come from a Glacier Freezer meeting...we've rescheduled their commercials from Wednesday to today. They're anxious to get started."

I dropped my sandwich. "Surely you jest! Martha, tell me you're kidding...I've written my spiel but I haven't begun to memorize it."

She pinched off a piece of my sandwich and dismissed my objection with a wave of her hand. "No problem, you'll do fine...you always do." And three days grace on my schlock debut walked out the door with Martha.

The word *problem* seemed to crop up with unwelcome regularity these days. All hope of memorizing the script departed; I'd have to fake it. As I looked helplessly around the room, my eyes lit on a stack of Bunny Hop contest posters. We'd been stuck with several hundred of the notices (urging teen-agers to audition for band leader Ray Anthony's Bunny Hop dance contest) because after the posters had been printed with the originally planned audition date, Ray postponed his contest.

I decided I could make "idiot" cards on the blank side of some of those posters. I proceeded to write in large red letters the beginning sentence of each paragraph and its key words. Lamar Gene, our all around handyman, agreed to hold them for me.

I read the copy over and over in the forty-five minutes before commercial time. It didn't help when Martha Lord decided to visit my office. "Fran, I'm really counting on you to wow Glacier's prez... Mr. Fitts'll be here watching the balloon go up. He's bringing his wife and sales manager, too."

"Ouch!...I wish you hadn't told me that."

Ignoring me, Martha burbled on. " Mr. Fitts'll want to see you after it's over. We'll wait 'til then to bring out the champagne."

"I need it now, not later," I said and left for the studio, clutching my notes to my forehead in the hope the words would somehow penetrate my brain.

I stepped into position beside the large white freezer chest that had been wheeled into the studio, and deciding that one more reading would be futile, I placed the script down in the bottom of the chest. Although my nearsighted eyes couldn't read the words from where I stood, I took comfort in the knowledge they were there.

Then the director signaled we were on the air, and I launched into the commercial. At one point I glanced at our studio clock, which was large enough for even a bat to see, and realized with relief I'd been going strong for more than ten minutes. Only five more to go. Picking up a package of frozen peas from the freezer, I paused for breath and smiled at the people in the glass sponsor's booth. Mr. Fitts held up his hand in what looked like a V-for-Victory sign. At least I hoped that what it was. He wouldn't be smiling if he were sending me some other signal.

Lamar Gene had been doing a smooth job of holding the cue cards and changing them at appropriate times. But two cameras were being used for the show and when Red's camera was supposed to move closer for a shot of the inside of the chest, *both* cameramen received instructions from the control booth to dolly forward. The hapless Lamar Gene was caught in a pincer movement and my cue cards were scattered to the four corners of the studio.

I blanked out. I couldn't even remember the name of the freezer company, much less what I was doing standing there with a box of peas in my hand. I stuttered for a few seconds trying to get my bearings and saw the Glacier president's smile turn upside down.

Out of the corner of my eye, I spotted my life raft—the script which I'd placed in the freezer. So near and yet so far. It wasn't going to come to me; therefore I must go to it. With the microphone still hanging around my neck, I leaned over, put my hand on the paper, lost my balance and fell into the freezer.

Though out of sight on my hands and knees inside the chest, I desperately continued talking. "This is your Glacier Freezer speaking to you...let me tell you what a treasure I am...and how I can make *your* life easier, more economical...."

In the bottom of my freezer well, I couldn't judge when my time was up so I kept going until I saw Lamar Gene's moon-face looming over the chest. "Fran, you can get out now."

The freezer hadn't been plugged into an electrical socket, so I wasn't cold, and with the exception of a couple of ersatz steaks poking me in the shins, I was quite comfortable. "Lamar Gene, I think I'll stay here for awhile...in fact, I may make this my permanent home...and be buried in a Glacier chest."

"You won't have to see anybody." He held out his hand to pull me out of the chest. "Martha and her gang ran for the elevators."

No champagne celebration for Frances tonight.

Discouraged, I went out to my old green Nash and drove home.

Twilight came earlier these October days. It was almost dark when I turned into our driveway. I breathed the pungent autumn smell of burning leaves even before I saw flames from the pile Will had raked too close to the garage for comfort.

"Will, you watch those leaves 'til they've burned out, you hear...we've lost one house by fire."

From the kitchen window, the lighted pumpkin Al and Cora Lee had carved in preparation for Halloween greeted me with a lopsided grin. For a moment, I stood in the driveway, a sadness coming over me. So many of the things I wished to do with Al, someone else did. He never lacked for love and attention but I often felt guilt over our not-so-normal way of life. Most of Al's school-mates appeared to have the idealized version of the fifties family— a Mommy who stayed at home and a Daddy who went to work.

Later on, at the kitchen table, I picked at a plate of shrimp creole Peace had warmed up for me.

"The creole was good two hours ago, but it's dried out by now," she fretted.

"It's not the creole, Mother, I'm just not hungry. I lost my appetite along with my freezer commercial." I went on to tell Peace of my schlock disaster; and going to the refrigerator, I began my favorite counterirritant of hitting my head on it.

"So that's where Al gets that. Stop it, Frances. Every time I tell Al to do something he doesn't like, he runs in here and bangs his head on the Kelvinator."

I sat down again, rubbing my forehead. "This hasn't been a good day for refrigerators all around. Remember back when an ice man delivered blocks of ice and you had to empty the drip pan at the bottom of the chest?"

"Yes," Peace said, "I also remember living at Crape Myrtle Farm, and when the block ice in the ice-house melted too fast, I had to keep things cool in the spring-house half a mile away. Believe me, if I had to go back to those days, I'd be knocking my head on the Kelvinator, too."

Back at the office, Martha Lord didn't come near me for two days, and I assumed my career as a fast-talking, highly-paid pitch woman for the Glacier Freezer Company had evaporated. Yet, as much as I liked the idea of more money, I thought of myself more as an entertainer than a carnival barker. Except for my chagrin at literally falling down on the job, I wasn't too unhappy with the outcome. I turned my thoughts to our regular show. For the month of December, management was talking of adding a daily Fran and Dick Christmas show, which would be very demanding on us. I hoped Dick would fatten up a bit during his visit at home. He seemed to get taller and thinner by the week. As for me, I'd been given so much of the new wonder drug, penicillin. for the chronic sore throats I'd had this year, that I'd become allergic to it—and had to fall back on Peace's sadistic iodine throat-swabbing.

Thursday morning, Martha finally came by my office. "Fran," she said, "your freezer commercial wasn't exactly what we had in mind. I'm sorry I couldn't stay afterwards but it was all I could do to keep a dialogue going with Mr. Fitts. He was furious and blamed me for selling him such a damn-fool idea...his words, not mine."

"Martha," I held out upturned palms, "I know I let you down... you gambled on me, but Betty Furness, I'm not."

Then Martha added she'd kissed the account good-by until this morning when Mr. Fitts called to say that, much to his surprise, the commercial had been a hit. Every one liked the clever idea of the freezer speaking for itself and he wanted to continue the series."

"You mean I'm to crawl in that chest every week? You can't get Dick to do it...he has claustrophobia in the worst way." But the odd rasping noise I'd heard in my car engine this morning prompted me to add, "Oh well, okay, I'll do it on one condition—if I have to throw the acrobatics, I ought to get more money."

"Well, actually, Fran....Martha looked at her feet, then the ceiling and finally got around to me. "Ah, er...to tell the truth, Mrs. Fitts convinced Mr. Fitts that they don't need a woman announcer. They're going to film the talking freezer with a male voice-over...and with the frozen foods popping out of the chest."

I knew the answer before I asked the question, but around this madhouse, it didn't hurt to let someone know when they owe you one. "Do I get anything for the idea? Say a free freezer?"

Martha gave one of her tight half-smiles and didn't bother to reply. "Just as I thought," I said to her departing back, "I'll have to keep hitting my head on the Kelvinator."

CHAPTER 30

HELPFUL HARRIET

The holiday season in 1953 loomed ahead of us like unscaleable mountain peaks. A daily fifteen-minute Christmas show had been added to our already overburdened *Music Shop* preparations. Alas, our long-time pleas for office help didn't accompany the new show. *The Christmas Show* itself wasn't a real show, but one long toy commercial. At least we didn't have scenery changes. Our set for the show stayed the same; fake fireplace, an ornamented fake tree and a fake Santa Claus, all of which matched my mood of fake gaiety.

Each day, Dick and I sat around the tree, demonstrating toys and games and exchanging childhood Christmas memories. One day, Dick said his best gift was a magic set when he was ten years old.

I teased, "Is that the same one you use now?" Dick was a frustrated magician and often asked office visitors to watch while he practiced his disappearing coin trick. "Dick, why don't you show our audience your coin trick before we read today's letters to Santa?"

It was those letters that contributed to the fact that I was growing to dislike our Christmas show. At first, the letters seemed harmless until they began arriving by the hundreds for our television Santa. Some letters brought tears to my eyes as I surmised the children hadn't a prayer of having their requests granted. The commercialization of Christmas had begun long before television, but the medium was escalating the trend. To tantalize children too young to understand why Christmas wishes couldn't be fulfilled seemed cruel.

We culled some of the more touching letters for the Atlanta Fire Department's Toys for Tots drive. As designated Santa's Helpers, we announced that St. Nick might have difficulty filling all orders. Children who wanted to share their toys to help Santa make this a happy holiday for all of his boys and girls were asked to send or bring them to WLWA-TV and we'd pass them along to Santa.

Toys arrived by the truckloads. A doll factory donated 500 imperfect dolls (they looked perfect to me), and individual response was overwhelming. And all those packages had to unpacked, sorted out and delivered. Our delivery problem was solved after I ferried a car packed with toys to my neighborhood fire station. The firemen helped me unload and thanked me for our *Christmas Show* help. Then they asked if they could enter me as their station's contestant for the title of Miss 1954 Fire Prevention. I said I appreciated the honor but had no time to do it justice. Instead, I'd prefer delivery help with our toy deluge.

"Shoot, Miss Fran, give us a holler whenever you get a truckload...we'll scoot old Engine 36 down to pick 'em up." For the next few weeks it gave me a delightful sense of power and satisfaction to call for a fire truck to pick up toys instead of to douse a fire.

Holiday season or no, our regular show went on as usual. Dick and I pantomimed Christmas records and the Swingbillies played Christmas tunes, but we felt we needed something special.

"How about doing Dickens's *Christmas Carol?*" Dick suggested.

I gave him a disgusted look. "Certainly. Shall we pull out all the stops with a Cecil B. DeMille production?"

But Dick insisted that even with our bare-bones budget, he could work out a script.

When we finally had it ready, our production of *A Christmas Carol* wasn't reviewed by the *New York Times* critics but the boys in the control room said it was effective. Dick played Scrooge, behind a false gray beard, wire-rimmed glasses, a black stove-pipe hat, and a long woolen scarf; I wrapped myself in one of Peace's bed sheets and clanked Al's bicycle chain as I played the Ghosts of Christmases Past, Present and Future; and Al hollered out, "God bless us every one" with the best of Tiny Tims.

It was with relief that we said good-by to the Christmas show and settled back into our regular routine. We filled much of our initial January 1954 *Music Shop* show by reviewing some firsts for the medium in its infancy. Thanks to television, Eisenhower's inauguration as the 34th President of the United States was the first to be seen by millions throughout the country—instead of by just a fortunate few in Washington. The movie industry, which had long ignored television, had allowed the Academy Awards to be televised in 1953; and in June of that year we saw a once-in-a-lifetime historic event, Queen Elizabeth's coronation, on the very day it occurred.

The television debut of a Grade B movie actor, Ronald Reagan, as host of the GE Theater which had begun on February 1, 1953, elicited no recognition from us. Closer to home, we mentioned the recent formation of our fan club, with requests to date for 4,000 Fran and Dick buttons.

On Tuesday, Carter Sever, station manager and notorious neatness freak, paid one his rare visits to our office. He'd been overheard to say he preferred to walk all the long way around the various offices rather than expose his twitching nervous system to the sight of our *Music Shop* rat's nest. His favorite question—other than the rhetorical "Why, oh why, did I leave the peace and serenity of radio?" was "Fran (or Dick) why, oh why, don't you clean up your office?"

When he walked in, both Dick and I looked up from our desks in mild surprise and said in unison, "Why, oh why, don't you clean up this mess?"

Carter gave a faint smile of resignation and looked around. "Maybe if I had Lamar Gene build some closed cupboards instead of those open shelves...."

Dick interrupted him. "Carter, we need everything out in plain sight, not poked away in cupboards...sometimes just seeing one of these treasures sparks an idea."

Carter picked up the curled remnant of a pastrami sandwich from the edge of Dick's desk and disdainfully held it at arm's length. "You can't tell me this piece of garbage is sparking anything but the appetite of your talking rat."

"Certainly I can," Dick said. "It's an important prop for today's Music Shop drama, *The Curse of the Curious Cat.*"

"What does a pastrami sandwich have to do with...." Carter hesitated in mid-sentence. He wasn't any better than I was at knowing when Dick was serious or teasing. On the surface Dick was unfailingly polite and friendly in an impersonal way, but there was a feeling that complexity and reticence lay underneath that veneer and kept people from getting too close. "Oh hell," Carter continued, "I'll never understand the creative mind. Seriously though, our Board of Directors is touring the station soon, and steps must be taken.

We felt comfortable enough with Carter to first-name him, unless a special occasion such as a Board of Directors tour, warranted a more formal approach. We assured Carter we'd be on our best behavior for the gentlemen and that by the time of the tour, we'd have done something to the office.

"That's what I'm afraid of," Carter said with a raised eyebrow, "but today the real reason I steeled myself for exposure to this junkyard was to bring glad tidings...your piteous cries for help have finally touched my heart."

I gave him a look of disbelief. Carter held up his right hand in the Boy Scout oath position. "On the level, starting next Monday morning, this office has a secretary."

Oh joy in Mudville, Dick and I couldn't believe such a bonanza after being put off for so long. We barraged Carter with questions— What's her name? Where'd she work before? What does she look like?

"Whoa there, you two, I'll explain what led to your rescue...my only sister fell in love last spring."

He went on to explain that his sister, Harriet, a sophomore at the University of Florida, had developed tender feelings for Ronald Ratchett, a senior from the state of Michigan. Fortunately, those feelings were returned, and Ronald and Harriet made plans for a June wedding after his graduation.

The Sever family was held in high esteem by other citrus growers in Florida, and many wanted to honor the young couple before the wedding date. The eight bridesmaids invested in yellow organdy dresses. Invitations were mailed to half the population of the state for the reception at the Orlando Country Club. The Uniquely Yours Bridal Shoppe delivered Harriet's white-lace wedding gown, with its train long enough to serve as Michigan's first winter snowfall.

The combination of graduation preparations and a constant round of prenuptial parties proved too much for Ronald. His timing was poor but it could have been worse. He might have chosen the *exact* day of the wedding to bolt instead of three days before the ceremony. For rejecting one of their own, the citrus growers talked of organizing a lynching party but Carter told us he thought that idea had pretty much petered out by now.

Yesterday, Carter's dad had called from Orlando to say sister Harriet hadn't snapped out of it yet. She was spending a lot of time crying under the grapefruit trees.

"Dad says they couldn't even get her in during the last frost, and Mom is so upset she sits out there in the orchard with Harriet half the time. The whole family is pretty much in a state."

I couldn't see where we fitted into this tale of blighted romance until Carter said he'd had the sensible idea of putting two needs together...Harriet needed a change of scenery and we needed office help.

I asked the $64 dollar question, "Can she type?"

Carter frowned, "Well, I'm not sure."

Oh great, I thought, a love sick sister who can't type...and if we don't like her, we can't fire her. The more I shook this gift box, the emptier it sounded.

"Oh, yes," Carter brightened. "Yes, she can type.

"I remember now she used to type her high school homework."

"Don't worry, Carter," Dick assured him, "we'll keep her so busy, she'll forget that Ronald Rats-his-face in no time."

But after Carter left, I voiced my thoughts on sister Harriet to Dick. "Look, even if she's a zombie, she'll have two hands and can do some of the scut work—peel the potatoes, mail contest prizes. You always complain you don't have any nails left 'cause we don't have a shipping department."

Still, I felt uneasy about the prospect of a blind-date secretary. If we could have passed on her first, my gratitude might have been less tepid.

"Ah, come on, be happy It is written that wise woman do not peek under gold dish or overturn jade goblets."

"Yeah, I know, don't look at a gift horse's mouth—and *you* have been in the control booth watching too many Charlie Chan mysteries."

In preparation for Harriet's arrival, Dick searched through the station until he found an unused typewriter, table and chair. I put Lady Cedric's cage behind me by the window. If Harriet was allergic to white mice, we'd have a problem as there wasn't any other place to store Lady Cedric and her two 'cousins', George and Louie.

We were all set to make Harriet's reception into the *Music Shop* family a warm one.

On Monday morning, Carter brought Harriet to our office, introduced us, gave her pudgy waist a fond brotherly squeeze and left her with us. Carter was such a good-looking all-American-boy type that for some reason I assumed that the Sever genes would be more consistent. Nature is tricky sometimes. The boy gets the million dollar looks and the girl gets the loose change. Sister Harriet hadn't done much to shine up what little change had been spared her. She had straight waist-length brown hair and she wore absolutely no make-up.

"Y'all are nice to find a place for me and I'll do my best to help," she said. Then, with a sweet smile, she sat down in her corner, tucking her unbecoming brown jumper around her knees and looking as if she wished she were back with her mother and the grapefruit trees.

In spite of her homesickness, she was eager to please and we set about finding tasks to keep her busy. At least I did. At the end of her second week with us, while the Swingbillies were playing "On Top of Old Smokey", Dick and I had a whispered conference.

"Dick, please make some use of Harriet. You haven't asked her to do anything since she's been in the office...I'm running out of busywork."

Dick whispered back, "Okay, I'll try to think of something?" But I don't think he tried hard enough. Harriet learned to cut a stencil, but I had to type out what I wanted on it first. She opened our fan mail, but both Dick and I missed doing that. And she wrapped and mailed the constant output of contest prizes. Other than that, much to our surprise, we didn't know what to do with her. I spent more time thinking of things she could do than I spent on the show. The problem was compounded by my realization that I couldn't concentrate knowing Harriet was waiting for me to throw another assignment her way, like a trained seal expecting a fish.

Furthermore, she didn't wait quietly. Grief overcame her often, particularly during the daily phone call from Mother Sever in Orlando. I tried to ignore the conversation, punctuated by Harriet's audible sniffles, but I was more fascinated by her dialogue than any I was trying to compose. In addition, her lugubrious reaction to our clowning and rehearsing of lively musical numbers made me wonder if the rest of our audience felt the same.

In desperation, I found myself seeking sanctuary in other parts of the building. I tried the large ladies, room, only to realize what weak kidneys our female staff had. The interruptions were never ending.

Impatience solved the problem for me on the day I became tired of waiting for a slow elevator. I made for the exit to the stairs, and off the landing below I saw a door marked 'Storage'. It was ajar, and curiosity prompted me to peer inside. I saw a gloomy but spacious cave filled with mops, pails, brooms and ladders. There were no windows but the room had several air vents. That private quiet space was dark but a white flash of an idea went through my mind. Searching until I found Purdue Mills, the building superintendent, I asked if he used the room often.

Purdue gave me the welcome news that he used the room only in the early morning hours and again in late afternoon. I could use it as much as I liked during the day.

My Remington typewriter was too cumbersome and noticeable an object to carry up and down the stairs; so I left it in the storage room, resulting in my spending more time there than in our office.

A few days after my find, Dick asked, "Where've you been lately? Every time I want to rehearse, you've vanished."

"Well, it may sound silly to you," I began a reluctant explanation, "but I can't work with Harriet hanging over my shoulder all day."

"I can't either," Dick whooped. "She drives me crazy, sitting there like a benign white elephant. Besides, I'm no good at dictation if someone is staring at me like I'm a space alien."

He asked me again where I'd been hiding and said one day he'd even asked Candy to see if I was in the ladies' room.

In a poor imitation of Charles Boyer in the movie *Algiers*, I crooked a finger at him and said, "Come wiz me to ze Casbah."

Mystified and curious, he followed me down to the storage room. Thereafter, whenever we had any serious creating to do, we'd scuttle off to our temporary haven.

CHAPTER 31

AND THEN CAME BRENDA

It was not long after my discovery of the storage room that I came home one evening to an unpleasant surprise. Dragging myself up the stairs to my bedroom, I dumped my things on the bed and was slipping off one shoe when I heard a voice behind me say, "You must be Frances?" I whirled around and saw a colorless middle-aged woman standing in the doorway.

I gave a nervous laugh. "You startled me, but my guess is you're a new lodger. Which room are you in?"

"Hasn't Mrs. Peace told you? This room is mine now...Cora Lee moved your things downstairs today."

Five seconds later I was downstairs asking Peace for an explanation. It seemed the intruder, a Miss Hodges, was a long time friend of Peace's neighborhood bridge partner, Marie Liede. Miss Hodges was in Atlanta on a two-month assignment from Washington's Department of Commerce, and she'd asked Marie's help in finding a boarding house. Of course, Marie immediately thought of Peace.

Peace said her rooms were occupied, but Marie insisted on coming over anyway—to introduce her friend, and let her see the house in case an unexpected vacancy might occur. Miss Hodges fell in love with my pretty blue room with its white eyelet curtains and four-poster bed and temptingly offered Peace several times her usual charge for a two-month stay.

"The poor lady needed a place and it's only for a short time and besides, Fanny, she's giving me so much money, you won't have to help for awhile...isn't that wonderful?"

It was far from wonderful. Not only was I working out of a dark, inconvenient broom closet at the office, but I was homeless at home.

"Peace, you're turning into the Hetty Green of Fifteenth Street ... money mad. Two months seem a long while to me...and where'd you put my things? I can't room with anyone."

When she told me that she'd moved me into the little room off the kitchen, I shrilled, "But that's nothing but a store room...I'd be better off camping in the back yard." In spite of Mother's protests that it wasn't so bad, I continued my objections. "So much water pours in the windows when it rains, I'm liable to drown...and my hair dryer gives out more warmth than that postage stamp heater in there."

Threats to move to another boarding house were useless since we both knew I'd never do that because of Al. Still I was furious. Peace had a generous nature but one of our bones of contention was that her *largesse* was often at my expense.

Only last week, I retrieved my best used-only-on Sunday pocketbook before it went out the front door wrapped as a birthday gift for Marie Liede. Peace protested, "But Fanny, you use it so seldom, I didn't think you'd miss it."

Furthermore, she made a habit of promising her many friends, acquaintances and even strangers at the grocery store check-out, that of course her daughter would contribute a guest spot on the *Music Shop* or a personal appearance, or whatever else might pop out of Peace's impulsively altruistic mouth. Promises I was not always able to fulfill.

What a miserable way to begin 1954. How had I let myself be squeezed out of my comfortable nests at both office and home? I was a shoo-in for the Miss Spineless award of the year.

Meanwhile, at the studios, Dick and I limped along, going back and forth from our office to the black hole off the stair landing. One day, I walked into the storage room and firmly closed the door behind me, not realizing that Dick was already there.

A loud clatter startled me. Dick had knocked over a pail as he jumped up to yell, "Open the door! Quick! You know I have claustrophobia." Untangling his foot from the pail, he looked dejectedly around, "And this place aggravates it."

"Something's got to give." I said, trying to suppress a giggle. "We can't go on like this! OOPS, that line sounds like B-movie dialogue. But, really, this is stupid...here we are, working in this dark cave—and there sits Harriet upstairs."

"Yeah." Dick said, kicking the offending pail to one side, "Come to think of it, she's in that *big* well-lighted office with nothing much to do but cry on the phone to Mama."

"Okay, here's what we'll do." I sat down on the bottom rung of a handy step ladder. "You go to Carter and explain the situation."

"What happened to 'what *we'll* do'? Suddenly I'm the patsy. Why me?"

"'Cause Carter'll take it better from you."

Dick was a nice guy who hated confrontations, but when he felt strongly about something, he usually had his way. A few detractors thought his tactics at times were underhanded because he'd agree when he really disagreed. Later, it would be discovered he'd convinced someone else to do his chestnut-pulling rather than do it himself and cloud his nice-guy image.

In this instance, though, Dick consented to a man-to-man talk with Carter and was going to get it over with immediately. We went back upstairs, and were not surprised to find Carter in our office. Familial loyalty had forced him to overcome his aversion to our office chaos so that he could give Harriet steady doses of encouragement.

"How're things going?" He looked at us while patting Harriet on the back with brotherly affection.

"Well, Carter, as a matter of fact," Dick cleared his throat. "I wonder if I might see you in your office about a little matter?"

"Sure, come along now, if you like...by the way, Harriet's been telling me how happy she is here with you people, and how great you've been to her." Carter beamed. "See, I told you things would work out just fine. Okay, Dick, let's go."

Dick said that on second thought, we had too much work to do right now...maybe he'd try later. We were back to our starting position.

Not long after our failed plan to get Harriet transferred to another department, I was reading aloud to Dick one of Bill Colvin's daily memos. Some were more mysterious than others and this one fell into that 'more mysterious' category:

"Memo to Fran and Dick from Bill Colvin—Subject: Guests On Tuesday, Jan, 24, Mr. Everett Olson, Southeastern Distributor for Paramount Pictures will bring two Hollywood starlets to be guests on Music Shop. Inasmuch as these two guests have a press conference in the afternoon, they will arrive after the show is on the air. Please watch for these guests and please interview them on the air."

Dick said, "We could save ourselves work by reading Covin's memos on the air. They're funnier than anything we write...where else does he think we'd interview the unknowns—underground Atlanta?"

"He's put an extra 't' on starlet, do you suppose that's because there're two of 'em. For starters, you could ask their names...or they'll never reach the heights of film stardom."

I had paused my reading to search for an opening in our schedule for the interview with the starlets when a P. S. at the bottom of Bill's memo caught my eye: "Don't forget to save a spot for Brenda Hollis on next Monday's *Music Shop*. Miss Hollis is interviewing Mr. Paul Royal, Superintendent of Fulton County public schools, and shall be a regular on your show for awhile."

"Dick, what's a Brenda Hollis? Have you heard anything about this, or her, or what?"

No, he had not. I went to Bill's office to see if verbal communication could shed more light on both the Hollywood hopefuls and the ominous phrase "and she will be a regular on your show for awhile." How long was 'awhile'?

Under my quizzing, Bill's non-stop pepper mill of words deserted him. He became uncharacteristically clam-like on the subject of Brenda, which left me more puzzled than ever. He insisted Carter's instructions stated merely that beginning Monday, Brenda Hollis was to have a daily ten-minute interview spot on the *Music Shop*. The interviews would be with various principals, teachers and board members of high schools throughout Georgia— until presumably they ran out of schools.

"Fran, it's wonderful public service."

"That's the worst idea I ever heard...it's no public service if no one's tuned in. Our song-and-dance show can't survive something that deadly plunked in the middle of it every day. And who's Brenda?"

Bill suddenly remembered an important phone call he had to make and waved me out of his office with a "I'll talk with you later."

When I reported back to Dick, he agreed with me on the awkwardness of adding the interviews to our show. "We'll lose our audience and never get it back," he said. "One might as well try to fit ten minutes of Wagner into Gilbert and Sullivan. "Then he was on the way out of the door to find out more information from Carter.

Upon his return, I couldn't wait to ask, "What'd he say?"

Dick pointed downward toward our retreat and mouthed, "I'll tell you later." Another drawback of the rampant nepotism in our office was not knowing how much sister Harriet confided in Carter. This uncertainty put a muzzle on our once freely expressed opinions on some of the more inane ideas management produced. We felt cribbed, cabined and confined these days, and in turn, the spontaneity of the show suffered.

Later on in our cave, Dick repeated what he'd gleaned from Carter re Brenda Hollis. Carter had confessed to being in a tight spot as Brenda was some sort of relative or close family friend of one of the station's major stockholders. Mr. Major Stockholder had rescued the station last year when it was headed for bankruptcy, so his request to employ Brenda had seemed a small return favor.

"But why the *Music Shop*?" I griped. "Surely there's a better spot for her."

Dick had asked the same question, and Carter had told him

it was one of Mr. Major Stockholder's favorite shows—and his personal choice for Brenda's debut. Carter also had assured Dick that Brenda was no amateur. She had an extensive background in public appearances which had involved constant travel, but now she wanted to get into a more conservative business.

"Good Lord," I muttered, "if Brenda thinks television is a conservative business, what's she been doing up to now?"

"My guess would be target woman for a knife-throwing act," Dick replied.

Now we were going to have not one, but two, unwanted people in our office—Harriet and Brenda.

"Whatever was I complaining about before we got all this help?" I asked Dick. Obligingly he reminded me I had been complaining about *not* having any help.

"I guess that proves the old saying," I sighed, "'be careful what you wish for, you might get it.'"

CHAPTER 32

THE BIBLE ACCORDING TO BRENDA

Late, late, late—I was feeling more like the White Rabbit in *Alice* these days. There was never enough time to fulfill the claims of each day, and this Monday morning was no exception.

My first stop on the way to the station was at Capitol Records on Courtland Street. The record companies gave us as many complimentary new releases as we wanted in return for the exposure we gave them. Rumors surfaced from time to time that some of the radio disc jockeys received more substantial inducements than just complimentary copies. You couldn't prove it by our *Music Shop*. Only a handful of the hundreds of records given us were suitable for pantomiming—or listening to, either, for that matter.

After picking up the records, my next stop was Wittenburger's Costume Rental. Today we were going to attempt one of Kipling's *Just* So stories, "The Elephant's Child." I was to read aloud while Dick pantomimed the journey of the little elephant, who full of insatiable curiosity, was on his way to the great gray-green greasy Limpopo River to find out what the Crocodile was to have for dinner.

It turned out that the only elephant head in Mr. Wittenburger's stock was a small one that had been made for a grammar-school play. He suggested a handsome rabbit head instead.

"Mr. Wittenburger, I can't change Kipling's story to "How the *Rabbit* Got Its Trunk", so I'll take the one you have...maybe Dick can make do by holding it in front of his face."

When I reached the station, I made it to Candy's reception desk just in time to put my armload down before I dropped it. From her desk, there was a clear view of our glassed-in office and I had been momentarily startled when I glanced that way.

"What are all those people doing in the office? Omigawsh...it's probably the Board of Directors, and Carter will be furious. We haven't done a lick of cleaning up."

Candy yawned. "Relax, Fran, it's only the welcoming commit-tee for the new addition to your show...Brenda somebody. Boy, are you in for a surprise!"

"That bad huh?"

Candy had a call on her switchboard, so she didn't answer.

I picked up the records and the future elephant's child and said over my shoulder, "Horn-rimmed glasses and support hose will be most suitable for the Board of Education."

Arriving at my office door, I was relieved to see the familiar faces of Colvin, Red, Martin and Dick—and *no* Board of Directors. The only stranger in the room was a woman holding court behind my desk. When I came in, she stood up and stretched out her hand, saying, "I'm Brenda...you must be Fran."

If you like the over-ripe flamboyant type, you'd like this one. She was wearing a black silk-jersey dress, so tight she almost split it getting up from my desk chair. Judging by the sappy looks on the men's faces, it was obvious some people do like. The woman was gorgeous. The relative-or-family-friend story Carter had dished out went by the boards...this was not Mr. Major Stockholder's Aunt Prunella.

For the first week after Brenda joined the *Music Shop*, traffic through our office was so heavy, I was grateful for our secret hideaway. Every male employee in the building thought of some excuse to visit our office for a look at the latest attraction. If you see it every day, however, even the thrill of viewing Mount Rushmore becomes routine, and traffic gradually trickled down to normal.

My former friend and now arch-enemy, Sheila LeClaire, made a half-hearted attempt to renew our buddy status for the sole purpose of pumping me about the latest staff addition. Before I could escape her, Sheila had me cornered in the ladies' room. "What did Brenda do before coming here?"

"Carter says she'd had experience...some sort of lecture circuit."

"With that New Joisey accent, my foot." Sheila scornfully rejected my vague explanation.

I laughed. "Sheila, one look at Brenda and she could speak Swahili for all anyone cared."

Brenda couldn't help it. Nature had gone into overdrive when she put Brenda together. The woman made the rest of us, including Sheila, look anemic. I, with my 'what God has forgotten, we stuff with cotton' figure melted into the wall when Brenda walked by, and Candy's Miss Gum Spirits' crown was threatening to slide off her head.

Dick was his usual polite self and seemed to take Brenda in stride, but something niggled at him.

"Fran, it's bugging me, I've seen her before but I can't think where."

"Well, you've played in a lot of clubs...why don't you ask her if she was in a show somewhere."

Dick did ask Brenda, but she said she was certain if she'd ever seen Dick before, she would have remembered.

Things rocked along for a couple of weeks. I didn't have time to show our new cast member the ropes so I turned her over to an unlikely guide, our unhappy mouse, Harriet. "Brenda, Harriet's been with us for several weeks, and anyone who's been in TV for a week is considered a veteran. She can show you around as well as anyone."

Perhaps it was because they were both new at the station and a bit lonely, for Harriet and Brenda began to lunch together every day.

One noon hour, after the two of them had walked arm-in-arm out of the office, Dick commented, "That's bound to be the oddest couple since Laurel and Hardy...what on earth do they talk about?"

"I have no idea." I shook my head. "On second thought, maybe it's good for both of them. Brenda can lighten Harriet up, and Harriet might tone Brenda down." I was more prophetic than I knew.

We were constantly searching for fresh sources of humor for the *Music Shop* but soon realized Brenda's contributions wouldn't do for the strait-laced moral code of the fifties' television. One morning she began one of her endless off-color jokes. "Say, have you heard the one about the circus midget who married the circus giant and when...."

"Brenda," Dick interrupted by holding up his hand, "if that's the story I think it is, remember, children are present," and he pointed to Harriet.

He made the remark in a facetious way, but I noticed Brenda watched her language more carefully after that. She also talked Harriet into getting a stylish hair cut and adding some color to both her face and her clothing. And she was a fresher, more sympathetic audience for Harriet's broken "left at the altar" record than the grapefruit trees—or me.

In the beginning, I had barely tolerated Brenda but a few incidents made me realize that underneath the flash, she wasn't a bad sort at all. One day she came up to my desk with a hurt look on her face and asked, "What's with the Madame Queen down the hall...I invited her to go next door for a cup of coffee and you'da thought I said a cup of cyanide."

"You mean the tall brunette who's tap dancing in the hall?"

"Yeah, that one...what's she practicing for?"

I explained that Sheila was tired of doing her *Shopping with*

Sheila program and was practicing to take over my job. She'd by no means given up her campaign to replace me on the *Music Shop* and had begun tap lessons with Jack Eppley, Atlanta's Busby Berkeley, at his studio near our station. I took brush-up lessons from him whenever I had time, but Sheila made a big production out of her lessons and practiced her tap dancing in the hall where no one could miss her budding terpsichorean abilities.

After I told Brenda about Sheila's anonymous letters to me, she became so indignant on my behalf, I began to warm up to her. And the advent of the filming of a religious program at our station was to further the thaw.

Whether it was Dick's remark which made Brenda think twice before indulging in her raunchy jokes or the daily sight of the Reverend Jason Winbourne Hill and his wife at the station, I don't know.

The couple were temporary tenants in WLWA's Studio B. The Reverend Hill had founded a fundamentalist church located near the Tennessee-Georgia border but he and his wife used Atlanta's TV facilities to film their popular *What's Troubling You?* show. The TV series was filmed (a rarity then) and shown on seventy-five stations, and it featured the informal approach of a minister and his wife at ease in their living room.

I wasn't familiar with the Hills program, but it was hard to imagine their series could be any better than our local *Frontiers of Faith*, conducted by Dr. Lionel Barfield and his wife. The Barfields had been with WLWA since day one, and were such warm, friendly people that everyone liked them. They had garnered a reputation for listening patiently before giving wise words of comfort. Many station employees took advantage of their generous nature with requests for advice on their own problems. The Barfields deserved wider coverage but seemed content with the status quo.

I assumed the Hills were cut from the same cloth as the Barfields until my favorite cameraman, Red O'Brien, (who filmed their show) commented that they bickered so much before the cameras rolled, he thought he was filming a Dick and Fran feuding husband and wife skit. He added that he had difficulty in reconciling their high-minded advice and smooth professional performance with their beforehand quarrels; but decided show business was show business, no matter what form it took.

I had too much on my own plate to pay the Hills anything but fleeting interest. The few times I passed Grace Hill in the halls, I nodded with a smile, but the permanent half-smile on her face was ambiguous. It was hard to tell if it was in answer to my greeting, or if it was something she habitually wore—like a hat for Sunday church service.

The first time we sat side-by-side at the ladies' room make-up table, I gave her a tentative bob of the head but received no return recognition. Unlike the extroverted Mrs. Barfield, perhaps Mrs. Hill was shy away from the camera.

Out of the corner of my eye, I watched as she took out a complete line of cosmetics from an expensive-looking alligator case and began slathering make-up on her face. I wondered why she used the dark shade abandoned long ago by television performers. During the early experimental days, anyone in front of the camera was thought to photograph better under a heavy coat of Max Factor's theatrical pancake make-up and brown lipstick. Both men and women used the unbecoming and messy clown paint which ruined skin and clothing. Fortunately, the phase passed after cameramen discovered that ordinary flesh tones photographed just as well.

As befitted her calling, Grace Hill, was an ethereal-looking woman with pale silvery hair, water-blue eyes and skin the color of whipped egg whites. As a result, the contrast between her coloring and the dark foundation make-up bordered on the grotesque. I heard that the fundamentalists didn't approve of the use of cosmetics, but perhaps the rule was bent for special occasions.

It was on the tip of my tongue to remark that I hadn't seen the experimental make-up of earlier days used in a long while, but Grace's aloof demeanor didn't encouraged girlish chit-chat. On the other hand, our show wasn't filmed for seventy-five stations so what did I know. Perhaps she enjoyed the elaborate preparation because it allowed time away from her overpowering husband.

During the second week of the Hills' tenure at the station, I was munching a Milky Way at my desk when the door to Manager Carter's office burst open and Grace Hill came flying out with Carter hard on her heels. Our glassed-in office gave us scant privacy but it did provide a front row view of lobby action. Grace's face was no longer pale, but red, and it was puffed out like a blowfish.

With some elephant's child insatiable curiosity prompting me, I stuffed the rest of the Milky Way in my mouth, grabbed a pile of papers and got to the door in time to heard Carter say, "Mrs. Hill, you must be mistaken...no one in this station would take something like that."

"I beg to differ...it's gone and that phony redhead was the last to see it.,.

Candy dropped her ear phones and grabbed a handful of her persimmon hair. "Who're you calling a phony redhead...I'll have you know it's natural." Candy was far more interested in protecting the good name of her hair than wondering as to what infamous deed she was accused.

"I don't mean *you*," snapped Mrs. Hill, "I mean that other one, Brenda-something."

My pretense of being en route to an important business meeting forgotten, I stood gawking at the scene. I was dying to know what "it" was, and Mrs. Hill's next words told me. "All I know is my alligator make-up case is missing. I forgot and left it in the ladies, room...I hadn't been gone five minutes when I remembered and went back to get it."

Carter looked perplexed. "But what makes you think Brenda took it?"

"She was the only person in the room, both when I left and when I came back. I could tell she was lying when she said she hadn't seen it."

Carter tried to calm her down by telling her he would look into such a serious accusation immediately, but Grace flounced off down the hall.

The story spread throughout the station as quickly as chicken-pox in a kindergarten. The swiftness of its travels was aided by Sheila, who made certain the news reached to all ears, even to Brenda herself.

It was Sheila who stopped me in the hall the following day and gloated. "I knew all along there was something fishy about that woman."

"Sheila, don't be ridiculous...why would Brenda take a case full of tacky old dark make-up she can't even use?"

"Maybe she's a kleptomaniac," Sheila said gleefully, for she had no intention of giving up such a choice morsel. "A minister's wife wouldn't say something like that if it wasn't true."

"Preachers' wives can be just as wrong as any other kind of wife," I said with emphasis.

After our conversation, I decided that if Sheila had it in for Brenda, Brenda had a lot going for her. Harriet and I did our best to smooth over the incident, but Brenda was not to be comforted.

"I've done a lot of things I'm not particularly proud of," she said, dabbing her eyes so hard one of her false eyelashes came off on her Kleenex, "but I've never been a thief."

Harriet got up from her desk to give Brenda a hug, and Brenda gave her a grateful look. "It's awful to be accused of something you didn't do ... that hurts bad."

A couple of days went by with nothing more said about the theft. Carter wasn't in any rush to further upset Mr. Major Stockholder's friend, in spite of his assurance that he'd look into the matter. If there was to be a showdown between Brenda and

Grace, Brenda held the winning hand. Moreover, the Hills were transients.

On Friday morning, when I came to work, Candy took a long look at me as I got off the elevator. Then she peered out of the window. "Fry-an, there's nary a cloud in the sky...why's your hair dripping wet?"

"Candy, if I told you, you wouldn't believe it. Please hold my calls while I'm in the ladies' room drying out."

My hair was wet because I was still camping out at home in my Cinderella room and bath behind the kitchen. This morning I'd forgotten that the bathtub had a trick faucet which you pushed down for a bath and pulled up for a shower. I pulled when I should have pushed.

I'd brought a towel and hair dryer with me and settled down at one end of the long mirrored make-up counter to repair the damage done by my unexpected shower. A few minutes later, Grace Hill came in. I peeked at her from underneath my towel and watched as she went to the other end of the counter and placed an alligator make-up case on it. Opening the case, she began her lengthy preparations for the camera.

I did a double-take and remarked, "Oh, congratulations, Mrs. Hill, I see you found a duplicate of your missing case...or did the old one turn up?',

In silence, Grace continued to sponge on the cake make-up for so long that I thought she either hadn't heard me or didn't want to. Finally she replied, "Yes, I found my case behind the couch in the studio...*that* woman's guilty conscience made her slip it back there."

"Mrs. Hill, isn't it likely you'd forgotten you left it there yourself...it's inconceivable that Brenda took it."

I continued toweling my wet hair. Here I go again, I thought, butting into things which are none of my business. It's a bad habit, and I'd better stop before I get a punch in the nose, or worse.

My tongue paid no attention to my cautionary thoughts, however, and acted as an independent organ by blurting out, "I think it would be kind of you to tell Brenda you found your case... and to apologize for shaming her in front of the whole station."

Another long silence while Grace intently applied her brown lipstick. Finishing, she gathered her arsenal of cosmetic jars and placed them carefully back inside her precious case, then closed it with a firm snap. She stood up, shook her tightly marcelled head at me, and said, "She took it...and I have no intention of apologizing to that tramp for anything." And out the door she went.

I dropped my towel, pushed still-wet hair out of my eyes, and dashed out the door after Grace. She had already passed the accounting department and was about to turn the corner at the end of the hall when I yelled after her, "'Let us not therefore judge one another...Romans, Chapter 14, Verse 13.' You're not the only one who can quote scripture. And how about good old 'charity suffereth and is kind'...Corinthians, Chapter er, ah."

Grace had disappeared by then, which was just as well as I wasn't sure if my last quote really was from Corinthians. In any case, it was myself I was reminding of those truths as well as I was reminding Grace Hill. As for the women in the accounting department, they didn't even bother to look up from their work as I ran down the hall yelling scripture quotes. They had long ago concluded that everyone in the talent department was deranged.

In the afternoon, after Brenda had finished her stultifying ten-minute air pocket in our show, Grace came into Studio A and whispered something to Brenda. They went out together and I had to wait until we were off the air to find out what *that* was all about.

"The poor skinny little thing said she wasn't herself these days with the strain of all the film work," Brenda explained. "She said she hadn't expected to be in show business when she married the Reverend.

Ordinary mortals find it difficult to admit when they are wrong. It must be doubly hard for a revered and professional advice-giver. Suddenly, my heart went out to Grace Hill; she didn't seem to be a very happy person.

"Anyway," Brenda continued, "she said she was sorry and I told her I appreciated the apology...it showed she was at least *trying* to live up to Corinthians I, Chapter 9, Verse 14."

My face must have mirrored my stupefaction for Brenda let out one of her donkey-bray laughs. "Fran, you should have hollered this one down the hall, too: 'Even so hath the Lord ordained that they who preach the gospel should live of the gospel.'"

After I had arranged my face back to normal, Brenda said, "Don't look so surprised, honey. My papa was a preacher, but about the only thing us eight kids got from him was the leather strap and Bible quotes."

CHAPTER 33

BRENDA'S ANIMAL KINGDOM

The day we saw our first Neilsen ratings since Brenda had joined the *Music Shop*, I wailed to Dick, "She's ruining the show... that ten-minute dead spot in the middle should be declared a national disaster area."

My feelings toward Brenda had changed but they didn't carry over to what she was doing to our show. For the first time since the *Music Shop* went on the air, we weren't number one in our time slot. We blamed that discordant note on Brenda's dull interviews with a series of earnest high school principals. Some of the men may have been effective speakers under different circumstances, but a lack of familiarity with television shows plus Brenda's Las Vegas persona, left most of them tongue tied.

Brenda's interviewing technique drew little from the men except uneasy stares at almost anything in the room rather than at Brenda herself. Although she'd taken Harriet's suggestion, that for the interviews a conservative shirtwaist was more appropriate attire than a silk jersey showing a generous amount of cleavage, nothing could camouflage Brenda's natural resources.

The situation was becoming impossible, yet we could see no relief for us. The good ship *Music Shop* sailed along with our two barnacles, Harriet and Brenda, still attached to its side. Even if we proved Brenda was the cause of our audience decline, our manager was between a rock and a hard place because of Mr. Major Stockholder's interest in Brenda. I was saving all the unfavorable-to-Brenda letters with the idea of convincing Carter to shift her to an evening program where she might be more appreciated. Fans of our own daytime show were mainly women, children and shut-ins. Viewing one of nature's miracles was wasted on them.

The subject of Brenda was one thing, but neither Dick nor I had the gumption to speak to Carter about sister Harriet. It wasn't personal, but we did long for the good old days when we had the office to ourselves and could concentrate on getting the show on the air. I realized I wasn't cut out to be a boss lady and preferred to do something myself rather than take time to instruct someone else.

Furthermore, I had a special way of doing things which may have looked like a lack of system to Carter, but I could usually find what I wanted in my jumble.

All that changed one Monday morning when I came into the office and immediately made an about face, ready to leave. I thought I'd entered the wrong office. Harriet's smiling face assured me I hadn't made a mistake.

"Surprise, Fran! Isn't it great?"

I was stunned. The office looked as if Mary Poppins, the English nanny of the classic P.L. Travers stories, had spoken her magic incantation and put everything back in place. Harriet had obviously inherited the same yen for tidiness as her brother Carter. Maybe it came from growing up among hundreds of precisely placed grapefruit trees. She'd arranged everything in the room into neat piles.

She gave me a tour accompanied by a running commentary. "Now here are the Bozo the Clown contest drawings, and over there the charade letters...and look," she gestured with pride, "look at the bulletin board.,,

I looked. Gone was our collection of irreplaceables which had draggled off the board onto a good part of the wall.

"I sorted it all out and took down everything dated last year."

"Oh, Harriet," I moaned, "you don't understand...I knew where everything was." I began pawing through the squared-off piles. "Tomorrow's if-men-played-bridge-like-women skit was right here...now I don't know *where* it is."

She reached into one of the stacks and pulled out a sheet of paper. "Simple. It's right here...underneath tomorrow's date."

"Harriet, I don't file that way."

"You don't file at all," said Harriet, and huffed out of the office.

Carter was the only person happy with our new look. Now he could show off the station to the visiting Board without cringing when he brought them to our office. When the time came for a visit from the Board, Dick and I had planned to toss painters' cloths over everything and plant some cans and brushes on top of them. Harriet's zeal now made that unnecessary, but it did serve to make *Harriet* necessary—at least for the time being since we couldn't find anything without her.

A few days later, in our cave off the stair landing, Dick and I had a serious conference. Self-preservation was becoming stronger each day and we agreed that we wanted our own space again—somehow, some way.

"Short of pushing both Harriet and Brenda out of the window

onto to Forsyth Street, we've got to think of something." I had to pant that out between breaths because Dick and I were busily practicing some dance steps to fill in the instrumental part of the Mary Martin/Bing Crosby duet "Lily of Laguna."

Dick did a couple of time steps before saying, "Maybe Ronald Rats-his-face will have second thoughts and realize he wants to marry Harriet after all."

"Well, he does."

Surprise in his tone, Dick asked, "How do you know? Harriet's never said that."

I looked a trifle ashamed, but not much. "Her mother forwarded Ronald's letter from Big Rapids, Michigan. Harriet read it and threw it in the wastebasket."

"And you fished it out! Why didn't you just ask her; she's hardly been silent about Ronald up to now?"

"I was afraid she'd think I was being nosy."

"Nosy, nosy, you're worse than the elephant's child."

When I proceeded to take the letter out of my purse and hand it to Dick, he looked uncomfortable. "This is against my better judgment," he protested and started to hand it back to me. "On second thought, I guess we'd better know what's going on."

"My sentiments exactly...read on MacDuff."

Dick cleared his throat self-consciously and said, "I feel like a peeping Tom but here goes, 'Dearest Hat...' Hat? If Ronald thinks she's a hat, maybe she's well rid of him."

I explained that Hat was a nickname for Harriet, but he looked unconvinced and began again: "'Dearest Hat, Can you forgive me? I can't explain why I panicked. Maybe it was all those parties and plans for a big wedding, plus graduations and job decisions. Everything crashed down on me and my feet turned to ice blocks.',

"Poor fellow," Dick interrupted himself. "I'm beginning to have some sympathy for the guy." He continued reading. 'I'm home now and have decided to join Dad's corrugated-cardboard business. Can't we consider the wedding temporarily postponed and try again? Give me another chance to prove that I love you with all my heart and soul. Ronald.'"

When Dick returned the letter, I said, "Don't you think it's a wonderful letter. Why do you suppose she threw it away?"

He shrugged his shoulders. "How should I know, maybe she doesn't like snow and corrugated cardboard."

My suggestion that I write Ronald with an encouraging reply and forge Harriet's signature made him look at me with incredulity. Men and women do not look upon affairs of the heart from the same viewpoint. I argued that Harriet was still in love with Ronald but her pride wouldn't allow her to accept his first overture. After all, his flight from the wedding had been unbelievably ill-timed and he'd rejected her before all her relatives and a good portion of the state of Florida.

"No, no, no," Dick said. "Are you crazy? With that harebrained scheme you'll end up in jail."

I gave up the idea with reluctance and popped the letter back into my purse.

As for Brenda, we didn't even have a harebrained scheme. We could only hope she'd tire of the daily grind and return to her former career. She was outgoing and outspoken except on the subject of what she did before beginning her non-intentional wrecking of our show. Our subtle and then not-so-subtle questions gleaned only what we already knew-something to do with the public which involved travel. Our two barnacles were both so well-meaning it made scraping them off all the more difficult.

Brenda's interviews, intended to be dignified material, instead were often ludicrous. Knowing nothing of Georgia geography, politics or history, she was constantly putting her foot in one briar patch after another. Untangling Brenda's misinformation provided her guests with plenty of conversational fodder.

She wrote extensive notes for each interview, but if her notes were lost or scattered, she had no floating branches of inner information to rescue her.

One of our ploy, to schedule Brenda's segment at the end of the show, failed. The front office insisted her portion be inserted in the middle of our hour to give her every advantage. After Dick introduced her, we usually spent the interval quietly preparing for the remainder of the show. On rare occasions, Brenda's misconceptions were so far out, no one in the cast could keep a straight face. In the name of professionalism, we'd all have to dash out into the hall before bursting into laughter.

Brenda was in particularly good form the day she said, "Let's see, Mr. Hanson, you're the principal of the Lumpkin Junior High School, and from all reports, you're doing a splendid job down there in southeast Georgia."

Mr. Hanson opened his mouth to speak but Brenda had already turned full face to the camera to continue her introduction.

"Folks, Lumpkin is noted for Westville, a re-created village of twenty-five buildings. It is an exact replica of a village from the pioneer Georgia days before 1850. They have a blacksmith's shop and a potter's shop...well, I'll let Mr. Hanson tell you more about his charming town."

By that time Mr. Hanson was about to bust. "Miss Hollis, you have the wrong location. My town isn't in the southeastern part of Georgia, it's...."

Dick and Fran in The Christmas Show

Drawing cartoons to music—
Dick's left-handed and Fran, right, so they'd meet in the middle.

Reading from the American People's Encyclopedia, a sponsor.

*Fran as a
John Robert Powers model.*

*Fran with
Bozo-the-Clown dolls.*

Don't know the name of that pretty girl
who is coming between me (fourth from left) and Bob Hope.

Dick, band leader Ray Anthony, Bozo the Clown and Fran.

Fran and Dick with the Swingbillies:
Randy, June Bug, Paul, Ruel and Harry.

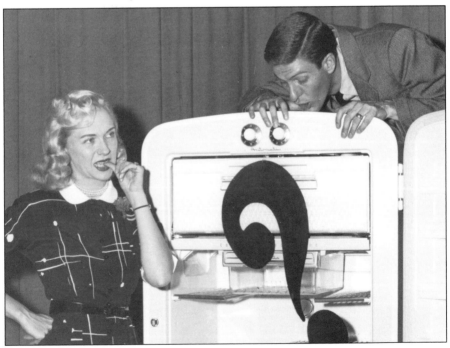

The "Guess how many cubic feet in this refrigerator" contest,
one of the many contests we ran.

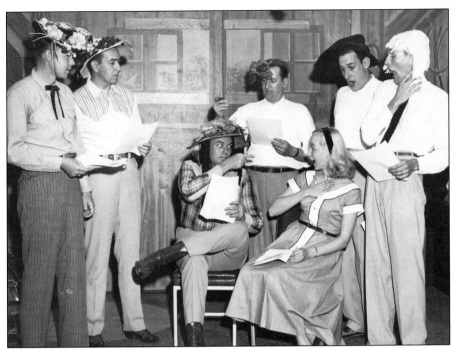

*The Swingbillies with Dick (in wig) and Fran
on Music Shop dramatic society days.*

Dick borrowed my purse for the skit. But I refuse to claim that hat!

Day before the Dog Show.

Helen Hayes, "First Lady of the American Stage,"
visited Dick and Fran's Music Shop.

Another contest!

Why is Fran looking happy? She has to open and sort all that mail!

Dick, Fran and Ilona Massey in Atlanta's first Telethon—June 1953.

Dick and his imitation of Piano Red.

College prom set for pantomiming "G'Bye Now."

Dick is obviously wondering what we're going to do next
to fill that long, long hour.

Dick as Kipling's Elephant's Child with insatiable curiosity.

Pantomiming under a tropical moon.

The Swingbillies with Dick and Fran—blowing bubbles!

Fran and Dick reading our feature story in Radio-TV Mirror.

Fran and Dick on set at The Music Shop.

The Music Shop adopted Darlene Moore.
The cast paid all her expenses at the Jolley Home for orphaned children.

When Swanson's Frozen Chicken pies first came on the market.

Fran and Dick promoting Swanson's.

"Fun with Fran" entertained pre-schoolers and their friends on their birthdays. This live TV show aired daily at 9:00 a.m.

Paul Whiteman "The King of Jazz" and Fran.

Fran pantomimes the song, "He Loves Me"
while picking the petals from a daisy.

Fran interviewing the Atlanta Humane Society representative.

*Fran pantomiming Marilyn Monroe in
"Diamonds are a Girl's Best Friend."*

"Mr. Hanson, my map must have a misprint." Brenda turned around to the large wall map of Georgia which was used as her backdrop. "See, here it is," she said, pointing a triumphant finger to the spot. "Lumpkin...right here between Columbus and Cuthbert."

The gentleman could no longer be contained. "Miss Hollis, that's not where my town is." He moved closer to the map and did some pointing of his own. "Here's my town, in northeast Georgia, Elberton. We have a lot of things we're mighty proud of, but an 1850 village isn't one of them."

Brenda did her best to recover. "Mr. Hanson, I know you're doing just as good a job in Elberton as you would if you lived in Lumpkin."

Mr. Hanson knocked her recovery in between the eyes like a hammerhead shark when he said gently, all things considered, "Furthermore, Miss Hollis, my name isn't Hanson, it's Wellborn."

Such confusions happened to all of us at times, but Brenda came in for more than her share as she was such an unlikely choice for her assignment. Although the *Music Shop* cast thought it funny, it wasn't amusing to Mr. Wellborn or some of the other guests she'd scrambled. You saw it when it happened, or the moment was gone forever—unless it was filmed, a costly process seldom done on a local level.

Before television became as ordinary as the telephone, it was a personal triumph to appear on the screen. In 1954, Mr. Wellborn's guest appearance on WLWA-TV was a happening in Elbert County, population 18,500, and a great many inhabitants of that county had gathered around a set to see him. To have the high school principal of Elberton mixed up with some fellow from Lumpkin didn't set well at all.

Whether her lastest blunder had anything to do with her decision or whether it was a coincidence, I don't know, but the next day Brenda announced that she'd had an offer from her former agent which she couldn't refuse.

She gave Carter notice that she was leaving to return to her dancing, even though it meant going on the road again. "I miss being a headliner with a live audience," she said, "so when my agent, Sammy Minckler, said he had this great opportunity for me, I jumped at it."

"Gosh, Brenda," Dick said, ever gallant, "the *Music Shop* won't be the same without you." If I'd been standing nearer, I'd have kicked him.

"You guys have been great to me, and I hate to leave you up to your ass in principals...but there's just not enough excitement for me here."

Since I had enough excitement to last me a lifetime in just one day around this place, I wondered what her offer had been. "What's this great opportunity, Brenda? C'mon, give."

"Sammy says that Druscilla wants to sell her dove act, 'Druscilla and her Disrobing Doves.' It's the best act on the exotic dance circuit," Brenda said. "She's getting married," she added, with what sounded like an envious sigh. "Sammy thought of me first thing 'cause he knows I'm good with live props."

"That's it!" Dick jumped up from behind his desk. "Yep, that's it...it's been driving me crazy...Brenda, the Blonde Bombshell. Brenda, with all due respect, I may forget a face but that figure of yours is not exactly a Chinese dinner, it *stays* in the memory."

Brenda said she knew she'd never played in the same club with Dick.

"No, we were across the street. Phil Erickson and I were playing a week in Miami at Martha Raye's Five O'Clock Club and you had your name in lights across the street at the Torchlight Club...'Brenda, the Blonde Bombshell.'"

"Yeah," said Brenda, "that was before I got the act with Bumpsy."

"Bumpsy?" Harriet, who had joined us, found her curiosity overcoming her astonishment. This was a long way from grapefruit trees.

"Bumpsy was my boa constrictor. We had a great act—'Brenda and Bumpsy, the Boa.'"

I looked at the woman with new respect. Just seeing a picture of a snake gives me nightmares for weeks.

Brenda went on to tell us that working with doves was going to be a breeze compared to the boa constrictor. Her Adam and Eve number with Bumpsy had been a big hit until he outgrew his babyhood. He'd always been so gentle she knew he didn't realize his own strength the night he almost loved her to death. After that, she was in a receptive mood when her great good friend, Mr. Major Stockholder, suggested she try another facet of show business.

"But this dove act is wonderful," Brenda said. "It's very artistic. The doves are trained to pick off each piece of veiling on cue. Sammy has the act booked in the best clubs from Miami to Las Vegas."

"Oh Brenda," Harriet sighed, "I'd give anything to see your act."

Our Bombshell said she'd been saving her big surprise for last. "You're all invited to my opening night—right here in Atlanta. It's two weeks from tonight at the Domino Lounge."

A large group from the station attended Brenda's opening, including Dick and Marge Van Dyke, Carter and his wife, and

Harriet. John Whitney escorted me, and after the show, he commented, "A very aesthetic performance. I see why you insisted we meet at *my* office instead of yours all these weeks."

Brenda's act *was* artistic. The doves and Brenda were complete professionals. She'd been wasted at our station all buttoned up and trying to make sense out of the Georgia Department of Education.

CHAPTER 34

A DRUM ROLL FOR MEL TORME

About a week after Brenda's departure, Harriet and Dick left me alone in the office. Harriet was headed for the post office to mail a carton full of contest prizes, and Dick offered to carry it for her. He was going in that direction anyway to check out the after-Christmas sale at John Jarrell's men's store. Even in the early struggling days, Dick was always well turned out and wore his clothes with an air. (He was the first man in Atlanta I ever saw wear black loafer-type shoes with tassels.)

It was pleasant to have the office to myself. I was taking full advantage of the opportunity so I wasn't pleased to be interrupted by the sight of a tall, fair-haired, bespectacled man peering uncertainly into the room.

"Yes?" I said to the stranger in a discouraging tone of voice.

"I'm sorry to bother you but the receptionist said I might find Harriet Sever here...maybe it's the wrong office."

I leaped up from my chair, raised both arms in the air and shouted, "Hallelujah, it's Ronald Ratchett." I went over and grabbed his hand. "Come right on in."

The young man seemed understandably startled by my change of attitude and vigorous welcome.

"How'd you know my name?"

"Ronald, if we were a post office, your picture would be on the wall with the 'Most Wanteds.'"

Ronald's confused look made me change the subject. "Harriet will be back any minute, so sit down there." I pointed to her desk chair. "Now, tell me how you had the good sense to come in person rather than leave it to a letter."

"Somebody named Brenda called me from here and said the same thing...if I wanted Harriet back, I'd better show up myself."

Instead of trying some idiotic scheme involving letters and forged signatures, Brenda had picked up the phone and gone straight to the point. Perhaps her chosen profession taught her how to get down to basics with more efficiency.

"Gee, I didn't think...maybe you're Brenda?"

After I shook my head, he said, "Well, I'd sure like to thank her. I wouldn't have had the nerve to make the trip without her encouragement."

I thought a minute before answering. "Ronald, Brenda isn't with the station any more, but Harriet'll take you to meet her at the Domino Lounge tonight. I guarantee you'll see more of Brenda than you could have dreamed possible for a first introduction."

Ronald gone or Ronald back, I didn't know which was worse. Within a few days, whatever fantasy we had of a blonde Viking riding out of the North on his white charger and carrying Harriet away had to be discarded.

In order to encourage Ronald to settle matters with Harriet, his father had asked him to spend two weeks in Atlanta researching the city's corrugated-cardboard carton market. The only hitch to this time table was Harriet. Instead of falling into Ronald's arms, she was having second thoughts and couldn't make up her mind.

Harriet's initial shyness with us had gradually worn off. With her confidante, Brenda, unavailable, I was now the recipient of her stream-of-consciousness thought wrestling.

"Fran, what should I do? Sometimes I think I was more in love with being a star in a big wedding than I was with Ronald. In my mind, the walk down the aisle in my beautiful dress was as far as I got...did I ever tell you about my wedding dress?"

Harriet and I were seated at my desk sorting out the 2,883 Bozo the Clown drawing contest entries which had arrived last week. Most children like to draw and the *Music Shop* encouraged them. Bozo was expected on our show next month and we were looking forward to thanking him for the generous supply of clown dolls, records and record players he gave us for prizes.

The sorting was tedious so I decided to let Harriet talk for awhile—perhaps it would help her reach a decision. "Yes, Harriet, you *have* mentioned it from time to time...a lace dress on special order from New York, I think."

That's all the encouragement she needed. During my years on fashion-show runways, no commentator had ever given such a detailed description of a piece of wearing apparel.

"Fran, it was taffeta with a Venice lace overlay...with a high crown-lace collar covered with pearls and sequins. The yoke inset had lace appliqués and more pearls and sequins...."

Mercifully, the phone rang. It was Bill Colvin asking if we could squeeze in more guests on the show today—a Mr. Lloyd Mason and two boys from the Atlanta Congress of Model Airplanes. I checked the format. "Sure Bill, we'll put 'em in between the sequins and lace appliqués...no, no, I'm teasing...we'll use them instead of the charades at 4:45. It's okay."

Harriet was still going on. "and my full skirt went into a chapel train. The fingertip veil was French illusion with a silk headband and a big pouf in the back with seeded pearls."

I thought her recital must be over but Harriet was just getting warmed up. "Oh, and my bouquet was going to be a cascade of phalanopsis orchids, white roses and stephanotis tied with white moiré ribbon and..."

She droned on, describing everything including the brides-maids' dresses, and I was trying to think of some urgent errand to send her on when she said, "And my floating hostesses were going to wear pale green satin."For the first time since she started talking, I was caught and wanted to know more.

The phrase "floating hostesses" had conjured up for me ethereal green ladies hovering near the ceiling, or perhaps seated on an ice swan floating in a punch bowl. I'd never heard the expression before and was disappointed when Harriet gave the prosaic explanation that it meant a few friends who flitted around the reception seeing that everyone was introduced.

"Harriet," I said, "the actual wedding has nothing to do with whether you love Ronald enough to marry him. A wedding fit for Queen Elizabeth isn't going to guarantee a happy marriage. Case in point—in the forties, Dick and Marjorie Van Dyke were married on the 'Bride and Groom' show in Los Angeles because it was a good way to have a wedding if you didn't have any money."

That information diverted Harriet into abandoning the subject of her aborted wedding plans. "Oh, I wish I'd known that, it's one of my favorite programs. It's on Channel Five at 3:30 so I don't get to see it anymore."

"It was on radio then, but the format was the same...free honeymoon, furniture, appliances, cash, a trousseau. Dick was making the magnificent sum of $80 a week as a nightclub pantomimist...well, at least for the weeks he and his partner, Phil Erickson, had work. Marge had a much steadier job as an x-ray technician."

"Oh, Fran, go on about Marge and Dick's wedding."

"Well, you'll have to ask Dick the rest of the story as that's about all I know, except fifteen million people heard their Valentine's Day ceremony. Dick said they'd have been married on a flagpole for that kind of start. I hope other 'Bride and Groom' marriages turned out as well as theirs has. The Van Dykes are one of the most devoted couples I know."

Harriet said she'd noticed that Dick talked with Marjorie on the phone every day.

"On the other hand," I went on, "I was married in traditional regalia at the First Presbyterian Church here and it didn't work out...so you'd better think of life beyond walking down the aisle."

Harriet admitted one reason for her indecision was the prospect of attempting another big wedding in the same town with the same cast. The loss of the wedding pageantry, added to the loss of face in her home town, still seemed to take precedence over the loss of the now reincarnated bridegroom.

I got up from my chair, began to stretch, and then stopped in the midst of it. "Harriet, I've an idea. Why don't you and Ronald have a quiet wedding here in Atlanta?"

She looked horrified. "Oh, I couldn't do that, my mother would die of disappointment."

"Nonsense, your mother wants you to be happy. Your parents could come from Florida, and Carter and Karen could have it at their house." I began to work up a lot of enthusiasm for the idea, particularly since I wouldn't have to do anything but attend the ceremony. "Ronald's a nice looking, well-mannered man with a good sense of humor." From our short acquaintance, he seemed to have a better one than Harriet. "And, a rosy financial future," I added. "If you don't want him, somebody else will."

Harriet's dilemma guided my choice of a record to back up our daily pantomime. Taking the fragile '78 RPM out of its cotton nest, I said, "Harriet, you remind me of my Dorothy Shay record of 'Jenny'".

"Who's Jenny?"

I was surprised by Harriet's question, but explained that the song "Jenny" was quite popular and had been sung by Gertrude Lawrence in an early '40s musical *Lady in the Dark* and later by Ginger Rogers in the movie with the same name. With the young though, even a year or two can create a musical generation gap.

I'm a walking encyclopedia of popular song lyrics because of the hundreds of songs I learned to pantomime. Once a record began playing, I could create the illusion of being the singer on it, word for word and breath for breath. Many people in our audience thought I was actually singing, and never stopped to question why I sounded like Rosemary Clooney one day or Patti Page the next.

Strangely enough, though, without the record backup, I could barely remember the songs. A favorite practical joke of the engineers in the control room was to cut off the sound in the studio in the middle of one of my pantomimes—just to watch my panic-stricken face.

"Harriet, Jenny was the heroine in a song about making up your mind." It was while I was struggling to recall some of the "Jenny" lyrics that Dick came into the office. "I've discovered there's a missing verse on the Park Avenue hillbilly's version of 'Jenny,'", I said. "Do you remember the one about Jenny at twenty two?"

He thought a few seconds. "Sure. 'Jenny made her mind up at twenty two, to get herself a husband was the thing to do. She got herself all dolled up in her satin and furs...Jenny got a husband, but he wasn't hers.'"

"See, Harriet," I said, "that's another plus for Ronald. He's all yours."

Secretly, I was thinking that some part of Harriet's vacillation was due to her enjoyment in being the center of her own drama. Ronald was courting her again, with dinner every night and frequent visits to the station for lunch dates. Brother Carter was solicitous and concerned, but didn't know whether to treat Ronald as a future brother-in-law or a reject. Her mother called every day from Orlando, but there was nothing new about that. I think Harriet sensed that as soon as she came to a decision, some of the ego-boosting attention focused on her now would fade.

I'm not certain whether the push Harriet needed to make up her mind came from singer Mel Torme's drums, the Bunny Hop, or the dog contest. However, the drums were a start.

It began with Mel Torme having a singing engagement at the Sans Souci nightclub on Peachtree Road. The young singer, with such MGM musicals as *Good News* and *Words and Music* to his credit, was a big recording star and a favorite with the 50's bobby soxers. A New York disc jockey had dubbed him 'The Velvet Fog', and when he visited us at the *Music Shop*, he confessed he loathed the sobriquet.

In 1954, he was well known, but had yet to acquire his formidable reputation as the complete showman, songwriter, instrumentalist, arranger—and gifted author.

On the day of his *Music Shop* appearance though, we hadn't known he had other talents besides singing until he asked, "Did the Sans Souci deliver my drums?" He wanted to rehearse a drum solo for when he played with the Swingbillies.

When Ruel Parker, the Swingbillies' leader, learned that Mel had played drums for such bands as Artie Shaw, Stan Kenton and Tommy Dorsey, he asked him not to tell Junebug and the rest of the boys. "It'll make them so nervous, they'll never stay on key."

But no one had seen any drums. A call to the Sans Souci revealed that Mel's drums had been delivered to his hotel, the Dinkler Plaza, instead of to the station as he had requested.

"No problem, Mel." Dick turned to me. "Fran, see if you can rustle up Lamar Gene. It'll only take him a few minutes to run up to the hotel...it's not that far from here."

Harriet followed me around in my agitated search for Lamar Gene. When we learned that Roger had sent him to the airport to pick up a film delivery, Harriet offered to get the drums herself.

What a relief. I went back to the studio to report that the drums were on their way. Mel was going to pantomime his own song, "Careless Hands." It would take too long for the Swingbillies to rehearse a live arrangement with him even if they'd been capable of such sophisticated fare.

Time passed. No Harriet.

Candy rang the hotel for me to see if she'd been there. The desk clerk reported that per Mr. Torme's instructions, a bellman had helped the young lady bring the drums down from his suite to the lobby where she was now.

I didn't waste precious time on the phone; I grabbed my coat and ran the six blocks up Forsyth Street to the Dinkler. Sure enough, there sat Harriet in one of the lobby's green leather armchairs, surrounded by the largest set of drums I'd ever seen. Heretofore, my only view of drum sets had been from a dance floor.

The three different size drums came with a great deal of equipment including cymbals and a stand. I realized why Harriet hadn't raced back to the station with them.

"Harriet, why didn't you call me?"

"Oh am I glad to see you... I didn't know *what* to do. If I left these things, I was afraid somebody would steal them." Harriet gave one of the drums a loud thump. "I'll bet every one of those 7,000 Shriners for the Southeastern Convention is checking in here now. I couldn't get anyone's attention."

Although a sea of red fezzes should have clued me, I'd forgotten today's reminder from Colvin that one of the convention's Imperial Potentates was to be a *Music Shop* guest.

"I don't think anyone can lift these monsters, much less steal them." I looked at the drums with dismay. "Come on, let's see if we can manage together." We could not. But a passing bellman pushing a rack filled with luggage gave me an idea. I asked the head bellman if it would be possible to borrow one of the luggage racks for a short while. A hotel guest, the well-known singer Mel Torme, needed his drums for our four o'clock *Music Shop* show. The name Mel Torme meant nothing to the bellman but he recognized me.

"Sure, be glad to. Tell the Swingbillies 'Hi' for me, they're my favorites. Boy, that Junebug kills me." He helped us load the drums onto a rack and waved us off.

We began rolling the apparatus down Forsyth Street, but due to a cross-eyed front wheel, we had to stop several times to redirect the rack's course. My tolerance for embarrassing situations had improved through daily public appearances, but when a sudden stop caused Mr. Torme's assortment of drum sticks to scatter over the sidewalk, I realized I had a way to go.

By the time we'd picked them up, we'd gathered a good-natured but vocal audience consisting mainly of the visiting red fezzes. One wag hollered, "Hey girlies, I'll let you beat my drums any time."

Under the circumstances, dignity, although not easy, was not impossible. Harriet made the mistake of trying to explain to the oaf in some detail that the drums didn't belong to us.

"Harriet," I barked, "front and center."

We'd gone another half a block when Harriet said, "I never in this world imagined I'd be pushing Mel Torme's drums...it's fun, isn't it?"

To me, serving as draft horse for a heavy luggage rack with Mel Torme's heavier set of drums on it, to the accompaniment of hoots and cat-calls from a street full of playful potentates, hardly seemed the epitome of show biz glamour.

"At least it isn't raining," I grumbled.

"Oh, Fran, if I marry Ronald, I'll miss the station something terrible."

"You won't have to give up the business, Harriet. Big Rapids must have a television station...and you're experienced now."

"No," she said sadly, "it wouldn't be the same. And I think you've gotten your Rapids mixed up. Ronald isn't from big ol' Grand Rapids...he's from little ol' Big Rapids. People like Mel Torme don't come to Big Rapids."

We'd finally mastered our chariot's erratic sense of direction, and I spent the rest of the trip telling Harriet an old chestnut of a joke her remarks brought to mind.

"A young man got a job in the circus cleaning out the elephants' cage. One day the owner of the circus gave the president of a large firm a tour. They stopped to watch the elephants, and the executive was impressed with the hardworking young man and decided his firm needed such a dedicated youth."

Just then we had to struggle to get the rack across the street. Once on the other side, Harriet said, "Fran, go on with the story... but I don't get it...half the time I don't know what you or Dick are talking about."

"Wait'll I get to the punch line, then you'll get it. So the company president offered the young man a position in his firm with a handsome salary and future. The young man shook the president's hand and replied, 'Sir, I sure appreciate your fine offer but I couldn't possibly give up my career in show business.'"

By then, we'd arrived at the entrance of our building. While I went upstairs for help, I left Harriet by the rack still wondering what elephants had to do with her wanting to work in TV.

The judgments we passed on transient celebrity guests perhaps weren't always fair. I recall an observation I made to Big John Whitney upon seeing the sky from an underground passage while touring the Lookout Mountain caves near Chattanooga. Catching a glimpse of a tiny patch of blue sky through a chink in the dark cave, I said, "John, that must be the way the sky looks to a gopher or a mole...how can they know what the sky really looks like by such a sliver of a sample?"

Now, decades later, I'll say I adored Caesar Romero and Andy Griffith, not only because I admired them as performers, but because for the fraction of time our paths crossed, they were polite, enthusiastic and gave more than necessary to our insignificant local show.

In the case of some of our other guests, I can only assume they were having a bad day when we met. As for Mr. Torme, I'm happy to say he seemed most grateful for our efforts in rolling his drums.

CHAPTER 35

THE BUNNY HOP FLOP

The Bunny Hop contest nudged Harriet further toward a firm yes or no to Ronald. Although during our *Music Shop's* promotion of the latest dance mania, several incidents gave her more of a rough shove than a gentle nudge.

She'd already left for lunch with Ronald the day that Dick, Bill Colvin, and I were in our office going over the contest plans.

"Bill, this Bunny Hop thing would do much better around Easter than January," I argued.

"You're not listening, Fran...I've explained that Ray Anthony's the key. He's determined to have every teen-ager in the country buy his Bunny Hop recording...and you know how fast dance crazes whiz by."

Dick nodded in agreement. "By Easter, they'll be doing the Kangaroo Krouch or the Simian Swing."

"If Ray's in such an all-fired hurry, why'd he postpone the contest after you'd ordered that pile of December 19th posters?"

I walked over to the waist-high stack of garish red and yellow posters, and pulled one out. "I saved them cause they make good cue cards and emergency umbrellas. See," I said, holding the poster up, "cross out December and write in January...that ought to please that miser in accounting."

Bill stamped paid to that idea; it was too cheap even for our low-standard station. He wanted new posters, same circus colors, with only the date changed.

"Fran, be a love and get the order to the printers this afternoon for me...I'm swamped with work."

I looked at him with exasperation. "Bill, you have more *chutzpah* than anyone I know...if you were in a bread line, you'd ask for your bread toasted. Does the sight of this desk indicate I have nothing to do?"

Bill threw himself down on one well-padded knee in an Al Jolson 'Mammy' pose. That man belonged in front of the camera, not behind it. He was basically a southern gentleman, but he tried to emulate the abrasive, hard-boiled public relations man image fostered by the theater. It was difficult for him, however, to sustain his self-created role for any length of time.

"Oh, get up!" I couldn't keep from laughing. "You look like one of Betty Talmadge's hams."

"*Hams*, glad you reminded me," Bill said, momentarily diverted from his original question. "The Governor's lady is scheduled for another guest appearance on *Music Shop* next Wednesday."

"Governor's wife or no," I lamented, "she's been on the show nine times in the past three months for her farm ham business." I scribbled a reminder on my notepad. "And for all that free advertising, we've never even been offered a ham sandwich."

"Speak for yourself," Dick said. "Betty sent Marge and me a ham last month...maybe it's your turn next."

"I guess we're lucky she's attractive and smart as they come," I admitted grudgingly. "She's probably tired of sitting in that dreary gray stone mansion pouring tea for the United Daughters of the Confederacy. Still, I'd be happier to see her if she'd pay something for her commercials."

"I'm not about to tell Herman's wife she'd not welcome—even if she wants to join the cast full time," Bill said. "Hey, hams have nothing to do with printers...are you trying to make me forget what I asked you?"

"Okay, Bill, I give up...either Harriet or I will go to the printers for you. Wait a minute, though, see if my facts are right."

I read back my notes. "Bunny Hop auditions at WLWA-TV on Saturday, January 23rd, at 10 a.m. All teen-agers, 18 and under, welcome. Dick and I choose three couples. The following week on the Music Shop, Ray Anthony will pick the winners of the grand prize—two free round-trips to Hollywood with an extra ticket for a suitable chaperon. A week's stay at the Hollywood Roosevelt, plus an appearance with Ray's band, currently playing at the Dinkler Rainbow Roof."

In all our *Music Shop* history, we'd never had such a glamorous and expensive prize so we expected the Bunny Hop to top our recent record of 7,800 entries in one week for the Gold Bond paint contest.

I put the Bunny Hop information on Harriet's desk so she could file it to her liking when she came back from lunch. Harriet's by-the-date filing system had never been clear to me. I back-slid so often that the untidy piles on my desk sprouted once again like mushrooms after a spring rain.

Before Harriet and Ronald had left for the restaurant in Rich's Department Store, I had suggested to Ronald that he steer Harriet through their furniture department on the way. He had laughed and given me a friendly wink.

The more I saw of Ronald, the more partial to him I became.

The more I saw of Ronald, the more partial to him I became. If Harriet turned him down, he wouldn't stay single for long. At first, I thought it a coincidence when Melba, our program director's secretary, showed up each time Ronald dropped by our office to see Harriet. After awhile though, the pattern became obvious and I wondered if Melba had the gift of second sight as far as Ronald was concerned. I dismissed that thought when I remembered Candy, our one-woman secret service, was Melba's good friend and probably helping Melba's occult ability via the switchboard.

As I left Harriet's desk to walk back to my own, Bill gave a parting shot. "Plug this contest on the air as much as you can...if we hit the jackpot, lots more where that comes from."

I made a moue. "Yes, yes, we'll do our best...we'll do the stupid dance on today's show." I did a couple of Bunny-hop steps behind the desk—one, two, three and hop like a bunny. It was easier than the Hokey Pokey.

On Friday, a week before the Bunny Hop auditions' day, Bill Colvin blew into our office in a more hyper kinetic state than usual. "It's a damn good thing I called the Minuteman Printers...some idiot gave them the wrong date for the posters."

I heard a low squeak coming from Harriet at her desk. I swiveled my chair around to give her a shush sign before I faced Bill with a sweet smile. "Ah me, William, I fear you read your Dale Carnegie lesson upside down this morning. Is this the same groveling beggar who was down on his knees in front of *this* idiot a few days ago?"

"Never mind that...it means the printers have to change the date line on the posters and can't deliver them tonight."

"Why tell us? Unless you're asking Harriet and me to tack posters on telephone poles tomorrow. Sorry to disappoint you, Bill, but I shinnied up my last pole when I was showing Al how to do it for a Cub Scout merit badge."

Bill said that of course he wouldn't ask me to do something so ridiculous, but he did want a favor. He was leaving town for the weekend. Would I remind Lamar Gene, who had a short memory, that he and our maintenance man, Purdue Mills, were being paid Saturday's time-and-a-half to plaster Atlanta with the Bunny Hop posters.

After he hurtled out of the office, Harriet apologized. "Fran, I'm so sorry, I had the Bunny Hop in the January 30th file instead of the 23rd."

My assurance that no harm done and that Bill should have tended to it himself made her feel better. I couldn't resist one tweak though.

"Harriet, see how dangerous a filing system is? People expect perfection from you. On the other hand, if Auntie Fran finds what she's looking for, people applaud the miracle."

Late that afternoon, I stood looking down on Forsyth Street from the office window, amazed at the presence of so many red-fezzed Shriners pouring in and out of Rich's Department Store across the street. I could almost imagine I was in Casablanca instead of Atlanta.

Their big parade was scheduled for 2 p.m. tomorrow. More than 3,000 uniformed Shriners, many bands, including the Chattanooga Bagpipes, a Dixieland Band from Jacksonville—plus drill teams, horses, and clowns would be marching down Peachtree.

When I reached the sidewalk, a group of the oriental-capped men walking directly in front of me contributed to the Mardi Gras atmosphere in the streets.

They were gaily playing with water pistols, spraying each other and everyone else within range. I narrowly missed a drenching before I sprinted into the haven of the garage where I'd left my car.

I smiled as I remembered the time-honored definition of an expert—a damn fool away from home. These Shriners were, for the most part, dignified community leaders in their home towns, yet here they were acting like ten-year-olds at summer camp.

Atlanta took the harmless, good-natured fun in stride. I thought once again how lucky I was to live here and be a part of a new and fascinating business, television. The city was large enough to have something interesting going on all the time, yet it kept its small town flavor. I vowed never to leave this spot in Georgia I loved so well.

Because of the Shriner's Convention, my homeward route along Peachtree Street during heavy traffic hours would be more crowded than usual—an opportune time to test a back way home which Big John had shared with me. But he must have left a secret ingredient out of his traffic-avoiding treasure map because I became hopelessly lost. The last familiar landmark I passed was the Union Bus Station on Cain Street, and the next thing I knew I was half way to Birmingham on the Bankhead Highway.

The delay, plus the good news waiting for me when I finally made it home, made me forget my promise to Bill to remind Lamar Gene about the posters until later in the evening.

The good news I got was the prospect that I might be reclaiming my room over the weekend. The usurper, Miss Hodges, had fallen out of love with my dainty blue and white bedroom as fast as she'd been smitten; and she carped non-stop. The smell of our art students' oil paintings made her ill; my tap dancing gave her a headache; why couldn't Al practice on the piano shen she wasn't home?

And Al forgot sometimes that I was no longer next door to him. This morning, he'd run into Miss Hodges's room without thinking. She was in her nightclothes but that was no excuse to scream "Get out of here, you nasty little brat,"—as if a seven-year-old was going to attack her!

Al had gone crying to downstairs to Peace and Cora Lee for comfort. Cora Lee threatened to quit and take Al with her if Peace didn't get rid of "that ol' Miss Hedge Hogges."

Peace fortified herself with one of Cora Lee's fly-away butter-milk biscuits for breakfast before tackling the diplomatic mission of asking Miss Hodges to leave. Armed with a refund check, Peace went upstairs to explain that her daughter Fran needed the room back sooner than had been expected. Miss Hodges didn't want to leave. She said she merely wanted the consideration befitting someone in an important government position. Peace protested that her whole household couldn't revolve around one person; and suggested Miss Hodges would be happier somewhere with more personalized service.

Miss Hodges had said, "I've paid next month's rent in advance and have no intention of leaving...that's final."

Further details of Peace's encounter was interrupted by dinner, but afterward I went into the kitchen to hear the rest of the story. I sneaked another sliver of Cora Lee's lemon pie and said, "It sounds like y'all got my hopes up for nothing...how can you promise me my room back if she won't move?"

Cora Lee's two dimples made a parentheses around that wonderful smile of hers. "We has ways." She and Peace let me in on their plan.

Miss Hodges would be at home tomorrow, Saturday; and so would the art students, who were in on the plot. It was Cora Lee's plan to vacuum the hall outside Miss Hodges's room very early in the morning and to continue as long as the ancient Hoover could hold up without burning out its motor. It was Betty Sue and Gretchen who suggested working on their paintings in Al's room and wafting the turpentine fumes next door with a hair dryer. As for Peace, she'd decided it would be a good day for Will to wash the upstairs windows from the outside, starting at 5:30 a.m.

"Why you devils! I think you're enjoying this," I said, wiping tears of laughter from my eyes. "I'm beginning to feel sorry for poor Miss Hodges...but it would be nice to get out of that Cinderella room and into my own bed. I think I'll bring my tap board upstairs to Claudine's room...my new routine needs at least a full day's work on it."

As a result of so many diversions, I didn't remember to call Lamar Gene until late in the evening. Fortunately, I did remember my promise to Bill since good old Lamar Gene had forgotten all about the next morning's job. "Lamar Gene, the printers are delivering 600 red and yellow posters...you can pick them up in the morning at the reception desk or in our office."

A week later on audition day, Dick and I met in the large, now empty space off the first floor lobby of our building. The recent merger of Atlanta's two newspapers, the *Atlanta Constitution* and the *Atlanta Journal* had resulted in both newspapers moving into the same larger building two blocks away.

The contrast, between the former ceaseless activity and noise, the crowded desks which we habitually walked past on our way to the elevators, and now this silent, deserted expanse, was depressing. Not only did we miss the excitement of having many well-known *Atlanta Constitution* figures* around, we missed a practical bonus as well.

Often, someone on the paper would alert us to potential guests and activities. The paper was still only a short distance away from us, but that sense of sharing had gone.

Now, as Dick and I viewed that huge bare room, its melancholy atmosphere was accentuated by the overcast weather and a penetrating chill. This was to be the proving ground for our Bunny Hoppers.

We kept our coats on while setting up my record player, the Bunny Hop record, and hundreds of entry blanks Harriet had mimeographed on our eccentric copy machine. Dick had raided his boys' pencil boxes.

"I wish we'd thought to bring some chairs," I complained. "The newspaper people didn't even leave a stack of old papers for us to sit on."

"Here, we can sit on a window ledge." Dick hoisted himself up on one of them, and then lifted up his hand and looked at it with a grimace. "Watch out, there's an inch of dirt on mine."

We spent the next minutes cleaning window ledges with Kleenex and entry blanks. Then we waited for the horde of hoppers to burst through the revolving door.

"We're lucky the paper moved after Christmas and Ray Anthony postponed...otherwise we would've had to rent the Biltmore ballroom," I said, peering out of the window in search of our first contestant.

* Doris Lockerman, Celestine Sibley, Jack Tarver, Jack Spalding, Photographer Kenneth Rogers, Lee Rogers, the legendary Ralph McGill, Dixon Preston, Maynita Gerry, and others too numerous to mention.

like buzzards we swooped down off our ledges and welcomed them—only to learn they were lost out-of-towners looking for Rich's Department Store.

At 10:15, Dick returned from his fifth trip to the sidewalk to see if anyone resembling a teen-age bunny hopper was dancing our way, and then said, with a shrug of attempted nonchalance, "Well, you know kids, no sense of time."

At 10:25, I said, "Dick, be back in a minute...I saw one of the posters in the garage cashier's cage...maybe the printers goofed and put 11 o'clock instead."

I ran next door to the garage and got close enough to the cage to read the poster. The ten o'clock time was correct so that wasn't it. Then I gasped—the *December 19th* date jumped out at me with as much force as if it had been alive. Those rejected posters, which had lain undisturbed in the corner of our office for over a month, were now decorating telephone poles from one end of Atlanta to the other.

"How could those clowns have tacked up 600 posters and not noticed the date." Dick hit his head with his hand in frustration.

"Lamar Gene and Purdue were paid to put up the posters, not read 'em. It happens. Once twenty members of my Atlanta Fashion Group mailed out eight hundred incorrect invitations to a polio benefit at the Driving Club. Not one of us noticed the mistake— right day, wrong date."

The comparable anecdote didn't give Dick any solace.

"But Jeepers, a whole *month* off is different."

"Dick, I hate to point this out, but the posters were only part of the promotion.. we gave the right date on the air plenty of times."

We lapsed into silence. The only sounds were from the muffled traffic on Forsyth Street and a freight train rumbling by underneath the windows. We'd been in that cold empty room for an hour and hadn't see another soul except the lost couple—not even anyone going upstairs to the station offices.

Finally I broke the silence. "Old Bill's going to be mighty disappointed, he wanted a big one on this."

As we sometimes did, Dick and I had the same thought at the same time. Gossip sheets and fan magazines use titillating headlines on their covers to lure readers—"Lucile Ball Caught Looking at Hubby Desi Arnez's Love Nest"—only for them to discover an innocuous story inside about Desi finding a robin's nest filled with baby birds and being hardly able to wait to show it to Lucy.

Our headline could read, "What Dark Secret did Fran and Dick Swear to Keep Forever?" Our Bunny Hop contest was a complete bust, our first failure. Not one teen-ager had shown up for the most expensive prizes we'd offered in *Music Shop* history. The mystery was the number *zero*. We could have understood a low turnout; no one at all was inexplicable.

We had no Bible to swear on but did everything short of cutting our wrists in Indian blood-brother fashion to seal our vow of silence. After agreeing on that, we moved on to the next problem—where to find three sets of agile Bunny Hoppers to present to Ray Anthony on Wednesday next.

"It wouldn't do any good for me to search Al's Spring Street school...no teen-agers," I said,

Dick remembered that the Druid Hills High School was near the house he and Marge had recently bought on Oxford Road near Emory University. He'd go there first thing Monday morning and lasso some Bunny Hoppers.

The poster mystery was easier to solve. Keith, the Georgia Tech engineering student who sometimes manned the switchboard, had been on duty last Friday evening so I questioned him.

His explanation was simple. On that evening, a man had delivered several brown-paper parcels addressed to Bill Colvin. Keith locked them in the storage room where he usually stashed weekend deliveries. By the time Keith arrived on Saturday morning, Lamar Gene had already gone into my office, grabbed the only posters in sight which fitted my description, and left for his telephone climbing.

On Monday, Dick and I were prepared to relate stories of a glowing triumph instead of our lonely watch, but no one mentioned the contest except Bill. He stuck his head in the door in passing to ask if we had a good turnout, and simultaneously Dick said, "Swell," and I said, "Jammed." Much to our relief, he was gone before we had to elaborate.

On the day of the Ray Anthony appearance and judging, no one thought to question why the three finalists came from the same high school, Druid Hills. Dick handled that smoothly. He waited until the winners were chosen before he mentioned their school. And we couldn't be accused of rigging the contest because no one had entered it.

Back then, we had no time to ponder on why something worked or didn't—we had no research or marketing department, no in-depth studies by advertising agencies to fall back on. Trial and error on the air was the state of our art.

CHAPTER 36

LOSE SOME, WIN SOME

The week after we'd buried the Bunny Flop, it was time to begin planning our next ambitious promotion, the dog contest. We couldn't blame Colvin for the idea this time since it came from our office. We had a new sponsor, the Ideal Dog Food Company, and were trying to think of something special to launch their commercials.

I suggested, "Let's do something with dogs."

Dick gave me a 'Lord, save me from fools' look and replied, "Brilliant, Dr. Watson."

"Oh, you know what I mean—show lots of dogs. Nope, we already do that for the Humane Society...it's got to be something different."

"That's it, show dogs, pedigrees." On second thought Dick discarded that idea. "Nope, not enough time. The Kennel Club works all year for their big week."

Harriet listened to us noodle back and forth and then timidly said, "When I was a little girl, I entered Woosie, my sort-of cocker spaniel in a pet shop contest. It wasn't the formal kind...but things like longest ears, shortest tail, curliest coat...."

Dick gave a boxer's handclasp over his head. "Hot dog, Harriet, that's a winner.. we ought to make you head of the idea department."

The three of us agreed it was a natural for the Ideal Dog Food Company, and for even more good-will, perhaps the company would donate cases of their product to the Humane Society.

"The station's new mobile unit means the show can be outdoors," Dick said and added, "Harriet, why don't you scout for a shopping center willing to loan us parking-lot space for a couple of hours."

Harriet blushed with pleasure at our compliments, but was unusually quiet for the rest of the afternoon.

The next morning, instead of her customary sharing of chatty details of the latest date with Ronald, she was so silent and preoccupied, I asked her if something was the matter. Tears came to her eyes, and she groped in her purse for a tissue. "Ronald went back to Big Rapids last night."

I leaped out of my chair and began pacing back and forth behind the desk. "Why that dirty, rotten, low down jack-rabbit, he can't do that to us." (I'd long since given up the role of disinterested spectator in this hearts and flowers drama.) I've a good mind to... oh, what's the use."

The steam went out of me and I sat down, thoroughly disheartened by the thought of living through several more weeks of Harriet on her second rejection from the same fellow.

"No, no, you don't understand." Harriet was still sniffling and blowing her nose, but I caught the gist of her words. She herself had sent Ronald back to Michigan—without either a yea or a nay.

My sympathies immediately changed back to Ronald. If I was exhausted by her see-saw, I could imagine how he felt.

"Well, Harriet, I suppose you know what you're doing...better to be like the Jenny in that song...all her troubles came from making up her mind."

"But I have made up my mind." Harriet went on to tell me that she'd decided to finish her last two years at the University of Florida. Ronald wasn't overjoyed with her decision but had accepted it gracefully. They planned to visit each other as often as time and distance would allow.

"Fran," she regretted, "I feel awful about leaving you with all those dogs...and it was my idea."

When I learned she was leaving at the end of the week in order to register for spring quarter at the University, I was surprised at my reaction. When I looked at dear Harriet, it dawned on me that I'd grown most fond of her. We'd been through so much together since she first came to us; the early irksome days were forgotten.

Her time in our pressure-cooker had matured her and she wasn't the same girl who first walked into our office. With Brenda's make-over and her new hair style, she even looked different. We'd kept her running so hard that she'd shed some of the weight she'd picked up sobbing under the grapefruit trees.

One trait remained constant...Harriet's tendency to weep upon any occasion, happy or sad. During the rest of her time with us, even the brilliant winter sun couldn't dry out our damp office. On her last day she controlled her farewell tears long enough to smile into the camera. We had flanked her with our two movie star guests: Audie Murphy, World War II hero and holder of the most decorations in history, now turned western movie hero; and actor Richard Long of *Big Valley* fame. our good-by present to Harriet.

After the show, she was emptying her desk drawers and packing up her *Music Shop* memorabilia. When she walked over to the wall shelves to retrieve her Bozo-the-Clown doll, she tripped over Lady Cedric's cage.

"Ugh... that's the only thing I won't miss about this place. Yesterday when I poked a piece of lettuce in the cage, one of those varmints bit me on the finger."

"Which one?"

She held up her hand, "My poking finger."

"No," I said, "I meant which mouse. Lady Cedric or one of the cousins?"

"Fran, you can't tell those mice apart." She gave me a look of disbelief. "Or can you?"

"I'll bet it's cousin Louie, he's the big flirt."

Since the talking mice's initial appeal to our audience had dimmed and they were receiving little fan mail now, I was searching for a gentle solution to terminate their employment. Al had long since lost interest in the creatures, and Peace complained she already had enough mice gnawing underneath the floorboards of our old house for her to welcome any more in plain sight. Brown or white, mice were mice to her. I was their only champion and even I was wearying of their care. Now Harriet's comment had squelched my idea of presenting them to her as a going-away gift.

That evening, at the Terminal Station, the Severs and I put Harriet on the train for Orlando. As soon as the train began to move, she ran back through the lounge car onto the vestibule. As we were turning back toward the Terminal's entrance, we saw her waving good-by and holding her photo taken with Audie Murphy and Richard Long high over her head.

I asked the Severs, "Do you suppose Ronald and Harriet will eventually marry?"

Carter didn't know, but Karen gave her opinion. "No, I don't... in fact, I always felt Harriet was more in love with the idea of being the star in a big wedding than she ever was with Ronald."

Carter draped an arm over Karen's shoulders. "Hon, maybe having her up here brought her out from under a lot more than the grapefruit trees."

After Harriet left, our only reminder of her was the arrival of two large crates of grapefruit from Orlando. My efforts to keep her elaborate filing system as a kind of memorial had failed. I found it impossible to stay with a process so alien to my own nature, and once again our bulletin board regained its individuality.

Mixed-emotion memories of Harriet and Brenda cured my desire for full-time help, but I was pleased when we lucked into a part-time assistant, Regina Belflower.

Regina, a wholesome-looking blonde was one of the contestants Dick had lassoed from Druid Hills High School for the Bunny Hop contest. She'd been my choice for winner even though Ray Anthony voted for another couple. Ray agreed she was the best dancer but her klutz of a partner had ruined her chance. She later confessed that her steady beau had chickened out at the last minute, and her study hall seat-mate had offered to substitute— neglecting to tell her that one, two, three, hop like a bunny, was too much for his size-twelve pigeon-toed feet.

We were so grateful to have any contestants at all that I looted the contest-prize room and presented the losers with a basket full of everything from T-shirts to electric mix masters. It was while Regina was helping me divide the haul that she asked if any part-time work was available.

"Can you type?"

"Yes, I got all A's in it last year."

We settled on her working three afternoons a week. Not only could she type like a Georgia tornado but she did everything else with the same speed—and she had no romantic problems. I'd have hired her for that reason alone.

One day, when Regina had left some neatly-typed stencils on my desk but wouldn't be in until tomorrow, I reluctantly headed down the hall to wrestle with our copy machine. As I passed by our program director's office, I remembered his offer to have his secretary Melba demonstrate her proficiency with the copier. Deciding to gamble he'd forgotten his two-day advance notice clause, I entered Roger's office.

Melba had her neatly cropped dark-haired head buried in a large yellow Atlas of the United States. The only out of proportion element in her pleasant features was a slightly protruding, over-sized jaw. She was so tiny, barely five-feet, that she kept pillows in her desk chair to raise her height. In contrast, her brain was far from tiny. Roger, her amiable boss, was a former band leader, and would have a thin time of it if Melba ever resigned.

She didn't hear me until I stood beside her. She closed the atlas hurriedly, and in the process of turning her chair around, knocked several colorful travel brochures off her desk.

I stooped to help pick them up. "Melba, I didn't mean to startle you." I glanced down at one of the brochures in my hand. "Mackinac Island, Michigan...isn't that the place no cars allowed, only horses...are you going to vacation there?"

Melba opened the atlas again and pointed to a spot on the map.

"Big Rapids, Michigan, why would anybody want to go there."

"Well, I've never been North...and that seemed a good place to start."

The saga of Harriet and Ronald had been dismissed from my mind and I wasn't prepared for a sequel. Nevertheless, the sight of Melba's determined jaw-line gave me forewarning that if Ronald stayed on ice during the winter months, he was going to get thawed out this coming summer.

"Melba, the best of luck to you...I have only one suggestion. Plan a small family wedding...the idea of a big church wedding makes Ronald very, *very* skittish."

CHAPTER 37

NO MORE DOGS

At the end of one of the longest Saturdays of my life, the day of the dog contest, I needed to sit somewhere before I fainted. My only seat choice was the cold concrete of the now-deserted parking lot, but no matter how uncomfortable, anything was better than standing. I flopped down with a sigh of relief.

From a distance, I watched Lamar Gene, our handyman, and Purdue Mills, our building superintendent, help the very last departing dog owners squeeze their animal into a toy-size red Hillman Minx. Son Al was standing on the sidewalk beside them. He'd begged to come with me to see the dogs and I was happy that, against my better judgment, I'd agreed. At least one of us had a wonderful day.

It was taking Purdue and Lamar Gene an unreasonably long time to settle the winner of the Ideal Dog Food contest's Largest Dog award. But then St. Bernards do not fit into small cars with ease. By the time the dog's owner had driven off, with Hugo, her St. Bernard, jammed into the back seat, I'd dismissed all curiosity as to why people who owned miniature cars also owned mammoth-sized animals. I was also thinking that fond as I'd become of Harriet before she left for the University of Florida and her family's grapefruit trees, at this moment, I wished she'd gone before coming up with this dog contest idea.

In the past, Dick and I had performed in theaters and auditoriums, but we'd never attempted an outdoor show, away from our Studio A womb. WLWA's recently acquired mobile unit had made possible today's classic textbook case for Murphy's law— that anything that can go wrong, will.

Two months ago we'd begun preparations—time enough to do it right. No more error-filled Bunny Flop posters plastered over town, and our main concern, a suitable outdoor location, was solved by our publicity man. Bill suggested using a vacant parking lot owned by the station. In the fall of '53, WLWA had bought land, located farther out on Peachtree Road, as a building site for more spacious quarters. So far, the paved parking lot next to a grove of trees was the only completed step of that project.

With the date, time and location settled, and the Ideal Dog Food Company's sponsorship, we felt confident that all was under control. In our organizational zeal, we even arranged a substitute plan in case of rain. We would show a Kennel Club film on prize-winning champions.

Bill Colvin, Dick and I were in our office going over the final details. Now, all we need are judges...can we do that ourselves?" I asked.

"Not unless you want to be pelted with Ideal dog food cans," Bill warned. "Dog owners are a touchy breed."

Heeding his advice, we invited Mr. Yarborough of the Humane Society and Mr. Eubanks of the Atlanta Kennel Club to act as judges.

When we called Mr. Eubanks, he said, "I've never judged anything but purebreds, but this sounds like fun."

All the big decisions had fallen into place, but Bill wanted to know about the categories, and Dick showed him a tentative list. "We've got prizes for the largest dog...smallest...dog with longest tail...best costume...and best trick dog."

I opted for more categories. "Why not add the prettiest and the ugliest?"

"Fran," Dick objected, "every kid thinks his dog is beautiful."

"You're right, bad idea."

We left it at five categories and decided the cut-off number for entries would be sixty animals. And from then on, the show developed as smoothly as a successful bank robbery.

The Saturday of the contest was clear and sunny, and the morning paper indicated no spring showers were expected. I was looking forward to the day, and was in such a cheerful mood that I didn't panic even when Marge Van Dyke called to say Dick would not be there.

"Fran, he has a high fever and much as he hates to be a no-show, I'm not going to let him get up. He wouldn't be a bit of help anyway, he's lost his voice."

I sympathized. "I thought he sounded funny yesterday...tell him not to worry, we planned things so well, he can relax and concentrate on getting better."

The show was scheduled for 2 p.m. but the crew was due to arrive at 1:30. Al's pleas to come with me had been granted after he'd promised to be quiet and stay out of the way. He would have promised anything to spend the day with a parking lot full of dogs. After the demise of his own dog, Rusty, Al had yearned for another, but Peace had firmly said, "No more dogs."

When I reached the parking lot at one o'clock in order to greet the early arrivals, I realized I hadn't thought to bring a card table for my paper work or some folding chairs for the judges. That's the last coherent thought I had the rest of the afternoon.

I also found that it's impossible to be in two places at once—before the camera and behind the scenes. During the hour before the show began, dogs of every size, breed and color poured into the lot in overwhelming numbers. Our announcement over the air limiting the contest to sixty dogs had gone unheeded.

Early in the proceedings, a friend of Ideal's Atlanta manager arrived with his small son and the boy's dog—a black and white mutt dressed in a clown suit. Although they hadn't signed up ahead of time, I accepted the dog with the thought that one or two extras wouldn't matter.

Exceptions, exceptions. Once I let that barrier down, I was obliged to take all non-registered comers. Instead of the anticipated sixty dogs, the count soon reached over a hundred.

The carnival-like atmosphere generated a high level of excitement which was catching. My shouted instructions could barely be heard over the din of chattering children and barking dogs. The Humane Society's pound was a haven of serenity by comparison.

The dogs were so keyed up that dog fights spouted like small geysers from one end of the lot to the other. Martin Magnus, our director inside the mobile truck, ordered the cameras to follow the fights until I relayed the message to him via cameraman Red.

"Martin, quit calling for shots of the warfare...you're lousing up Ideal's claim that their food makes ideal dogs."

Furthermore, our choice of location adjacent to a wooded area might not have been wise. After several parents disappeared into the foliage, I chastised myself for not thinking to provide a comfort facility until cries of "Here, Skeeter" or "Here, Blackie" came floating back from the woods. Then I realized that many a dog had escaped the clutches of a youthful owner to head for those tempting trees.

Some of the children were crying because of their straying dogs, while still more took up the chorus after the judges announced the winner of the 'largest dog' category. No other dog was as huge as Hugo, the St. Bernard, so none of the other dogs could even be in the running; but as an appeasement, I allowed the children, with their dogs, to march by the camera and wave to their friends at home.

In the smallest dog category, the choice between two mongrels, one of which looked like a cross between a Chihuahua with a touch of toy poodle. The other appeared to be a toy poodle with a touch of Chihuahua.

Mr. Yarborough and Mr. Eubanks picked up each dog several times, and after they held a lengthy discussion, Mr. Eubanks came over to say, "Fran, it's a tie so far...the only way to break it is to weigh the dogs...did you bring a scale?"

"Of course I didn't bring a scale," I said with some degree of tartness. "The last thing on my mind this morning was a scale."

Mr. Eubanks stood there waiting for me to come up with a solution. "I know, call it a tie... they both get prizes."

He looked relieved and went away, only to come back after the 'longest tail' judging was over. "Fran, did you bring a tape measure?"

True to form, I hadn't brought a tape measure either. The judges needed one to settle another squabble. After they'd chosen a long-haired dog's tail as the winner, a a short-haired dog owner insisted his dog had the same bone-length as the long-haired dog, and that it wasn't fair to include hair in the length of the tail.

The owners of the two dogs in question were bordering on the belligerent, so I called another tie with prizes for both and hoped the Ideal budget was sufficient to cover my generosity on their behalf.

The situation eased somewhat in the best-costume category. Even the losers applauded the choice of a black Scottie dressed in a kilt and tam-o-shanter, with his four-year-old owner in a matching kilt. The duo was so appealing I spent far too much time with them. This was my first experience with having *too much* to shoehorn into an hour, instead of the stretching we usually had to do to fill our *Music Shop* hour. A run-through would have been more efficient but was impossible under the circumstances.

Actually, the show was more of a totter-hobble-stagger and lurch-through. Before the contest began, I had no qualms about being able to keep things moving along by myself. Now I longed for Dick and appreciated how much it meant to have a partner.

But even Dick could have done nothing about the weather. Despite yesterday's assurance of no rain from Harvey Musslewhite, our weatherman, (he had sworn on his Georgia Weather Bureau man, his pointer, the Farmer's Almanac, and his great-aunt Velma's arthritis) we were suddenly being rained on.

A large cloud had floated over our parking lot and proceeded to shed enough dampness to terrify the cameramen with their expensive equipment and to send dog-owners back to their cars, dragging screaming children and yelping dogs behind them. The cloud passed so quickly that everyone soon came sheepishly back to the lot and we continued the contest. Precious time was lost, however, and the last category, the 'best trick' dog turned into a shambles.

We speeded things up by showing all the trick dogs at once. Although some of the dogs gave an excellent imitation of playing dead, it was hard to tell whether it was from training or boredom. A fox-terrier who lackadaisically ambled through a hoop won by default. Mercifully, the hour ended and I'd have to wait until later to discover if I'd made more enemies than friends for the Ideal company.

Meanwhile, by the time my son had left the men on the sidewalk and came to join me on the concrete pavement, my heart had stopped fibrillating. "Oh Mother," he yelled, "wasn't it great? I had the best time."

God love him, what would I do without his innocent eyes. Getting to my feet, I said, "Al, I'm happy you came along today—Mother really needed you—now do me one more favor." I pointed toward the trees. "Run over there and bring me my clipboard and things...then we'll head for home and you can tell everybody all about it."

Al trotted off to the other side of the lot. This time, I was so tired, I lay down full length on the pavement and wondered if I'd have the strength to drive the few blocks to Fifteenth Street. I drifted off for a minute and when I drifted back, a small black furry animal was sitting on my chest.

Al gathered the black blob in his arms. "Mother, look what I found, it was asleep on that stuff you told me to get."

I shook my head to wake up and asked, "What is it?"

"It's a puppy! Oh, Mother, can I keep it?"

Just then Lamar Gene and Purdue came over to us to say that they'd finally gotten Hugo and family off, and after I thanked them profusely for all they'd done to help me. I indicated the small puffball in Al's arms and said, "But somebody left this one, what'll we do with it?"

The two helpers didn't find my heartfelt thanks enough incentive for them to give suggestions on what to do with leftover puppies. They mumbled something about wives waiting for them for dinner and disappeared into the dusk.

"I can't imagine anyone forgetting such a cute little thing." I took the puppy from Al for a closer inspection. "To my untrained eye, it's a male of mostly French poodle...maybe three months old."

Al had no interest in minor details; his main question was "Can I keep it? I'm going to name it Fido."

Remembering that at his age, I'd named my pony Black Beauty, I didn't question the unoriginality of his choice. It didn't matter anyway, he couldn't keep it. "Al, this puppy belongs to someone and if they don't call the station, I'll mention it on Monday's show."

Al was not giving up. "But if nobody calls, *then* can I keep it?"

I couldn't let the child raise his hopes. "Al, you know what Peace said."

Last year when Al's dog Rusty died, our family went into deep mourning. We kept it from Al that we suspected our crotchety Wicked-Witch-of-the West neighbor, who disliked children and dogs with equal intensity, of luring Rusty to her back porch with her version of a poisoned apple. I had wanted to replace the dog immediately but Peace balked, protesting that she'd had more grief in her lifetime than she could handle without searching for more at the dog pound. "Fanny, our dog history has been dismal. Al will have to settle for cats and rats...we have more luck with them. No-sir-ee, *no more dogs*, and that's *final*."

But adamant as she'd sounded at the time, I didn't think she'd deny temporary shelter to our orphan. "Come along, Al and bring Fido. It'll be okay to keep him 'til we find the owner."

My assumption that Peace would be lenient about giving our lost puppy short-term hospitality until the rightful owner claimed it was correct. And on Monday's *Music Shop* I announced that we had a leftover puppy from Saturday's dog show and would the owner please call. For several days I made the same announcement. No one called.

At the end of the week, I decided to take the puppy downtown with me and put him up for adoption on the air. With Fido tucked under one arm, I was rummaging in the storage closet for something in which to carry him when Peace stuck her head around the corner.

"What are you doing in there?"

"Peace, I'm looking for a spare box. I need one for Fido...I'm raffling him off on the show today."

Before I knew it, Peace had snatched the puppy from me and was holding him up to her shoulder. From there, he began licking her face. "That's my sweet doggie," murmured Peace, "wassums that bad woman going to take you away...well, Peace won't let her."

"Honestly, Mother, you do beat all...what happened to all that sworn-on-the-Bible no more dogs resolution?"

When Peace answered, "I can't fight fate," and continued to stroke the wiggling bundle of black fur, I abandoned the box search and asked Peace to tell Al the good news.

Before I left for work, I heard them arguing in the kitchen. "Al, Fido just isn't a proper name for a part-French poodle."

"But Peace, the dog in my school book is named Fido...besides, when I call him Fido, he comes."

Peace capitulated. "Hum, changing his name now might give him a complex. Tell you what we'll do... you can call him Fido on one condition...if you'll let me spell it the French way, *Phydeau*."

CHAPTER 38

THE LOST SUPPER

On a blustery March morning in 1954 when I clattered into the office, Dick was on the phone. He gestured for me to quiet down and went on talking. "But Mr. Harris, I thought that *was* an allowable deduction...it always has been."

We each had a phone, which gave us some privacy, but we made a point of discreet withdrawal at the slightest indication such was desired. The March winds had blown me into a wild woman so I departed for the ladies' room to pull myself together. By the time I returned, Dick was bringing his conversation to a close. After he hung up, he pulled his hand down over his face and said, "Something's got to be done."

"About what?"

He still had the phone in one hand. "I've been talking with the IRS and...."

"Oh Dick, I *am* sorry." I could commiserate with anyone having dealings with that branch of the government as I was paying off an unexpected two-year misunderstanding. "I made a mistake on my return and I'm sure it cost them more to find me than they'll get...the IRS man told me I should pay my taxes with a smile."

"If you tried that, he'd still insist on cash." Dick replied. "But no, it's not the IRS exactly, it's Candy. I had to yell to her to get off the line...undignified, but better than having the whole staff know my tax business."

"I've warned Candy about her addiction. She smiles sweetly and keeps right on listening in."

Lazily drawing circles on his notepad, Dick was silent for a moment before he said, "Let's cure her for good.',

"Short of packing Miss Gum Spirits back to Waycross, I can't think of anything we could do...and in spite of sharing phone conversations, I'd miss her."

Dick had the same look on his face that my son Al gets when he's up to something. He told me his scheme. Every day until he knew Candy had overheard him, he would call me from a nearby phone and we would follow this scenario:

"Fran, I don't think we can sit on something this big any longer. Don't you think somebody ought to tell Candy?"

My response was to say, "No, no, it's too soon...let's wait."

"What if one of the Swingbillies lets it slip, they know, too—and more along the same line.

The second day our script was in action, Dick heard tell-tale clicks and faint breathing sounds during our conversation, and I was sure our fish had the hook in her kewpie-doll mouth when she asked, "We're friends, aren't we, Fran? I mean if you heard something like I was going to be fired, you'd tell me?" And she jerked off her earphones, a sure sign whenever Candy was agitated.

"Of course I would, Candy. But what gave you such an idea?"

She looked so worried, I was tempted to confess right then. Instead I repeated her words to Dick and we decided the joke had gone far enough. We worked out a new script.

Our next phone conversations would call for a meeting with the Swingbillies at ten o'clock on Wednesday morning to decide whether to reveal the mythical all to Candy that same day or wait another week.

At the appointed time, the five Swingbillies, Dick and I gathered in our office. Dick pointed through the glass partition to Candy and then to his watch. "A small wager...a dollar each in the pot...winner to guess the exact time she comes through the door."

Before he had time to collect the bets, Candy left her reception desk, ran across the lobby and burst into our office.

"Okay, you guys, what's all the hush-hush you can't decide whether to tell me or not?"

Standing there with her arms akimbo and her lip out almost as far as her bouffant skirt, Candy was such a picture of righteous indignation, we all laughed. When she realized that she'd given herself away, she reddened to match her hair.

We explained that the prank, with its message, was for her own good. She took it well, and was relieved that it wasn't more serious, and promised to go easy on the seven of us in the future. As she turned to leave the room, she rattled her bracelets and gave us a wink. "But I'm not promising as much for the rest of the bunch."

Our next problem came just a few days later when Dick found a box on his desk from our saleswoman, Martha Lord. Dick opened the box and lifted out a long oilcloth table cover. Oilcloth is a cotton fabric coated with vegetable oils and pigments that have been mixed into a clay filler. The unattractive material has since been largely replaced by plastic.

Martha's memo said the tablecloth was her only sample from a new mail-order account, and for us to please not lose it. A promotion would begin next week on the *Music Shop* and orders for the cloth were to be sent directly to the firm's Chicago office.

Dick spread the tablecloth out on his desk and we surveyed the horror gloomily. Reproductions of da Vinci's painting, *The Last Supper*, may be seen in hundreds of homes—but not on oilcloth table covers. Here the rich colors of the masterpiece had been cheaply copied in sickly hues dyed into the slick material.

Dick ran his hand over the slippery surface. "I didn't know it was possible to ruin a work of art this way. Poor Leonardo...he'd called this *The Lost Supper*."

I remembered a few things about the original painting from an art history course which I had taken. "Da Vinci began this painting in 1497, Dick, and finished it four years later. He used tempera which doesn't hold up as well as oil paint. And during World War II, a wall opposite the one the painting was painted on was blown away, so it stayed exposed to the weather for three years."

"I didn't know all that," Dick said. "It's a wonder it survived at all...and now some fast-buck mail-order house is adding insult to injury by stamping a great work of art on this ugly material—to catch ketchup."

"Look at the painting, Dick." I pointed to an area on the cloth. "See ... the salt spilled on the table points to Judas...I'd like to point it toward the people who thought up this repulsive idea."

"Sacrilegious," Dick said, "that's the only word for it."

"A sin against good taste, if nothing else."

A light dawned for Dick. "This has to be Candy's get-even joke ... and it beats our phone scam by a country mile" He grabbed the cloth and ran out to tell Candy that she had us going for awhile.

He returned in a few minutes to say the commercial was not a joke and that he'd already decided we wouldn't run it. "I couldn't face my Sunday-school class if I'd spent the week convincing our audience to buy one of those things." Dick taught Sunday school at his Presbyterian church and I admired him for it.

Although I had no Sunday-school class, the specter of my family's reaction to the appearance of such a commercial on our *Music Shop* was enough to deter me—that plus my own convictions. The battle of how far to go with ads was a constant source of friction. As WLWA-TV was on the air to make money, the sales department wielded much power.

On the other hand, a performer with the slightest conscience finds it difficult to smile in front of a camera, a piece of shoddy merchandise in hand, and entreat the audience to buy it. The idea of the tablecloth was so distasteful to me that I was pleased that

Dick, too, wanted to stand fast against presenting such a jarring product.

Our reaction to such a commercial must be considered in the context of the conservative climate of the '50s. The powerful billion-dollar electronic ministries with their high-profile high priests had yet to evolve.

In 1954, on Sunday mornings each week, our station tele-vised devotions from Atlanta's different churches as a public service. All denominations were covered.

Hovie Lister and his Statesmen Quartet, a popular gospel singing group, and Elvis Presley's idols when he was a young boy, were on at six Sunday evenings, followed by fifteen minute talks by the Reverend Billy Graham. These people hawked no religious articles and gave no pleas for money. Once the religious saviors discovered the power of television, however, they began buying TV time—and a new chapter began.

Dick, eager to have *The Last Supper* matter settled immedi-ately had left for the boss's office. When he returned, I asked if Carter had agreed with him.

"Not exactly...you know how hungry the station is and Carter hates to turn down business."

"So?"

"So I played my ace...insisted it was against my religious principles."

I raised an eyebrow. "How does a Presbyterian deacon get away with objecting to *The Last Supper*?"

"Funny...Carter asked me the same thing."

"What'd you say?"

"I told him that I'd recently converted to Judaism."

The outcome was a victory for our side. Carter threw the tablecloth tussle back in Martha Lord's lap. With Dick feeling that strongly about it, the manager didn't want an either/or situation to develop.

While folding up the eyesore cloth, I remembered that it was Martha's only sample and briefly considered trashing it. No, they'd send her another. Instead I hid it underneath a stack of drawing contest entries and hoped she'd forget about it.

That hope evaporated late in the afternoon. I was drawing a cross-eyed camel for tomorrow's show. One of our features was sketching cartoons while a popular record played. Dick was left-handed and I was right so we'd begin at each side and finish in the middle. We worked so rapidly it was necessary to prepare the newsprint paper with a light pencil sketch which wouldn't show on camera. At that time, Dick painted clown pictures as a hobby and was the better sketcher, but my drawings were adequate.

I was concentrating on the camel's expression so intently, I didn't hear anyone come in. I jumped when I felt a hand on my shoulder. Martha Lord said, "Excuse me, Fran, I didn't mean to startle you...I just came by to pick up my tablecloth."

Leaving my camel, I began searching the shelves until I found the cloth, and I said something banal about sorry things hadn't worked out.

She made no move to leave and instead said, "Do you have time to have a drink with me...we could walk up to the Owl Room."

Her invitation took me by surprise as it was the first socializing Martha had proffered to me during our many months of business association. Tired, I was mentally debating whether to accept, when the sight of a fine rain streaking the office windows helped in my decision to decline. Before I could tell her to invite me again some other time, she pressed, "Please, it's important."

Slipping her raincoat over her tailored suit, indistinguishable from all the other tailored suits with Peter Pan collars she habitually wore, she then put on one of her ever-present hats. The only incongruous brush stroke in this perfect career-woman picture were the ankle-strap shoes.

Somewhat unwillingly, I put on my coat and followed her down to the street. It was raining so hard by the time we passed the garage where I kept my car, I almost begged off. My 'elephant's child curiosity' won. I wanted to know what was important enough to inspire Martha's sudden urge to walk six blocks in drenching rain for a drink with me. Also I couldn't resist the opportunity to learn more about the person behind Martha's businesslike office armor.

The Ansley-Dinkler Plaza's Owl Room had been named for its frieze of plaster owls with lighted eyes. The bar was crowded at this hour, and although the term 'singles bar' had yet to be coined, the Owl Room was known as a place to meet that special mysterious stranger, and I felt self-conscious. I'd never been there without an escort; I wasn't at all certain Martha qualified in that respect.

The young maitre d' said we'd have to wait for a table, but before I could bolt, he took a second look and said, "Why hello, Fran, remember me—Ted Atlee from Chemistry One at North Fulton?"

I never thought a subject I barely passed would pay off one day, but my teammate in that perplexing study managed to find us a quiet corner table. We shed our sodden coats, and Martha removed her hat and straightened out its damp feather.

"I don't think I've ever seen you without a hat," I commented, and went on to tell her about my Aunt Sue, who also wore hats well, indoors and out.

Martha said she used them to give her height and dignity, and they were also godsends for a working woman who called daily on business offices—since hats concealed the hair that needed a trip to the beauty salon.

As we talked, we discovered common ground. She was a widow with an eleven-year-old daughter and we compared the trials of single parenthood. I asked her how she'd become a "time" saleswoman as at the time it was an unusual occupation for a woman.

"I was secretary to Mr. Moore, the sales manager at radio station WATG, and after I rescued an account one of his salesmen bungled, he suggested I try selling. I like the freedom...." The waiter brought our drinks and when he left, Martha took a sip of her Scotch and soda and said, "Ah, I needed that on a wet night... where was I? Oh, to sum it up, I could never punch a time-clock again."

As we continued to chat, other mutual interests surfaced, including a love of the theater. Recently, Martha had played the part of Crystal, the man-eating other woman, in a community theater's presentation of *The Women*.

"I wish we'd known that, you could have given a sample scene on the *Music Shop*. Remember that for your next play."

Pleased with the suggestion, she said she could have kicked herself for not mentioning it to me earlier, and catching our waiter's eye though a haze of smoke, she ordered another round. I'd been preparing my farewell as I hadn't called home to say I'd be late, and Martha had yet to reveal anything that could justify her earlier "Please, it's important" entreaty. And I didn't want another drink, for during the week I seldom drank anything stronger than tea or coffee. What was a harmless amount of spirits for some, was hangover time for me.

Whether it was the second drink or Martha's friendly interest, I found myself enjoying our conversation. The original purpose of her invitation had yet to surface but we did become better acquainted. We swapped stories about the difficulties of being a single woman in the fifties when most of our contemporaries were leading lives of domesticity.

She confided, "It's tough to be a female in sales...sometimes I have a hard time convincing advertisers to take me seriously."

I regarded her with new respect and sympathy. "Martha, now that I think of it, I don't want to change jobs with you."

Walking through the hotel lobby before parting company, Martha said casually, "By the way, Fran, since Dick turned it down, maybe you'd consider the tablecloth commercial...I'm going to lose the account if I don't find a choice spot."

"Martha, I can't believe my ears. The hacksaw job I did on your freezer commercial, even with its happy ending, surely proved that freezer commercial, even with its happy ending, surely proved that I'm not good with the hard stuff."

"As long as I get it on a good show, the company isn't fussy about who does the commercial...also," she gave my shoulder a pat, "I'll see that you get top dollar."

"What do you mean, *they* aren't fussy?" I squawked. It was one thing for me to be particular but not the other way around from some low-class mail-order house.

"Don't ruffle your feathers, I just meant that sometimes on the air when you get nervous, you stutter."

"Marion Davies stutters, but she manages okay."

"Yes, but Fran, you don't have a Mr. Hearst."

I laughed, but was secretly vexed by the proposal. Now I understood her unexpected hospitality. I'd thought the tablecloth matter settled, yet here it was on my doorstep again.

"You don't have to give me an answer tonight," Martha said. "Go home, dream about all that nice money, and we'll talk more tomorrow."

CHAPTER 39

INDISCRETIONS AND DESCECRATIONS

I had promised Martha that I'd sleep on her idea but suspected that sisterhood and greed were about to overcome any principle I might have that some things shouldn't be for sale. After all, what harm could a few commercials do? There were plenty of places the extra money Martha dangled so temptingly could go. Cora Lee needed new teeth, Peace needed a new coat, the old house needed painting—the list of needs was long.

When I came through the kitchen that evening I gave Cora Lee a cheery greeting but didn't get one back. She was either peeved with me for not calling that I'd be late, or it was one of her sore-blood days.

Cora Lee had two pet ailments, the sore-blood and the down-in-the-back. Other days she was plain tarred, which had nothing to do with the dark, sticky paving substance, but meant she was 'plum wore out' or tired. None of these conditions slowed her down but we tried to cosset her on her infrequent low days.

"What's the matter, Cora Lee, a touch of sore-blood?"

"No, Miss Fanny, it's that boy of your'n."

Oh dear, I thought to myself, when Cora Lee calls Al, *my* boy, instead of *her* Allison, it's serious. When I asked her what he had done, she instructed me to go into the serving pantry and take a look at the Lady Baltimore cake she'd made for Sarah Dent's birthday tomorrow. I looked, then came back to the kitchen and reported, "There's a big hole in the side... looks like somebody stuck a fist in it."

Cora Lee stuck her lip out even further. "Somebody did, and he's upstairs in his room."

I wondered all the way upstairs as to what had possessed Al to put his fist through Cora Lee's Lady Baltimore. He was a sunny child. I can't think of a better word for his disposition once he recovered from his first six months of infancy colic. A normal little boy, he had a fair share of mischief on his record. Last year, he and his best friend had thrown rocks at the Harper Florist greenhouse which backed up to our property. The perpetrators of the broken glass incident would have remained unknown without Al's conscience-stricken confession.

On the whole though, his misdeeds were minor and came as a surprise to us. In hindsight, I'm certain that being raised by three strong, albeit loving, women, often made him feel like putting his small fist through something, if only a birthday cake.

I found Al sitting in a chair in front of the maple desk Aunt Sue had given him when he started first grade. He was clutching Fig Newton, the tattered rabbit he'd had since babyhood. Newton had been consigned to the back of Al's closet (as befitted a second grader) and was brought out only for dire emergencies. Al's eyes were red from crying and even if Cora Lee hadn't told me the story, some white cake icing still stuck on his hands was a giveaway.

"Mother, is Cora Lee real mad?"

"Well, let's say she's not very happy." I pulled up a chair beside him. "She has so much to do and when she makes an extra effort like a birthday cake, it hurts to have it ruined."

Al didn't say anything so I continued. "Cora Lee is an artist in her own way and she made something special...the same as you did with my wonderful birthday collage. You wouldn't have wanted her to put her fist through that, now would you?"

Al shook his head, and I asked, "Al, do you know why you did it?"

He shrugged his shoulders and said he was running through the service pantry, the cake was sitting on the shelf, and before he knew it, his right hand shot out and when it came back to him, it was covered with icing.

I put my hand over my mouth to keep from laughing. "Al, do you want to hear a story?" As a story was the last thing Al was expecting, he quickly nodded yes.

"Okay, once upon a time when I was five-years old, we lived on the Prado at the other side of Ansley Park. My six-year-old friend, Charles Wagonhalls, lived next door, and we played together almost every day during the summer. That September, Charles started first grade at your school, Spring Street, and I went to kindergarten. After that, Charles wouldn't play with me anymore."

I stopped for a second and Al said, "That was mean of him."

"I understand now, but I didn't then. On day, as I was walking home from Miss Mamie's kindergarten, I saw Charles's bicycle parked at the top of a wooded hill...the one that leads down to the creek in the park. I went over to the bike, pointed it toward the creek, and gave it a good hard shove. Down the hill it went until it crashed into a tree and fell over into the water."

"Oh, Mother," Al gasped in empathetic response to the enormity of my act. "What did you do, did you run away?"

"No, but I wanted to. I was like you when you told us about the greenhouse. Nobody would know how the bicycle got smashed unless I told on myself."

"Mother," Al patted my hand and from the lofty age of seven granted me leniency for my youthful indiscretion. "You were only five."

"I was old enough to know that I'd done a bad thing and why— to hurt Charles. But I know you didn't mean to hurt Cora Lee, did you?"

"No ma'am, it was sorta like at the beach when we make sand cakes...and then we smush them."

He had a point but he'd have to learn the difference between a sand cake and Cora Lee's real cake so I asked him what he thought he should do to make it up to her.

We discussed some possibilities and finally we decided to use some of his Christmas money to buy Cora Lee a birthday cake at the Sugar Plum Bakery tomorrow. That way she wouldn't have to bake another one for Sarah.

Before he left the room to make his settlement with Cora Lee, I said, "Al, some day ask Peace to tell you the story about when Dotty Dimple pushed her blonde curly-headed cousin, wearing his Little Lord Fauntleroy suit, into the fish pond."

"Who's Dotty Dimple?"

"That's what her family called Peace when she was a little girl."

Al looked as if he doubted that Peace was ever a little girl—or me either, and after he left the room, I hoped I'd handled the cake thing all right. Nobody hands you a book of instructions when you become a parent. The idealized version of an unbroken string of happy childhood memories is seldom true. The mere telling of my Charles Wagonhalls story had give me a deep wrench in the pit of my stomach. Although the incident happened decades ago, in my mind I still heard the crashing sound of Charles's bicycle when it hit the tree and I could still see the twisted wheel spinning in the water.

But maybe that uneasy feeling in my stomach was related to the question of what to do about Martha's tablecloth offer. Although it gave us some advantage, at times I wished management wouldn't leave quite so many decisions to us. If Carter had presented Martha with an actual order to back off, I wouldn't have to make a choice now.

By next morning, the unshakable *Last Supper* was on my desk once more. It seemed to have been in our office longer than it had taken da Vinci to do the original painting. Dick, in passing by, said, "I thought we'd gotten rid of that thing."

I was ashamed to tell him I was considering going along with Martha's request and that he might have 'The Supper" around for some time. And presently, Bill Colvin stopped by and offered his unasked-for observations. "Hum, I heard Martha finally found a home for the tablecloth commercial...I knew Dick turned it down... imagine my surprise to hear it landed on *Music Shop* anyway."

Colvin was the male equivalent of Candy and knew what was going on at the station before anything *was* going on.

I didn't realize my mind was made up until I snapped, "It's simple...Martha needed a favor. As a single female parent, I can identify...selling 'time' is hard enough for men and even rougher for Martha."

Bill looked at me with amusement. "Where'd you get the idea Martha trails in the sales department? She sells the pants off Pete and Scott...and boy, do they resent it."

"Good for her," I said, and meant it.

Half an hour later Martha came into the office with a script in hand. She made no reference to our Owl Room visit but started right in on the business at hand.

"Fran, you can put this in your own words but here's a guideline from the company...'Leonardo da Vinci's masterpiece, *The Last Supper*, faithfully reproduced in all its moving glory on our famous wear-ever triple-ply oilcloth table covers. Yours for the unbelievably low price of $9.98, by calling this number...."

Martha plowed on without seeming to notice I'd put my hands over my ears. "I think it best to tack the tablecloth on the wall instead of showing it on a table. What do you think?"

"It doesn't matter what I think, I can't do it."

"But Fran, you promised! I was counting on you."

"Martha, I only agreed to *think* about it." I picked up the slippery oilcloth and the colors seemed even more distorted than they had yesterday. How could I have considered the matter for even a short while? Once again, I handed the cloth back to Martha, this time commenting, "I'd surely go to hell for convincing anyone to put something that hideous on their table."

Martha gave one last pitch. "Think of it from another angle...you'd be introducing a work of art into homes which might not have one otherwise."

"Oh c'mon, Martha, even you don't believe that. Somehow the idea of somebody slurping soup from a bowl on Luke's chest or having Christ being covered by a dish of beef stew doesn't seem the best way to introduce art into the home."

Martha laughed and took my refusal with good grace. She

tucked the cloth under her arm and said, "It's pretty bad, I know, but a buck's a buck. Anyway, no hard feelings...I've got another spot for it in case you turned me down."

After she left the room, I sat there shaking my head.

I felt I'd come to a right decision for wrong reasons. Still, there was a bright side even though Dick and I hadn't succeeded in keeping the commercial off the air with our small skirmish. Martha would probably leave the *Music Shop* off her list should her next account be a set of plates embossed with the bloody severed head of John the Baptist.

Dick and I were in our office the following Monday when I found a small package on my desk, with an accompanying memo from Martha Lord. 'The enclosed is to be advertised on *Music Shop*. Fran will model it while Dick makes the pitch, and this time Mr. Sever says it's an order.'

"Probably some tacky old housecoat," I said to Dick, ripping the paper off the package. "Oh, no! She couldn't, she...she...." I sputtered. "Not again."

I held up a neon-yellow T-shirt with the words "Jesus Saves" spelled out in purple sequins on the front.

Dick grinned and said, "As long as *I* don't have to wear it, it's not so bad. Anyway, you don't have much choice—Carter has spoken."

"I'll go naked down Peachtree before I wear this...this...this thing." I jammed the abomination back into its box. "I'm going next door this minute and tell Carter, 'No.'"

I was halfway out of the door when Dick yelled, "Hold it...wait a minute." He was doubled up so, I thought he had a cramp until I saw he was laughing. Finally he recovered enough to say, "I didn't know you'd blow so soon...Marge was hoping to get more mileage out of all that work."

"Marge?" I was still irate and having a hard time following his remark. "What's Marge got to do with Martha's 'Jesus Saves' shirt?"

Dick said that while he was telling Marge about our *'Lost Supper'* battle, and our cure for Candy's switchboard eavesdropping, Marge got the idea for a practical joke of her own. "She had more fun making that thing...she spent an hour sticking on those purple sequins."

"Lie to her a little," I said, smiling now. "Tell her I stewed all morning before working up the courage to holler to Carter."

I held the frightful T-shirt out at arms length and looked at it again. "At least Marge made an original desecration...not a desecration of an original."

CHAPTER 40

THE 'MILASHUN' of CORA LEE

Marge's 'Jesus Saves' work of art now held pride of place on our bulletin board. A colorful addition, and an inspiration because so many times we felt only divine guidance could get us through another show.

Subsequent events indicated that 'Love Thy Neighbor' on the shirt would have been more helpful.

One evening, when I entered our kitchen, Al greeted me with one of his 'knock-knock' jokes. He was at the riddle-and-joke age and had such an inexhaustible supply, I considered placing him on the *Music Shop* credits list as a writer, along with Peace's title of Prop Master. If Al was any example, Spring Street School was turning out more comedians than mathematicians.

My talents as a straight man were being honed daily by the role I played for Dick on the show, so I recognized my cue when Al said, "Mother, knock, knock."

"Who's there?"

"Doris."

"Al, we don't have a Doris here."

"Moth-urr, you're supposed to say, 'Doris who?'"

"Okay, Doris who?"

Al flapped his arms triumphantly and said, "Doris closed, that's why I knocked."

He began another but I held up my hand in mock horror. "No, no, don't torture me...save them for the dinner table and we can all guess."

Al was jumping from one foot to another with excitement. "We're not eating here...we're going to the Tenth Street Coffee Shoppe for supper."

Al was another Candy. His household news was sometimes garbled but always contained a germ of truth.

"What's up...why aren't we eating here?"

"'Cause Cora Lee's in bed with 'milashun.'"

'Milashun' was not one of Cora Lee's regular down-in-the-back or sore-blood ailments so I had no idea what he meant. I assumed it must be serious though for our stalwart friend to make one of her rare retreats to the sick bed.

Peace was so busy helping Will prepare a tray for Cora Lee's dinner that she only nodded confirmation to Al's announcement. Peace, Al, student Sarah Dent and I were dining out.

After we'd fitted ourselves snugly into one of the coffee shop's red plastic booths, I asked, "Why didn't the other girls come with us?"

"Betty Sue's with Warren and the other two went to a dance." Peace explained that Claudine's brother, Brandon, and his friend, Eric, premed students at Emory University, had invited Claudine and Gretchen to a Chi Phi fraternity house dance. All day the girls had been holding endless conferences beside themselves with anticipation.

"I've never been asked so much advice in my life," Peace said. "On what to wear, what to do with their hair, what to say...."

"Why in the world would Brandon ask his sister to a dance?" I asked. "Surely he could do better than Claudine."

Claudine Suggs from Plains, Georgia, came in last of the four art students in my estimation. When she kept her mean streak under control, she had a bluff heartiness which gained her a certain amount of popularity with her classmates at the Museum school. I secretly believed some of the attention was due to her relatives. Any young woman who has three tall, attractive, unmarried older brothers is not always loved for herself alone. To add to her winning hand, two of the brothers were going to school in Atlanta, one at Emory University and the other at Georgia Tech.

"Fanny, he isn't taking Claudine. She went with the friend, Eric. Brandon said he'd bring Eric for her if she'd ask one of our other girls to be *his* date."

Betty Sue Darby from Savannah wasn't a possible as she was enamored of Warren Daniels, the young lawyer who'd rescued her from the city jail, but Gretchen Rosser and Sarah Dent had yet to make any firm commitment to a local swain.

My choice would have been the quiet, intelligent Sarah Dent with her rare offbeat sense of humor. Sarah subscribed to the *New Yorker* magazine which the other girls considered the height of sophistication, and they were somewhat in awe of her.

Perhaps that's why Claudine chose the chattier Gretchen, whose whole personality was right there in the front window. And Gretchen's main interest in life was men. The art school was merely a time-filler until she met Mr. Right. Gretchen was outspoken about her goal, but all of us more or less shared the same thought.

In the South, in the '50s, marriage and motherhood were still thought to be the most suitable roles in life for women.

Once the coffee shop waitress had taken our orders, my next and more important question was "What's with Cora Lee?...Al says she has 'milashun'...that's a new one."

Peace furrowed her brow for a second. "Oh, I know what he means. He heard me say that Cora Lee had suffered a *humiliation*."

While she was relating the events of the day, I couldn't decide which locale was the scene of more daily crises, WLWA-TV or our home on Fifteenth Street. The latest home crisis involved the simple act of washing clothes.

Cora Lee did our laundry in an old Maytag which she filled with water using a hose. She emptied the washer in the same manner, but unable to find the customary long hose attachment, which let the water drain on Peace's flower beds, she had used a shorter length hose. But the short piece had reached only as far as the back porch steps and allowed the draining water to flow into the driveway, and on to the sidewalk downhill past our neighbor's house.

Mrs. Wexler, the shrew of the neighborhood, had been a source of great discomfort to us for years. Our list of her unneighborly acts was long, headed by the poisoning of our beloved dog, Rusty. Although we couldn't prove our suspicions, circumstantial evidence plus her known hatred of the animal made her the logical culprit.

Today she'd added one more malicious act to our list by reporting Cora Lee to the police. "That terrible woman!" I almost choked on my mouthful of meatloaf. "How could she call the police over a little water running down the sidewalk?"

"I came home from study club this morning just in time to see a police car backing down the driveway," Peace said, "and half the neighborhood rubber-necking in front of the house."

Since we seldom had a police car on Fifteenth Street, this one brought out the curious. The officers had merely given Cora Lee a warning not to empty the washing machine water on the public sidewalk in the future. Nevertheless, a visit from the police, and even such a minor reprimand, had left Cora Lee feeling she'd been responsible for a major lapse in respectability.

Peace sighed. "She was so undone she took to her bed with 'milashun.' Will and I spent the afternoon hanging out the wet laundry so I didn't have time to make dinner."

"Poor Cora Lee," I said, ""what can we do to cure her?"

"I asked her if she'd like to take a short vacation." Peace looked distressed. "That only made her cry harder...said I wanted to get rid of her."

Al gave his suggestion. "We could get her some buttercups."

Sarah laughed and asked Al what made him think Cora Lee wanted buttercups, even if they *had* been blooming in March.

Al said with conviction, "I know she likes 'em. She has a can with a picture of buttercups on the front-,,

"Al, where does she keep this can?" Peace tightened her lips.

"In the big kitchen closet, behind a lot of maple syrup bottles."

Peace said with exasperation, "So Cora Lee's been dipping Buttercup snuff again...she promised me she'd given up the habit. No, we won't buy her any buttercups."

During this conversation, Sarah had been absent-mindedly tugging on a strand of her dark, curly hair when suddenly she slapped her hand on the table. "May I suggest something?"

"Anything's better than vacations or buttercups, which is the best we've done so far," Peace said.

"Our cook at home, Norissa, has a beautiful voice, one of the best in Eufala...she sings in her choir the same as Cora Lee, and loves to have the family come to hear her."

"Sarah, a brilliant idea...a chance to show off for her proud 'family' should chase away a mild case of humiliation." Peace snapped her fingers. "We'll ask her if we can visit her church next Sunday."

"Well, if you do, don't embarrass her like Daddy did dear Norissa one time," Sarah warned.

"I can't imagine your father ever embarrassing anyone," I said. "What on earth did he do?"

Sarah smiled at the memory. "For starters, a deacon seated Daddy, Mother, Sis and me smack dab in the middle of the front row of the church. We were about as inconspicuous as four white giraffes. When it came time for the collection plate, Daddy dug into his pocket and put in a $20 bill for the four of us."

Peace observed that certainly seemed generous enough not to cause any embarrassment.

Sarah gave a half smile. "That was only the beginning. The minister announced that the church needed roof repairs in the worst way...so the choir was going keep singing and the deacons were going to keep passing the plate as long as it took to collect enough for the job. The second time 'round, Daddy didn't have any more cash on him so he borrowed some from Mother."

"I'd better tell our church they're missing out on a good fund raising plan," Peace said. "Go on, Sarah, your daddy hasn't disgraced himself yet."

"Well, the choir kept singing, the plate kept whizzing by, and Daddy kept borrowing money from Mother, then finally Sis and me. While all this was going on, Norissa began shaking her head and glaring at Daddy from the choir box. He hadn't a clue as to what he'd done wrong 'til the next day."

Sarah took a swallow of her iced tea while we waited expectantly. "Norissa told him she'd always bragged to her friends that her Mr. Dent was one of the most upright and successful men in Eufala, Alabama...and here he turns up on the front row of her church—borrowing money from his women folk. She didn't know when she could hold her head up again."

Al was getting restive with the heavy, for him, conversation so he asked, "Sarah, what has arms and legs, but no head?"

"Beats me."

"A chair."

"Okay, Al, you got me, but here's one for you. Why is the Fourth of July like soup?" Al shook his head so Sarah gave him the answer. "'Cause it goes best with crackers."

Al was delighted to find a kindred spirit and a new straight man. And we were delighted with Sarah's plan of action to combat Mrs. Wexler's mortification of our Cora Lee—just so we remembered to ask first if her church needed a new roof.

On the drive home, Peace inquired, "Sarah, you were the only person downstairs when the boys came by for Claudine and Gretchen. What were they like?"

"I only talked with them for a few minutes but brother Brandon doesn't look a thing like Claudine."

I thought to myself that was a plus for him already.

"They don't look as if they come from the same family. She's short, stocky and sandy-haired and he's tall, slender and dark-haired. His friend Eric smiled but never opened his mouth."

As an afterthought she added, "Brandon has nice manners... he shook my hand and said he'd enjoyed talking with me."

During the next couple of weeks, after the Battle of the Maytag and Cora Lee's 'milashun', life at home seemed serene. Dick and I were rushed at the studio for a Big Apple employee's show. Big Apple, a chain of grocery stores, was one of our biggest sponsors so we wanted to keep them happy. When we discovered our stage was to be one of their freight cars beside a warehouse loading dock, I wasn't certain I wanted to keep them that happy; freight cars have been known to move.

With so much extra activity at the station, I hadn't paid too much attention to home developments; but one evening at the dinner table the change in atmosphere was so palpable I noticed that all was not well. With the exception of Al and Sarah, our usual merry band was quiet and constrained.

Claudine sat at her place like a squatty sand-colored rock. Al's attempt to coax a smile from her with his latest knock-knock joke was met with sullen silence. The girls treated Al like a lovable young brother so that wasn't a normal reaction.

Gretchen wasn't silent, but we wished she would be. She rattled on about nothing in particular in a voice which hit the ear like a factory whistle. And the occasional tear sliding down Betty Sue's cheek into her spoon bread indicated misery of some sort.

Finally Peace couldn't stand the tension any longer. She asked the girls if she could try out the essay she'd written for her study club to see if they had any improving suggestions. As the paper was strategically placed on the sideboard within easy reach, I suspect she'd planned to read it, with or without encouragement, in the hope of diverting her charges' attention from whatever was troubling them.

Al and I loved my mother's stories so we clapped receptively and Sarah followed suit. Peace ignored the lack of response from the other three, cleared her throat and began reading.

After reading a few paragraphs of her paper describing her girlhood at the turn of the century, Peace looked up from her paper and realized her fifty-year backward look wasn't a success as a diversionary tactic. She put the paper down and said, "I'll finish some other time."

Once again silence reigned over the table, with only the sweet sound of ""Amazing Grace" wafting in from the kitchen. The message in Cora Lee's song fell on deaf ears and it was apparently going to take some time to discover what was troubling three of Peace's flowers, who were more like cactus plants tonight. I decided to take Marge's 'Jesus Saves' T-shirt off the office bulletin board and wear it to dinner tomorrow evening. Maybe that would spark the atmosphere up again.

In the meantime, nobody could keep a secret for long at our house. Would it be Peace, Cora Lee, or Al who would solve the mystery of why everyone was so out of sorts these days.

CHAPTER 41

MEAN STREAKS,
WEAK STREAKS

I didn't wear Marge Van Dyke's yellow T-shirt to dinner the next evening, but my description of the Big Apple employees' party coaxed a few smiles from the unsociable group.

Standing on top of a box-car, Dick and I had lip-synched the record, "We're Just Two Little Girls from Little Rock," with Dick as Jane Russell and me as Marilyn Monroe. I wore a leopard-skin hat, but that was before anyone realized leopards were becoming an endangered species.

We'd finished our song when a gust of wind carried the hat off my head onto the railroad tracks below. I lunged for it in an unsuccessful rescue attempt, and if Dick hadn't been quick-witted and agile enough to catch me, I'd have been an endangered species along with my leopard hat.

When my rescue story was interrupted by a phone call for Betty Sue, one mystery of the girls' strange behavior was solved. As soon as she'd left the dinner table, Sarah held up crossed fingers. "Let's hope that's Warren...Betty Sue hasn't heard from him in well over a week."

Peace looked concerned. "So that's it...I heard her crying in her room last night but until she says something, I don't want to pry."

A jubilant Betty Sue returned to the table with the news that she had a date with Warren for Saturday night. Her mood change left us with only two malcontents, Gretchen and Claudine, and the rest of us rose above their gloom.

Peace entertained us with the latest on Mrs. Wexler. "I was in the backyard showing Will where to plant Betty Sue's Silver Moon rose—the bush she gave me for Easter—when Mrs. W. pops out on her back porch like one of those little birds who come out of cuckoo clocks. She waves for me to come over."

"The dowager duchess granting an audience." I shook my head in disgust. "Why do you run over there every time that witch crooks a scrawny finger."

"She's an old lady and not well," Peace said with compassion. "And those two sons...."

I interrupted to explain the sons to Sarah. "They're contractors, and all that unsightly lumber and junk in Mrs. Wexler's back yard belongs them. We can't get a removal order out of the health department."

"The last official to give the mess a look-see said they didn't want to discourage small businesses." Peace raised her eyebrows. "Can you imagine? I told them the only small business in that pile was rat-raising."

I scolded, "I don't see why you speak to her after all the bad things she's done to us."

"Fanny, she's crippled with arthritis and might as well be alone for all the mind those sons pay her...rattling around in that spooky old house with nothing to do but worry her neighbors."

"Mark my words," I said with a frown, ,someday she's going to push your see-no-evil soul over the edge. If she calls the police for a little water running down the sidewalk, God knows what she'll do next."

Peace rejected my prediction and told us that this time Mrs. Wexler had made a pleasant request. She'd asked permission for professional gardeners to clip the privet hedge and trim the eight mimosa trees which served as a divider between her property and ours.

For years, Mrs. Wexler had claimed that the trees and hedge were our responsibility. Mimosa trees are beautiful but they shed like a pawn shop fox fur. Gratefully, however, we accepted ownership for the shade they gave the house through the long sizzling Georgia summers. Few houses then had air conditioning so we depended on electric fans, tree-shade and iced-tea to get us through the hot months.

From time to time Will had hacked away at the hedge, but he was like a barber who can't resist taking a wee bit more off the top. The results resembled a roller-coaster.

"Will can't trim trees," said Peace, "so I'll be glad for a professional touch." She began pulling her napkin through a china napkin ring, then paused, "Come to think of it though, she's never asked me for permission to do anything before."

Sarah commented that Peace was getting an olive branch in the form of a privet hedge from her irascible neighbor. I had a caustic observation on the tip of my tongue but thought better of it. Peace would only chide me for my pessimism.

In the week that followed, an unexpected change in the weather wasn't the only surprise we had. I arrived home Friday evening to find Peace waiting for me in my bedroom. She asked me to close the door. "Now I know why sorority housemothers often take to the sherry bottle...if four girls are this much trouble, imagine a whole house full of them." She took a deep breath. "I've asked Claudine to find another place as soon as possible."

I flipped over backward on the bed in astonishment. "For heavens sake, why?"

"Surely you've noticed how grim meal time's been this week."

"Yes, but hardly cause for such off-with-their-heads action. Why are they all in such a rotten humor anyway?"

"Claudine's mad at Sarah...but not half as mad as she is at Gretchen. The girls are bound to be at sixes-and-sevens sometimes...but today, Claudine went too far."

"What'd she do?"

"She emptied all the clothes out of Gretchen's closet, dumped them in the hall, and was about to pour a pitcher of water and a package of flour on them when I caught her."

Peace threw up her hands. "I can't tolerate such behavior."

Apparently the feud had begun the night the two girls went to the Emory fraternity dance. Eric, the friend brother Brandon had brought for Claudine, called a few days later with an invitation to a hay-ride—except he invited Gretchen instead of Claudine.

"From what Sarah tells me, Eric and Gretchen are a good match. She's the original long-playing tongue, never stops talking, and he never starts."

Shrugging off my coat, I threw it over a chair and asked Peace, "How in the name of Nowhere can Claudine get mad over that? It isn't as if Gretchen had stolen her steady beau."

Peace absent-mindedly picked up my coat and hung it in the closet. "Blind date or no, Claudine's behaving as though Gretchen's broken up Abelard and Heloise...or Romeo and Juliet."

"Sarah wasn't in on any of that...what's Claudine's beef with her?"

"She's furious because brother Brandon asked Sarah to that same hay-ride—instead of asking Gretchen, who was Claudine's choice for him the night of the dance. Remember?"

"Peace, none of this makes sense...but then I've always thought Claudine had peat moss in her head for brains."

All day Sunday, the ill-will emanating from Claudine was catching. I snapped at Al for no reason; Cora Lee grumbled from the kitchen about too much work; Gretchen and Sarah, co-victims of Claudine's displeasure, whispered conspiratorially in corners. Betty Sue added to the murky climate by hovering pitifully over the phone, waiting to hear why Warren hadn't shown up for their date last evening.

Late that afternoon neither Peace nor I could stand the sight of Betty Sue's suffering any longer. We sat her down on the piano bench and tried to put some spine in her.

I began with the suggestion that she call Warren. "Betty Sue, just pick up the phone and ask the ill-mannered bozo what happened to him...maybe he's had an accident."

Betty Sue's Savannah conditioning wouldn't permit her to do anything so forward. "Fran, he lives with his parents, so somebody would have let me know."

Impulsively, I went to the phone and called John Whitney. We'd been together last evening so I knew he had Sunday night duty at WQST. John reported he'd have heard if Warren was suffering from anything more serious than a two-sizes-too-large hat size for his pointed head.

"What do you mean, John? What's happened to balloon Warren's head all of a sudden?"

"OOPS, gotta go, record's almost over, air time coming up... talk with you later." The line went dead. I don't think air time was coming up—I think John joined the Benevolent Male Protective Society and didn't want to discuss Warren's transgressions with me. I returned, after our unsatisfactory conversation, in time to hear Peace's pep talk.

"Betty Sue, you're a pretty, sweet-natured and very talented young lady. If Warren doesn't realize what a gem you are, that's okay. Men are like the Peachtree trolley, if you miss one, another'll be along soon."

Betty Sue was not to be comforted. She whispered that Warren was the only man she'd ever want and walked sorrowfully up the stairs.

Peace watched her disappear around the landing. "She didn't give me time to suggest my sure-fire cure for all ills, a Technicolor musical. I'd planned to take her to the Tenth Street theater tonight...the movie, *Seven Brides for Seven Brothers*, is on."

I gave her a wry look and said, "Mother, in Betty Sue's present frame of mind, I don't think a movie with seven brides in it would do much cheering up."

"Well, maybe my prescription wouldn't do for Betty Sue...but it would do *me* a world of good after this dreary Sunday."

My Monday morning return to the frenetic but more cheerful ambiance of the television station was a relief. The discords at home didn't stay contained there, however, as a half-hour before show time, Cora Lee called. Her words were so hurried and excited, I had to ask her to calm down so I could understand her. "Miss Fanny, you gotta come home right now...Miz Wexler's cuttin' down our trees."

"I can't come home now, Cora Lee, we're about to go on the air. Where's Peace?"

"She's out somewheres, but Miz Wexler and two mens with big saws is in our driveway. Will and I can't stop her and you ain't gonna have no mo 'mosa trees without you coming home this minute."

"Did you tell her those trees are on our property?"

"Yessum, but today she say they're on hers and they sheds too much."

In spite of my reassuring Cora Lee that she'd done all she could, she hung up the phone with great reluctance.

Needless to say, the hour's show dragged by and I could only hope Cora Lee was unduly alarmed and had mistaken the men's trimming of the trees as something more drastic.

Upon leaving the station, I gambled once again on John's secret short route and this time was pleased to see how much traffic I'd avoided. My pleasure lasted only to the foot of our driveway, however, where I was greeted by a shocking sight—raw, sap-oozing stumps, the remains of three of our lacy mimosa trees. Moreover, the missing prizes had been in the most strategic location to shade our house.

When I came from the garage to the kitchen, I still couldn't take in what I'd seen. Peace was standing with one hand braced on the refrigerator door. Without a hello, she said, "I'm waiting for you to show me how to do it right-"

Al was holding her other hand. "Mother, I tole Peace I could show her but she said you'd had more practice."

"What are you two squirrelies talking about...practice in what?"

"Beating your head against the refrigerator door without cracking your skull...it's the only thing I can think of to do to keep me from strangling that woman next door."

At that point, Cora Lee handed Peace a glass of sherry. "Heah, this'll do you mo' good than that ol' door."

Later, at the evening meal, it seemed years to me since our sour silent group had been good-humored and friendly. After losing her trees today, Peace had lost heart in her efforts to spread sunshine. She was so preoccupied she failed to notice Betty Sue's absence until we were half-way through dinner. "Did anyone see Betty Sue come in this afternoon?"

No one had, so Peace said, "Al, run upstairs and knock on her door, maybe she's asleep...tell her it's dinner time."

Al came running downstairs in a minute to say that Betty Sue didn't answer and her door was locked. Peace threw down her napkin and hurried upstairs, only to return with a worried look on her face. "I yelled loud enough to wake downtown." She began searching through the sideboard drawers. "Where's that dratted skeleton key? Maybe she's too ill to answer."

Finding the key, she dashed back upstairs. A few seconds later, we heard her scream. We all rose as one and stampeded up the stairs.

Mother stood transfixed at the bathroom door. We crowded around her, craning our necks so see what she was staring at. There was Betty Sue, fully dressed, lying on the floor. At first glance, she looked peacefully asleep, but when we saw the small pool of blood on the floor beside her, we knew something was *very* wrong.

CHAPTER 42

THE VIGIL

Until the gravity of the situation sank in, everyone stood frozen as if waiting for a curtain to rise on the next act. Then suddenly, the scene changed to one of frantic movement, with no choreography except people milling around helplessly and colliding with one another.

Since we'd dashed upstairs following Peace's screams, she hadn't made another sound, or moved from where she stood staring down at Betty Sue's inert form.

"Maybe she hit her head on the basin," I said.

That seemed unlikely after sharp-eyed Sarah said, "Look," and pointed to an empty pill bottle which had rolled against the old claw-footed bath tub. Sarah maneuvered around Peace and was reaching for the bottle when she slipped on the bloody floor. She pitched forward, but caught the tub's edge in time to steady herself.

"Sarah, be careful," I urged, and I, too, ducked around Peace. By that time, Sarah grabbed the empty pill bottle, and read the label aloud.

"Nembutals...."

I was trying to pick Betty Sue up when Cora Lee and Will joined us. "Here, Will, give me some help...let's get her back to her bed."

When Peace saw what we were doing, she broke out of her trance and took command.

"Stop, don't touch her."

I was so startled I dropped Betty Sue's arm back across her chest, and asked in bewilderment, "Peace, why not?"

"Leave her there...we might be doing the wrong thing. Claudine, tuck a blanket around her, gently. Frances, go call the doctor."

I raced to the hall phone, fervently hoping our long-time family physician, Dr. Murray Lawson, was at home. His wife, Renee, answered and asked if it was important enough to interrupt his dinner. Fighting down my mounting hysteria, I moaned, "Oh, Renee, is it ever."

When Dr. Murray came on the line, I'd regained better control of myself and gave him the story as calmly as I could. I asked him what we should do.

He vetoed any inept first-aid attempt at the house and instructed me to drive Betty Sue the short distance to his hospital on North Avenue. He rapped out terse, explicit instructions. "Frances, see that she's kept warm and stays on her stomach. Hurry now, I'll meet you at the hospital in fifteen minutes.... I was about to hang up when he added, "Oh, more thing, at the slightest sign she's stopped breathing, you know your artificial respiration."

His last remark threw me into an even more overwrought state than I was already in. I didn't know if I could even remember the resuscitation technique I'd learned in a first aid course, taken the year Al was born. I ran back into the room praying to myself, "Please, dear God, don't let Betty Sue stop breathing."

After I'd issued Dr. Murray's instructions, Will picked up the small limp figure of Betty Sue from the bathroom floor and carried her down to the car. Gretchen, Sarah and I crawled into the back seat of Peace's black Chevy and got our laps in position to hold Betty Sue. Before Will could deposit her, Mother jumped out of the driver's seat and said, "Frances, change places, I'm too shaky."

I took over the driver's seat and hoped Peace's confidence in me would prove out. I called out, "Okay everybody, hang on, 'cause I'm pushing it to the floor."

"Fanny, hold it," Sarah shouted, "we don't have Betty Sue yet. Will, what in God's name are you doing?"

Will had placed Betty Sue only half-way into the car and now was down on one knee groping around on the ground. "Miss Betty Sue's done lost her shoes...they's right here someplace...nobody oughter go to heaven barefoot."

Everyone yelled at poor Will at once, except Peace who said soothingly, "Will, never mind the shoes...she's not going to heaven, just the hospital."

As I pulled out of the driveway, Will ran alongside the car waving Betty Sue's shoes. Nobody oughter go barefoot to the hospital either.

Waiting for us at the emergency entrance were Dr. Murray and a battery of interns and nurses. They placed our Betty Sue on a stretcher and whisked her away.

Then there was nothing for the five of us to do but wait, and we sat down on one of the long benches near the entrance. After two bloody emergencies had passed by in front of us, Peace was looking as white as Betty Sue.

Sarah seemed to have kept her wits about her better than either Claudine or Gretchen, so I asked her to hang on to Peace until I came back. "I'm going to the nurses' station for smelling salts...and while I'm at it, maybe I can scout a better place to sit."

Before I could get up from the bench, Claudine flung herself on Mother and cried, "Oh Peace, if Betty Sue dies, it's all my fault... I never dreamed she was so unhappy about my leaving."

The girl was sobbing convulsively, out of control. Claudine could make two of the slightly built Sarah, but that didn't stop Sarah from standing up and giving her a hefty slap. "You idiot, she's not here because of you...it's Warren. Honestly, Claudine, you don't think of anyone but your precious self."

That quieted Claudine down, but not before she sniveled, "How could she do that over some man?"

Sarah shook her finger in the girl's face and said, "Talk about the pot calling the kettle black...what about you?...turning on our darling Peace and your good friends over some man you only went out with once."

At this point, Peace collapsed in a dead faint between the two girls. Clearly, the loss of her precious trees had paled in comparison to Betty Sue's tragic condition, but the combination, plus this new squabble, was more than she could handle in one day.

We carried her to a quieter corner and a comfortable couch, and the receptionist held some ammonia under Peace's nose. We knew she felt better when she opened her eyes, saw our anxious faces, and quipped, "I feel like Marmee in *Little Women*. Oh, my Lord, that reminds me, I haven't called the Darbys."

Peace almost fainted again at the thought. "How'm I going to face her parents?" She rambled on. "I've always felt a mother was a success if she kept her children out of jail and the hospital...here I wasn't able to do either for that poor child."

We chorused that she hadn't been responsible for the results of Betty Sue's broken heart. We did wonder why Warren's failure to keep one date caused such a violent reaction until Gretchen said she thought there was more to it than that. When she had come home for her lunch break, she'd seen the mail on the hall table and noticed one of the letters was for Betty Sue from Warren. "I'll bet it was a kiss-off letter."

Remembering my unsatisfactory conversation with John Whitney about Warren, I was inclined to agree with Gretchen. We'd know soon enough, but the main thing now was to pray for the girl to recover.

During that long night's vigil, we occupied the time by breast-beating claims as to what we had or had not done, that might have contributed to Betty Sue's suicide attempt. I said I'd helped by ever introducing her to Warren.

Peace insisted she should have realized how deeply Betty Sue felt about the man and how devastating an abrupt rejection from her first romantic interest could be to a young girl. Her protected·

life in Savannah with two elderly parents had in no way prepared her for the outside world.

When to call the Darbys involved still more discussion. The consensus was that we'd wait until morning. At 1 a.m. there was nothing they could do for their daughter which wasn't already being done. They would be terribly worried—and we were doing an excellent job of that for them.

During the very late hours, the emergencies slacked off, and after our sporadic bursts of conversation, we lapsed into silence under the cold hospital lights. We were leaning against each other in various stages of half-sleep when Sarah sat up suddenly and said, "Wake up, Dr. Murray's coming down the hall."

The five of us leaped to our feet and moved toward him, eager for news. I could read nothing in his face except great fatigue. Standing there before us, he said, "Relax, ladies, all's well."

He stopped to slip off his surgical gown and cap before continuing, but we were hugging each other and babbling so loudly that we almost missed the rest of his speech. "The patient's stomach was pumped out...she's weak, but there's no damage. I congratulate you on your fast action...now go home."

That's all the encouragement we needed to head for our car. I was last in line as we filed out and was surprised when Dr. Murray tapped me on the shoulder and whispered that he'd like to have a word with me in private.

"Frances, your mother looks so worn out, I'd better have this talk with you instead. Number one...did you know of the girl's pregnancy?"

I stared at him. "No! I'm sure nobody did." I thought a second and then said, "That explains so much."

After I gave him a brief summary of the situation, Dr. Murray said, "Damnit, the naive ones are the most pitiful."

"That darling girl." I shook my head. "She must have been terrified."

I turned to leave but he held out a restraining hand. "Wait, Frances, I still have to write a report for the records. It won't take long...then you'll have a copy for her parents."

I advised Peace and the others to wait in the car, that I wouldn't be long, but the time it took for the doctor to fill out the necessary forms seemed to stretch into an eternity. Of course he had to report the case—and a double whammy it was, too. Betty Sue could easily end up back in jail. Attempted suicide and an illegitimate pregnancy. We certainly couldn't keep that from her parents, and she'd go home in disgrace.

At long last Dr. Murray returned with a copy of his report. Glancing quickly at it, I saw that it stated that Betty Sue Darby had been admitted the previous evening for acute gastroenteritis accompanied by profuse bleeding. The truth as far as it went but no mention that the former was self-induced and the latter a miscarriage. I gave him a grateful bear hug right there in the hall and sprinted out of the door to join the others.

The streets were deserted in the early morning hours and I was grateful for that, especially after I ran a red light on the drive home. Patches of ground fog we traveled through added to the atmosphere of unreality we had felt since we first heard those cries of Peace's from Betty Sue's room.

In my near-catatonic state, the only thing I remembered about the ride home was Claudine's whimpering question, "Peace, do I still hafta move out?"

My mother mumbled that she'd almost lost one of her girls tonight and she didn't want to lose another.

Sarah had the last word. "Claudine, you can stay if you mind your manners from now on...if I whacked you once, I can do it again." She gave a wicked cackle. "Besides, if Brandon and I get along on that hay-ride, I may end up being your sister-in-law."

CHAPTER 43

THE WARRENS AND THE WEXLERS OF THIS WORLD

Early Tuesday morning, Dr. Murray called to say Betty Sue could come home on Thursday, and Peace immediately called the Darbys in Savannah. She downplayed the incident but agreed that they should come take Betty Sue home for a long rest.

After her conversation with the Darbys, she asked me how much I thought she should tell them. "An overdose of pills is too serious a matter not to let them know. What if she tried again? I'd never forgive myself."

"Why don't we decide after we've talked with her? You're all ready to take her suitcase to the hospital this morning. You go on now and I'll join you on my way to work."

Peace agreed to that and as soon as she left, I ran to the phone and called Betty Sue's boy-friend Warren at his law office. He listened while I related last evening's hair-raising events. "Warren, I believe the least you can do is send Betty Sue flowers with a 'speedy recovery' wish."

He waited for so long before answering me, I thought the shock had been too much for him. At last he said, "Er, well, I don't know, Fran...I'm not sure that would be wise."

"I'm not suggesting *wise*, I'm suggesting *kind*," I retorted.

"Oh, hell, I'm sorry about what happened, but there's no good way to break it off...she'd just get her hopes up for nothing. Besides, Mary Ellen doesn't want me to see Betty Sue again."

"Listen here, Warren, there may be no good way, but some ways are worse than others. You could have been man enough to do it face to face...not some sneaky mean ice-cold letter, dictated to your secretary."

"Ah, er, as a matter of fact, I didn't dictate that letter...Mary Ellen did."

"That's the second time that name has come up in this conversation...who the hell is Mary Ellen?"

"Mary Ellen Griggsby. She says she knows you. Oh Fran, she's the most wonderful thing that ever happened to me. The minute I met her, I knew she was the girl for me."

I clicked in on Mary Ellen Griggsby; last year's President of the Atlanta Debutante Club. I thought for a moment and one particular facet of Mary Ellen's charm for Warren fell into place. "How convenient for a young struggling lawyer, Warren. Her father is head of one of most successful law firms in Atlanta. I guess 'Daniels' tacked on the end of 'Griggsby, Griggsby and Cole' sounds even better."

After a drawn out sputter, he said, "Hey, that has nothing to do with it. Mary Ellen is such a sweet, wonderful girl, I'd love her if her father was a bum."

"Okay, okay, but I'm happy you didn't have to step over the corpse *of another* sweet, wonderful girl to get to Miss Griggsby!" I slammed the phone down so hard I hoped he wouldn't be able to hear out of that ear for the rest of his life.

I sat there fuming for a moment, wishing I'd been able to find an older established lawyer for Betty Sue, in her hour of need in the Decatur Street jail, instead of a fresh-out-of-law-school hungry barracuda.

Come to think of it, the only critical comment I ever heard from John Whitney about Dorothea (his ex-wife and Warren's sister) was on the subject of ambition. I respected his reluctance to speak of her—enough to curtail my natural curiosity about the woman— but I clearly remember the scant remarks he did make.

The occasion of John's mildly disparaging comment was an evening we had together when I was so tired, I almost fell asleep in my onion soup.

"What's the matter, hon, do I bore you that much?"

"No," and I yawned. "But sometimes after our show, I feel like I've spent a week training tigers...whereas you, my fine friend, get paid a handsome sum to sit around all day with nothing to do but listen to music, make a few witty remarks, and drink coffee."

John gave a forced laugh. "Hah, you sound like my ex-wife. There's a hoary old story about the woman who wrote to an advice columnist to say she was about to be married but was afraid to tell her family. The woman's letter, which could have been written by Dorothea, said her family was scattered—the mother was in an alcoholic recovery center; the stockbroker father was under indictment for churning widows' accounts, and her brother was in the Atlanta federal pen for smuggling arms to Central America. Her question was, "How do I tell my family I'm marrying a disc jockey?."

"Of course I know there's a lot more to it than that," I said apologetically.

"You're damned right there is...I took every communications course the University offered, but nothing prepared me for my first job...."

"Which outsiders don't realize, 'cause you make it look so easy." I nodded my head in sympathy. "I'm sure you get some of the same stream of ill-equipped job seekers for radio as we do at the station. But John, at least you started out with a beautiful speaking voice."

"Are you kidding?" John laughed. "The first time I heard my voice on a tape recorder, I sounded like an Arkansas hog-caller, and kicked myself for not following in my doctor father's footsteps. That would have suited Dorothea since she never felt disc-jockeying was a proper lifetime occupation for a grown man."

"I expect you like it for the same reason I like working in television, it's exciting and mentally stimulating."

John went on to say there was no end to the developing knowledge his trade provided—not only of music, but current events, politics, fashions, literature, history and more. "I can't imagine wanting to do anything else," he said.

No more mention was made of Dorothea and we turned to other subjects. Despite John's reticence, I surmised that a self-serving ruthlessness ran in his ex-wife's family, especially after learning of her brother Warren's shabby treatment of our Betty Sue.

My phone call to Warren, plus late morning traffic and a stop to pick up some daffodils for Betty Sue resulted in my missing Peace at the hospital. I found she had gone on to a meeting, so I would be talking to Betty Sue alone. When I reached Betty Sue's room, she was propped up in bed wearing a soft blue flannel robe over her hospital gown. She gave me a weak smile of gratitude for the flowers and then asked me to help tie up her hair with the ribbon from the bouquet.

"There, that's fine, baby girl, but you're not supposed to look like a movie star today...no one would ever know you had us all scared silly last night."

"Oh, Fran, I'm so ashamed...I didn't for one minute think about what I would be putting y'all through. How could I have been so stupid?"

Her main worry now was what to tell her parents. When Peace was there earlier, Betty Sue had begged Peace to let her say she'd had an extreme allergic reaction to the capsules she'd taken—with no mention of how many. Peace agreed to say as little as possible— if Betty Sue would promise never to do such a foolish thing again.

If the girl dreaded confiding in her parents that much, I didn't think we ought to insist, but one loose end still bothered me.

Sitting on the edge of the bed and taking her hand, I said, "Betty Sue, Dr. Murray told me, and nobody else, one of the main reasons which must have pushed you into such...." What little color was left in her face drained away and she jerked her hand out of mine.

"Cross my heart, I'll never tell a soul," I promised, "but I want to be certain from now on you know how to protect yourself."

Betty Sue covered her face with her hands and the floodgates opened. Between sobs, the age-old story came out. Everything had come to a head at once—Warren's increasing coldness, the discovery of her pregnancy, and the devastating good-by letter.

"And Fran, honest, I don't understand," she said, looking at me with big puzzled eyes. "We never really *did* anything, just cuddled."

"Betty Sue, Dr. Murray once explained to me that you can be a virgin but become pregnant all the same...it only takes one little sperm that may slip past the barrier of the hymen to do the job...you'd have been better off if you'd gone all the way and used precautions."

While she was digesting what was astounding information to her, I said, "So *promise* me you'll have a good talk with Dr. Murray before you leave the hospital."

As I walked down the hall away from her room, I realized that not once during our visit had she mentioned Warren, and I certainly wasn't going to...him and his Mary Ellen!

The Darbys arrived from Savannah on Wednesday of that eventful week and they stayed at the Biltmore for the few days it would take Betty Sue to recuperate. On Saturday morning, Peace, Cora Lee, Al, and the girls gathered on the front porch to bid good-by to our shy lovable Betty Sue. She looked as virginal as ever, and none the worse for wear after her drama-filled months at Fifteenth Street.

Will, loading her luggage into the car, was having difficulty in finding room for all the paintings she'd done at school. No matter how he arranged and rearranged them, he still had a few left over. Peace saw his predicament and called, "Will, never mind, bring them back up here." She turned to Betty Sue to say she'd ship them to Savannah for her later.

Betty Sue protested, "No, no, Peace, if you don't mind, I'll leave them here 'til I come back for summer school."

At that remark, the Darbys closed ranks protectively on either side of the girl. That gesture, plus the happiness her parents showed to once again have their daughter with them, made me question her optimism. I suspected Betty Sue would have to be content with an art teacher in Savannah.

After many tears, hugs, kisses and assurance from Betty Sue that she'd write often, the Darbys drove away. The day was unusually balmy for March so we lingered on the front porch and chatted. Peace commented, "You know, out of all you girls, Betty Sue was the last one I'd have picked to have so many things happen to her."

I said, "And none of them good." But Sarah Dent reminded me I'd forgotten that one of Betty Sue's paintings placed second in the Museum school's mid-term exhibit. "She was so excited about that red ribbon...maybe it made up some for jail, wishy-washy Warren, and the hospital."

Peace and Sarah were sitting on the porch swing and I gave it a push which set it swaying back and forth. "At least Mama and Papa Darby don't know about the day their darling daughter spent in the Atlanta jail...they really would think we hadn't done right by little Nell."

Al, who had forgotten for the moment that he was a big boy and had been sitting in his favorite place, Cora Lee's lap, now suddenly slid down, skipped over to the swing and began pushing it with me. "Mother, yes they do."

"Do what?"

"They do so know... 'member how brave everybody said Betty Sue was. You always tells me to be brave, so I thought her parents would like that."

Peace caught on before anyone else did. "Al, what did you tell Mr. and Mrs. Darby she was so brave about?"

"I tole 'em how everybody said she was so brave that time she was in jail. They really liked that and asked me lots of questions... but I got scared when Mr. Darby started yelling." Al looked around at his mesmerized audience. "Did I do something wrong?"

Cora Lee sprang from her chair and walked over to ruffle Al's hair. "No, you little jumpseed, you done right. Miss Betty Sue is a brave one and it's time her Ma and Pa knows it." She took him by the hand. "Come on now, let's see what you wants for lunch." Hand in hand they left a speechless group of women.

For awhile Peace went into the doldrums after Betty Sue had gone. She pruned and puttered over the Silver Moon bush the girl had given her until we thought she'd coddle it to death. That, and looking at the big gap where the three mimosa trees had been, seemed to deepen her depression.

One morning, I had an idea which might remedy at least one cause of Peace's gray mood. I made a trip to the Garden Gate Nursery on Roswell Road to consult with Mrs. Gilbert, the owner and one of our station's sponsors. She recommended fast-growing bamboo plantings as a solution for the loss of our trees. She guaranteed our property would look like a jungle movie location in no time.

I couldn't wait to get home to show Peace the remedy for our plundered landscape. When I pulled into the driveway, I saw her sitting on one of the tree stumps with her head hunched over between her shaking shoulders.

Scrambling out of the car, I ran to her as fast as I could. "Peace, what's the matter?" When she looked up, I saw the tears first and then the smile; she was in a paroxysm of laughter. In between gulps for air, she managed to point to three small clay pots at her feet.

When she recovered enough to talk, she said, "Mrs. Wexler sent these around from Harper's Florist—with a note saying she wanted me to have something suitable to replace our trees which were *inadvertently* cut down."

The three pots contained some wispy plants which could have been anything from a spider fern to a cosmos. The possibility was very remote that those anemic bits of greenery would grow to shade anything larger than Mrs. Wexler's lumber pile rats.

I sat down beside Peace on the stump, put my arms around her, and for awhile we both rocked back and forth, laughing like loons. Then Peace, gathering the miniature pots in her arms, marched across Mrs. Wexler's yard, and placed the pots on her back steps. By the time Peace had returned to our driveway, Mrs. Wexler came out of her back door.

"Mrs. Peace," and she gave one of the Wexler 'Grand Duchess' waves, "come here a minute."

Peace grabbed me by the arm and walked me up our back steps and into the house without turning around. "Fanny," she said, "I'm sorry she's old and sick...but I swear on my mother's grave I'll never speak to that dog-and-tree murderer again."

And she never did.

CHAPTER 44

PIGEONS, PARAKEETS AND A PROPOSAL

"Will, move it moah to the middle," Cora Lee was on the back porch shouting instructions to husband Will for the placement of a scarecrow. "No, no, not theah...wait a minute, I'm coming out." She walked down the steps and waded out in a sea of red Georgia clay mud which now covered our back yard.

Our mud yard was the result of Peace's yearning for a proper Kentucky blue grass lawn rather than the ragged crab grass which had taken over. Last week, a man had come with equipment to break up the hard clay and Will had sown the precious seeds. When a soft April rain began the next day, we thought the heavens had been unusually accommodating to water the new lawn so swiftly.

Three days later, it was still raining and most of the seed had washed either onto Mrs. Wexler's yard or the Harper property behind us. But, when the sun had finally come out again, Will once more had covered the ground with the expensive seeds. Yet our troubles still weren't over. The morning after Will had scattered his seeds, Peace looked out of her bedroom window and thought she was back at Crape Myrtle Farm. Every pigeon for miles around had discovered that 33 Fifteenth Street was serving tender fresh grass seed for breakfast.

Peace commandeered grandson Al into shooing the pigeons away but it was a losing battle. "Now I know," she complained, "what Gertrude Stein meant in her poem...the one that goes 'pigeons in the grass, alas.' *Alas* isn't a strong enough word for how I feel."

That's when Cora Lee had said, "Never you mind, miz Peace, I gets Will to make us a scarecrow."

In his own way, Will was as essential in keeping our Noah's Ark afloat as she was. He was a paradox for Peace—as he was both a comfort and a frustration. Tools were left where he last worked with them and if given a can of paint with explicit instructions to paint a bathroom floor, likely as not, the adjacent bedroom floor received a coat of red paint for good measure.

And Mother insisted that in spite of his middle age, Will was still growing. No matter how many large-size white serving jackets she gave him for his infrequent dining-room duty, he invariably appeared in one which looked as if it belonged to Al. I suspect that he kept the ill-fitting one with its too-short sleeves in order to discourage Mother. He'd never gotten the hang of serving and offered dishes from the right side more often than the left, and he considered the knife a perfectly acceptable utensil for pie eating. As far as Will was concerned, coffee was coffee—what difference did it make whether it was served in the large stovepipe-metal coffee pot or the Georgian silver one.

Despite such minor slips, Will's comfort side far outweighed his frustrating side. Like an Atlas, Will kept the old house from falling down around our ears. He could repair almost anything and was never happier than when working on a lengthy challenge. This morning he had one worthy of his talents. A recent tornado-like wind had ripped holes in the roof of the garage, and he had been working on the roof when Cora Lee asked him to turn his attention instead to the building of a scarecrow to keep the pigeons away.

He frowned all the way down the ladder, but silently gathered the needed materials and went to work. Will was so quiet much of the time, some people thought he was a mute. He could speak when necessary but it was an effort to do so. Cora Lee had explained to us that when Will was three years old, he'd accidentally swallowed lye which his grandmother used for soap making. The corrosive substance affected his vocal chords and left a spray of liver-pink scars on the right side of his face. Aside from that slight disfigurement, Will was a good-looking man with skin the shade of Cora Lee's iron pancake griddle.

He fashioned a simple scarecrow out of two pieces of lumber, old work pants, and a discarded straw hat, and he and Cora Lee were now in the yard having a discussion about the most effective place to anchor it. As we watched them from the kitchen window, Peace and I deduced that they were not in agreement. They were standing toe-to-toe in the mud, pulling the scarecrow back and forth between them. "They aren't getting the scarecrow up," I said, "but as long as they're out there arguing, the pigeons stay away. What is it with me and birds?" I took a sip of coffee and made a face at the bitter taste—Cora Lee often had a heavy hand with the chicory. "As if these pigeons weren't enough, it's Kay's Jewelers' parakeet contest time again." my mind was already moving into the hours ahead.

"My Lord," Peace said with wonderment, "has it been a year since the last one? I thought you swore off and decided Dick would judge the next one."

"Dick said I've had more experience with parakeets...and I can't argue with that after last year's fiasco. Today's contest is bound to be better. Mr. Hammond promised no more of those glass boxes of his that scared the birds last time...and John said he'd be a judge again if I would."

Peace gave me an enigmatic look. "I'm certain that's the real reason you didn't object...how serious is that anyway?"

"Just hints. He hasn't actually proposed so I don't have to worry about an answer yet." I squinted up at the ceiling, noticed a large chunk of plaster missing, and made a mental note to tell Will about it. "Besides, I'm not sure I'd feel right about leaving you here to cope alone...on the other hand, I'd still be in hollering distance."

Peace seemed far away with her thoughts and gave me an apathetic wave when I went out the back door.

At breakfast I'd intended to discuss the disappointing results of a talk I'd had with manager Sever late yesterday afternoon, but Peace was too occupied with mud, pigeons and scarecrows. I'd wait until evening.

My interview with Carter had been prompted by a remark from Candy. Despite her promise to close the switchboard keys and her ears to station personnel's private conversations, Candy continued to be an unending flow of inside information. She considered me her best friend at the station so she meant well when she whispered, "Fra-yan, I think you oughtta know something."

Naturally, I was all ears. "What?"

I'd have been happier without hearing Candy's latest bulletin. "Dick's just gotten a big raise (she named the figure), did you?"

The look on my face answered that question. In those early days, no one would have dreamed of the astronomical salaries TV performers collect today. For example, Dick made $2,500 an episode in the '60s when he starred in his smash sit-com *The Dick Van Dyke Show*. It must have seemed a very big raise from his '50s *Music Shop* salary. In the fall of '88, he had an even bigger jump in salary for the Van *Dyke Show* that he shared with his son Barry. Although the series was deemed a failure, most people would have been happy to fail for the price of $125,000 per episode.

I'd been content with my salary until Candy's news. Then the unfairness of the now sizable gap between Dick's salary and mine, although we were both doing the same amount of work, hit me hard.

So instead of working on our program the previous morning, I had spent an hour composing a memo to manager Carter. I wanted to be on firm ground when I confronted him because I wasn't going to let this pass. I found that after meticulously listing everything I did to get the *Music Shop* on the air each day, I'd typed a single-spaced page and a half.

I ended my memo by reminding Carter that when Bill Colvin began selling 'I Like Dick Van Dyke' and 'I Like Fran Adams' buttons two months ago, the thousands of requests for them had run neck and neck, neither one of us ahead of the other.

Carter's secretary, Louise, delivered my memo to him promptly, and he been as prompt in asking me to see him before I left for the day.

After Carter's initial statement—"Fran, I knew you worked hard, but this detailed account is indeed impressive,"—the interview went downhill. He listened politely as I stated that since I was doing the same amount of work as Dick (more, I sometimes thought), and since I received just as much public support, equal salaries seemed only fair.

Carter protested, "Fran, it's the facts of life. Management takes into consideration Dick's responsibilities as a family man."

"Carter, I'm not Mrs. Wiggs of the Cabbage Patch but I also have financial responsibilities...a small son to raise and a mother who needs help."

"Oh pshaw, Fran, a pretty girl like you...why you'll be married in no time."

I was doing my best not to get angry—or shrill—so I kept my voice low and even. "Then you must know something I don't. Besides what's all that have to do with fairness? My talents and abilities won't disappear and my brain won't turn to mush if I become a Mrs. Fran."

Abruptly, Carter reached for a stack of letters on his desk. "See these?" He held up a handful. "We're inundated with requests for job interviews. Half the women in Atlanta would work for a television station without *any* salary."

I knew he spoke the truth. Every fair-size city now afforded a chance for bright-eyed hopefuls to fulfill a yearning for fame, if not fortune. Now, instead of making an expensive, risky and arduous trip to Hollywood or New York to gamble on making it in films or theater, or as magazine cover girls, star-struck beauties, trained or untrained, could start in their own backyard.

We sat there in silence for a minute. Carter was fidgeting with his pen set and looking distinctly uncomfortable. Intuition told me that if I continued to irritate him with that word 'fair', I was as likely to get a pay cut as a raise.

"Thanks for listening anyway." I got up to leave and headed toward the door. "You're the best manager we've had and I'm sure you'd buck the system if you could."

Carter looked happier, and gallantly said, "Fran, I know we couldn't get anyone else as bright, creative and popular as you... and later on in the year at the next salary review, I'll see what I can do."

I had to be content with that. The deluge of daily fan letters was beginning to make me feel that I was as adorable and indispensable as the writers said. Carter had not so subtly shown me that I could blunder out of television as easily as I'd blundered in.

On the drive to Kay's Jewelry store, where this year's contest was to be held, a great wave of weariness washed over me. I remembered how full of optimistic enthusiasm I'd been this same time last year. The work was play then. Now, the physical stamina required to keep the *Music Shop* going seemed on par with cleaning out the Aegean stables—and the demands as endless. Where, pray, I asked myself, was all this shoveling leading, if anywhere?"

On the other hand, the constant excitement and continuous surprises, good and bad, were addictive. I felt I was between Scylla and Charybdis as I couldn't imagine returning to a more mundane pursuit of livelihood.

Pulling up to Kay's Jewelers, I couldn't help but remember last year's contest site. The Kimball House, that architectural gem, had been demolished in spite of Aunt Sue's and the Historical Society's attempt to save that reminder of Atlanta's past glories.

It was a shame that the ancient hotel had to go but I was relieved that today's judges were to be spared the ordeal again of chasing a flock of no-talent birds around the spacious high-ceilinged Kimball House ballroom. Perhaps this year's batch would prove more talkative in the smaller room we would have at Kay's Peachtree jewelry store.

When I reached the conference room in back of the store, Mr. Hammond, Kay's manager, was standing by the door. "Hurry, Fran...Big John Whitney is already here. The contestants are in my office. Same rules as last time. I'll bring in the first bird right now."

Mr. Hammond's let's-get-this-over-with attitude was in marked contrast to last year's elaborate preparations and his solemn speech. Without the locale of the Kimball House and the concurrence of the community drive to save it, the press considered the second parakeet contest at Kay's store a non-event.

Recalling Carter's disheartening remarks yesterday, my lack of enthusiasm matched Mr. Hammond's. I wondered whether the experience in judging a parakeet's ability to screech "It's Okay to Owe Kay" would carry much weight on a future application for employment. If Mr. Hammond's demeanor this morning was any indication, my expertise in such a specialized field wouldn't be needed again—even on a yearly basis.

John, seated in a comfortable chair at one end of the long conference table, rose immediately when I walked in. Once again, I was impressed by his courtliness, outstanding even in Atlanta, where that quality was the rule rather than the exception. (He once had confided that Mother Whitney had expected him to seat her at the dinner table from the time that he was four.)

"Hi, honey...big improvement this year—chairs that don't give you the bends."

I looked around the room, expecting to see Paul Jones, the *Atlanta Constitution's* drama critic—and a fellow sufferer in last year's judging—but the only other person in the room was a little girl standing at the end of the table holding a parakeet cage.

"Where's Paul?" I asked. "I thought he was our third judge."

"I saw him yesterday," John answered. "He suggested I go back to Milledgeville...not the radio station...the mental hospital. He couldn't believe I'd let myself in for such punishment again." John gave my arm a slight squeeze. "I said I had my reasons."

I pointed to the little girl with the parakeet and whispered, "Who's that? His replacement?"

John gave me a look of mock reproof. "Fran, how could you forget Bobbie Lee Barber and her JoJo. Mr. Hammond got the idea from the Miss America contest...you know, where the former winner hands over the crown to the new champ."

A second glance jogged my memory. Bobbie Lee had the same self-possessed manner and poker face at ten years of age that she'd had at nine. JoJo, the only bird who'd repeated Kay's slogan last year, was confirming my prediction of the creation of a Dr. Frankenstein monster of a bird. Listening to him repeat the slogan over and over, I cast a hostile eye at the wretch. Why couldn't he have loosened up last year before I'd risked my life hanging out of the Kimball House window for him?

I gave Bobbie Lee a polite hello and said, "Bobbie Lee, we won't be able to hear the other birds if you keep JoJo in the room."

She said she'd take the bird to Mr. Hammond's office and leave him with her mother. She was back in a flash with a message. "Mama says if nobody's going to take pictures for the paper, there's no point in staying. 'Bye now."

John and I watched as she left. "I didn't like that child last year," I said, "and she hasn't improved with age. She never did thank me for saving her stupid bird."

Mr. Hammond returned to the room. He made no comment on our dwindling number of impartial judges, but gestured to the weedy-looking man accompanying him. "This is our first contestant. From Adel, Georgia...Mr. Pafford and his bird, Verdis."

John said, "After all the Honey Boys and Cuddles we had last year, I'm expecting big things from a Verdis."

Mr. Pafford barely had time to set the cage on the table when Verdis came through. Loud and clear, he squawked "It's Okay to Owe Kay"—not once but several times.

"Good boy, Verdis," Mr. Pafford blew a kiss toward the cage. "You've paid for the trip already."

John warned Mr. Pafford not to be too confident as there were eight more contestants to be heard. Privately, we remembered how last year's birds had clammed up on us and agreed that Mr. Pafford had very likely won.

An hour later, we were in a quandary. After we listened to the other eight Jonathans, Tweeties and Sweetums, five birds out of the nine had said, "It's Okay to Owe Kay" with the enunciation of a Rex Harrison. Feast or famine.

Mr. Hammond brought the five birds back in and said that now we'd have to grade each one on coloring, parakeet perkiness, enunciation, and overall personality. Too tired to argue about it, we spent another hour evaluating the birds. When we were finally done and waiting for him to total up our scores, I said to John, "Paul was the smart one...this is my swan song...'Quoth the raven, nevermore!' OOPS! Sorry, I can't seem to get away from bird talk today."

John was busy looking through his pockets and didn't answer me. Finally he pulled out a black velvet jewelry box.

I looked at the box with interest. "Well, look at you, Lucky Pierre...you've already received your goody for judging. What's in there? Cuff links?"

John handed it to me. "Open it."

I did, and gasped. "I didn't know Kay's carried anything so gorgeous...this ring looks more like Tiffany's."

"It's been over a year since you trusted me enough to dangle you out of the Kimball House window."

I bent over to get a closer view of all that sparkle and said, "Well, this does seem rather grand just to celebrate a parakeet contest."

John was in no mood for levity. He placed the ring, still in its box, in the palm of my hand and said, "Now repeat Kay's slogan after me with a slight variation, "It's Okay to—Marry John."

Although we'd discussed marriage from time to time, the idea had always been in the far-distant future. I was caught by surprise and said the first thing that popped into my mind. "John, did you know that the male parakeet is henpecked? The female picks on him unmercifully, except during mating season. Maybe we'd better choose another anniversary."

I held the ring up and was tempted to try it on, but I restrained the impulse.

John had a suggestion."Let's celebrate by going to the Biltmore tonight...we can make the night Jack Webb set fire to your dress our anniversary."

"Jack Webb didn't set fire to my dress," I contradicted, "he saved it. Still...I'm glad you have a romantic streak."

"I was teasing, but I'll save my *other* surprise 'til tonight."

It dawned on me that John was assuming a 'yes' answer. I slowly closed the box and handed it back to him. "John, such a big change in my life would involve Al—and Peace. I've got to be really sure of my feelings this time."

John nodded and was about to say something when Mr. Hammond returned to announce the name of the winning parakeet. It was Verdis, and Mr. Pafford was ecstatic. The other eight bird owners were sore losers and began to argue with Mr. Hammond, John and me that the contest seemed rigged. There might have been possible grounds for such an accusation so John and I bolted out of the door, leaving Mr. Hammond to the bird owners—and the birds.

John said that he'd pick me up at seven that evening, and I agreed. As I drove home, my thoughts were occupied with his words and all their ramifications.

Once home, I was walking from the garage to the back porch when something flew by my head. It wasn't a pigeon, and since Will was still repairing the garage roof, I thought perhaps one of his shingles had fallen off it. I had barely stepped inside when another unidentified flying object hit the door.

Cora Lee was stuffing an armful of muddy sheets into the washing machine and Peace was in the kitchen chopping onions on a chopping board.

"What's going on here? Something almost hit me a minute ago."

Peace wiped the onion-tears away and said, "Oh, Sodom and Gomorra, I told Will to quit that. He's up there trying to keep the pigeons off the grass seed with a slingshot."

"If his aim had been better, I'd be a dead pigeon by now," I complained.

Peace ran outside to tell Will to come down off the roof and bring his slingshot with him. Cora Lee huffed into the kitchen and said, "That's the second time today I'se washed them sheets and hung them in the yard...if the pigeons and the mud gets 'em this time, people jest gonna have to sleep on 'em."

When Peace came back, I asked her why Will was taking pot-shots with a slingshot when we had a scarecrow in the yard.

"The pigeons love the scarecrow, it's even more popular than the grass seed. I talked Will out of his first idea...but he didn't ask me about this latest."

"What was the first?"

Peace plopped a leg of lamb into the roaster and dumped the chopped onions on top. "He has a friend with a pet skunk...I told him the cure was worse than the disease. Will might have a friend, but we wouldn't—not with a skunk in the yard."

I told Peace then that I had some important news. She followed me to my bedroom and we sat down for a good talk.

After hearing my news, she was quiet for a few moments. "Do you love John? It's important that you both be reading from the same page—I don't want you to make another mistake."

"I have a big 'LIKE' for John...he's been such a good friend and I've grown to depend on him. I don't expect Ferris wheels and calliope music this time."

Mother patted my hand. "Well, one plus is that you and John would make a handsome couple—which is more than I can say for Maurice and me."

"Maurice?"

"Yes, now *I* have some news." Peace went to her bedroom and brought back a letter. "Maurice has invited me to visit Quebec this summer. He wants me to meet his family to see how I like them, and probably vice versa, though he was tactful enough not to say so."

I stood up and began walking around the room. Finally I turned to Peace and said in a tone of disbelief,

"Maurice, Maurice Duval, the syrup man from Canada...*that* Maurice?"

"Fanny, I've tried to teach you that pretty is as pretty does. Maurice is very pretty on the inside and a good person. If I married him, you could say yes to John without feeling guilty about leaving me."

At the moment, I had no rebuttal for dear Peace. My emotions had done more churning around today that Cora Lee's old Maytag washer.

CHAPTER 45

THE BEST LAID PLANS OFTEN....

That evening, John and I were seated at what appeared to be the same table overlooking the dance floor in the Biltmore's Empire Room as we'd had the evening of my dress fire. I held out my hand and said, "Show me the ring again, John, I'm dying to get another look at it."

"I don't have it with me." He reddened and seemed uneasy with my request. "Well, er, actually, it wasn't really mine. Mr. Hammond loaned it to me on a trial basis."

I threw him a quizzical look. "If I'd put the ring on my finger, thinking it was for keeps, what would you have done?"

"Mother's already offered me one of her rings...when things get settled, we'll go to Madison for it."

"That's certainly more sensible...family jewels mean more." I wasn't sure why I was disappointed. After all, John was being both practical and romantic...a good combination.

While he was absorbed with the menu, he made the habitual sound, through a small gap between his front teeth, that indicated deep thought. I was looking at the menu also but my concentration wasn't on a choice between chicken or steak. I had a more important choice to make. What was holding me back from an unqualified, "Yes, John, I'll marry you and try to make you happy."

The man had so many positive qualities—a good disposition, an easy way with Al, a sense of humor. Also, on our weekly dates, he was never out of conversation. If I analyzed our talks, they centered mainly on the daily happenings at WLWA-TV and radio station WQST, but that was only natural.

Marriage to John would solve so many problems. My home environment stayed in a constant state of confusion: pigeons, burst sewers and water heaters, lost trees, attempted suicide, and more. But most important, John would become a father for Al.

As for the office, I wouldn't mind the ceaseless treadmill if I were headed anywhere on it, but after yesterday's dampener from Carter, I felt insecure there as well.

Would I simply inherit a new set of problems if I became Mrs. John Whitney? I was so caught up in my thoughts I hadn't heard the first part of something John was saying to me. "Sorry, John ... you were saying something about Los Angeles?"

"I said I hoped we could marry sometime next month so you could go to Los Angeles with me."

The prospect of it filled me with excitement. "Oh, I've dreamed of visiting California for years...but John, neither of us could get away for that long a honeymoon." In my exhilaration over the prospect of such a trip, I momentarily forgot I'd been considering resignation plans.

"Not for a honeymoon...to *move* there. That's the other surprise I promised you." John beamed with satisfaction. "I've been offered a much better deal with station KABC in Los Angeles."

"Los Angeles?" I knocked over my water glass in my astonishment, and waited until the waiter had mopped up before I spoke again. "Los Angeles...you mean in California?"

"Of course, honey chile...that's the only Los Angeles I know. You sound as if I'm talking about another planet."

I was stunned. As far as I was concerned, he might as well be talking about another planet.

The waiter brought me a fresh glass of water just then, and that gave me a moment to recover somewhat. I stammered out some of the questions bothering me. "But John, what about Al's school?...and Peace, what about Peace?"

"Sweetie, they have schools in California just like here, probably better...and as for Peace, I like your mother very much, but it wouldn't work for her to come with us."

If Peace married Maurice, she wouldn't come anyway, but I wanted to leave the door open, just in case, so I asked, "Why not?"

John answered, "Because I've had enough in-law trouble for one lifetime. Dorothea's mother had a major role in our divorce."

"You never told me that."

"Her mother never thought I was good enough for her darling, and she finally convinced Dorothea of the same thing." Before I could interrupt John to say we were talking apples and oranges here, he continued, "The job may not work out, but if it does, we'll send for Al—but *no* mamas."

"John, Peace isn't Dorothea's mother, she's mine, and she'd never interfere...she's already on your side."

"Nope," he said with finality. I'd never before noticed how immobile and set John's face could look. "Most mothers are possessive and Peace is no exception."

Under normal circumstances, I'd be relating the news of

Dick's raise and my dispiriting talk with Carter, but all that seemed unimportant now.

Was *'in like'* enough to make me change my name, move three thousand miles away, yank Al up by his roots, and leave Peace and Atlanta? John and I had always been hurried and harried in our courting. Could more quiet time together turn my 'big like' into love?

We had been talking during the orchestra's break, so when Wade Creager waved his baton to the opening strains of "Just in Time", a song from the new musical, *Bells Are Ringing*, John said, "Let's dance."

After we'd taken a few steps, John squeezed my hand and whispered in my ear, "We'll go by my apartment on the way home and I'll do some serious convincing."

"No, not tonight, John, I think I'd better go home. Pigeons, parakeets and proposals all in one day are too much." I smiled, but I wasn't smiling on the inside.

We rode home in silence except for John's whistling through his teeth. It was a habit I once thought endearing; tonight my skin rippled at the sound.

Once I was home, I climbed the stairs and stopped by Peace's room. I wanted to sit on her bed and talk—the way I'd done as a girl after coming home from a dance. When I saw she was asleep, I went to my own room instead and crawled into my four-poster bed. I was too tired to think any more about the pile-up of the day's events.

My nightly ritual of listening to a miniature music box, given to me by my father for a long-ago birthday, soon had me floating into sleep.

By the following morning, all personal thoughts had to be temporarily shelved. My talk with Carter and the events of the weekend had stopped me from making my usual preparations for the *Music Shop* hour, so, for a change, I didn't groan when I received and read one of Bill Colvin's memos. It said the guest for today's show was the multi-talented Joel Grey, a nineteen-year old night-club and musical comedy star, and son of the famous Yiddish comedian and band leader, Mickey Katz.

I'd never heard of either of them but that didn't mean anything. Television had yet to homogenize the country, and New York was filled with talent whose names were unknown in Atlanta. Bill's memo pleased me because it said that Joel Grey was bringing his singing, dancing and comedic talents to Atlanta for a Community Chest benefit, and I figured if Mr. Grey gave us a sample of his talents, our *Music Shop* show would be a breeze. (Twelve years later, in 1966, Joel Grey was to make Broadway-musical history in the unforgettable role of the Emcee in *Cabaret*.)

In case Joel Grey was in a hurry and we needed another act toward the end of the show, I'd use Oomglick and Nudnick, the world's most lifelike puppets. It's no wonder they were lifelike—the puppets were Fran and Dick made up with mop wigs, red spots of rouge, rubber balls on our noses, and oven mitts on our hands.

I realized there wasn't time to write a fresh puppet routine so I hurriedly hunted through a stack of emergency scripts. I found one on a satirical safety rules for the road and knew Dick and I could ad-lib on the subject of safe driving until our red puppet noses fell off.

The script was entitled "How to Keep from Getting Old" and I glanced at a couple of the rules: 'Always race with locomotives to crossing. Engineers love it 'cause it breaks the monotony of their jobs.' and 'In rainy weather, see how close you can get to pedestrians. Dry cleaners appreciate it.'

Corny, but it would have to do; and hopefully we wouldn't even have to use it. I threw the puppet props into my carrying basket and ran down the hall toward the studio just as Carter came out of Bill Colvin's office. We collided and I dropped my basket. It was the first time I'd seen Carter since the ill-fated interview and he seemed to make an extra effort to be the same friendly Carter. But I realized I didn't feel the same about him. I was lying when I said I thought he'd done his best for me.

While he was helping me pick up the wigs and oven mitts, I faked a laugh and said, "Carter, I don't care how many girls you interview, you'll have a hard time finding one who can turn herself into a real live puppet."

Carter's smile disappeared. He turned on his heel, oven mitt still in hand, and almost ran to his office. If I continued to needle him, I was going to get the heave-ho before I had time to resign gracefully.

Things stabilized a little after that and by mid-May, the Kentucky blue grass had vanquished both the pigeons and the crab grass. Peace was expecting a visit from Maurice in the next week at which time they would finalize plans for her Quebec visit. And at last, after imitating Harriet and the song, "Jenny" for several weeks, I made up my mind. I accepted John's proposal.

I felt guilty about not being hat-over-the-windmill in love with John but comforted myself with the knowledge that many a successful marriage was based on mutual respect, need, and compatibility. Heretofore, my heart had always ruled my head. The other way around might bring me luck.

No one at the station, including Dick, knew of my plans as I intended to wait until the end of summer before giving the obligatory two-week notice. According to Carter's boast, my replacement could easily be found in the many interview requests on his desk; or perhaps Dick might prefer having his former male partner, Phil Erickson, with him once again. Phil, however, might not be available since he and his equally talented wife, Nancy, had recently opened a highly successful nightclub in town.

John and I had devised a special wedding-code for discussions of the subject as insurance against Candy's switchboard wire tap, and it was driving her wild with curiosity.

We'd chosen a date in early September before school for Al would open in Los Angeles. Aunt Sue suggested we have the ceremony at her Peachtree Street house with invitations for family and close friends only. After she'd learned that John's mother was one of the head dames in Madison, Georgia's Colonial Dames chapter, John could do no wrong in her eyes.

Furthermore, John made certain he stayed in her good graces by inviting her to record some WQST public-service announcements for the Humane Society. No more mike fright for Aunt Sue. She was now an authority on both mediums, radio and television; her daily phones calls to Peace were filled with advice to be passed along to me on ways to improve the *Music Shop*.

One fine May morning, I was enjoying my coffee and congratulating myself on reaching so many firm decisions. Peace and Al had left the kitchen, and I was on my second cup of coffee when my complacency collapsed so suddenly that a large swallow of hot coffee went down the wrong way. After Cora Lee had thumped me on the back a few times, I stopped coughing, but I was still thinking that in all this rearranging of lives and the semi-secrecy involved, I'd forgotten Cora Lee and Will.

"Cora Lee, you and Will will have to decide between California and Canada. Peace and I'll both want you so it's your choice." I was being diplomatic as I doubted that either Mother or Cora Lee would accept a separation.

Her answer came as a surprise. "No ma'am, Miss Fanny, me and Will stays rightcheer in this old house."

"You can't...if Peace goes to Quebec, she'll have to sell the house."

Cora Lee poured herself a cup of coffee and sat down at the table. "Baby, yore mama's got no more mind to go live in that there Kaybec than a cooter turtle."

"She could have fooled me," I argued. "She's sure talking like it."

"I'm not saying she might not go stay a spell jes' to talk that French she's so crazy 'bout, but me and Will, the girls, and your mama be here same as ever."

"Cora Lee," I accused, "you've been reading the cards

again...how do you know that?"

"Miz Peace is givin' you yard room now so's you can make up yore mind 'bout Mistuh John without worryin, 'bout her."

Her assessment made a lot of sense. Peace and Maurice were such an incongruous couple that I'd never reconciled myself to the union. As enamored as Peace was with the French language, I couldn't imagine her fitting into a large French-Canadian family... and all that snow! At least California was warm and sunny, and I was certain I could overcome John's objections to her joining us in time.

"How about me, Cora Lee, am I really going to move to California?"

"Yessum, you shore is, but not near as soon as you 'spect to."

Before I could ask her what she meant, she saw Will in the backyard and jumped up. She'd been trying to catch him all morning to tell him to take his too-lovable scarecrow down. I was left alone at the table with all the old indecisions in my mind.

The floorboards in our old kitchen made a comforting creaking sound when I walked over to look out the window at our now-flourishing yard. The pink, white and red camellia bushes next to the house were in bloom; the scent of Peace's pet lilac bush by the window was so strong, it even overpowered the smell of Cora Lee's chicory coffee brewing on the stove.

When Al came running through the kitchen a few minutes later, he came over and hugged me around my waist. Then he looked up at me. "Oh, Mother, don't cry. I like it better when you hit your head on the 'frigerator door 'cause you do that so funny."

It was the first of June when I drove John to the airport and waved him off to Los Angeles with many promises to write. He said *he* wasn't a letter writer but he'd phone as often as possible. We assured each other that the summer would go fast.

Even though John had only been gone a few days, I stayed at the office late on Friday to write him a long letter. He called on Saturday and we had a good chat.

The next week, I managed a shorter letter but before I mailed it, John called and I told him everything that was in the letter. His big news was the apartment he'd rented. "Fran, it's big enough for the three of us and near the station...a perfect location for me."

"How about schools, is it near a good grammar school?"

"Oh, er, well, I guess I didn't ask about that."

"And parks. Is there a park anywhere near?"

John rather crossly said he hadn't had time to go into a lot of details...after all, he'd just arrived in town.

I didn't want to start a long-distance quarrel so I changed the subject by asking how he liked the job.

"Crazy about it so far…radio work is about the same no matter what part of the country you're in."

"Are the natives friendly?"

I thought he hesitated before answering me, but then he said, "Oh yes, everyone has been wonderful."

"Watch out, John. I hear you can't tell the difference in Hollywood between a real movie star and an ordinary citizen… everybody looks like a star."

He agreed. "Yeah, you're right…even the waitress across the street at the ham-and-eggs joint looks like Lana Turner."

After that call, two weeks went by without further word from John. I'd sent him a couple of 'wish-you-were-here' cards and in spite of his avowed letter writing aversion, I thought it wouldn't have sprained his wrist to scrawl a few lines. Perhaps he had, but the mail was slow; and the time difference between coasts made it difficult to judge the best hours for phone calls.

About the middle of the third week, I began to wonder if he might be ill. I debated whether to call him at work, but remembering the constant interruptions we suffered at the station, and not knowing if he had night duty, I decided to wait until the weekend.

Several phone calls Saturday and Sunday were unsuccessful. No answer. I was now determined to talk with him no matter what. On Monday morning, I gave Candy the Los Angeles number for John at KABC. "Candy, keep trying until you reach him."

That was a mistake. She immediately wanted to know why he was in California in the first place.

"Candy, does everyone in this station tell you *why* the person they're calling is somewhere…just get the man on the phone for me, okay?"

After she said I'd certainly been hard to get along with lately…and excuse her for living, she returned to her switchboard. I was ashamed that I'd taken my bad humor out on her, but sometimes Candy's constant surveillance was annoying beyond belief.

It wasn't until after lunch that she buzzed my office and said in a frozen-popsicle voice, "Mr. Whitney on the line."

"John, are you okay?…I've been trying to call you all weekend."

He was apologetic but said he'd been away the past couple of weekends. The station owner and his wife had taken him under their wing and invited him to house parties at their Palm Springs's house. The invitations gave him too good a chance to know them better. He couldn't decline them.

"Do they have phones in Palm Springs?" I could have bitten my tongue off after that remark but it was too late.

"I'm sorry, Fran, but you know how it is. It's a whole new world for me out here."

"I know." I did my best to sound sympathetic. "If it's this hectic in Atlanta, I'm sure it's a thousand times more so in such a glamorous city. We were smart to wait 'til fall...a new city, a new job and a bride would have a lot to cope with...but I do miss you very much."

"Yeah, I miss you, too, honeychile...look, I've got to hang up...air time coming up."

"Well, at least that sounds familiar. Is there time for an 'I love you'?"

"Listen, I'll call you later from home...there's a Candy clone on the switchboard here."

"So what? I didn't know it was a big secret."

We said good-by and hung up simultaneously. I was left with the feeling that a long-distance romance had a lot of drawbacks. With the prospect of a dateless Fourth-of-July weekend coming up, I realized how much I'd grown accustomed to having John share most of my scarce free time.

For the Fourth, our program director substituted a documentary film on the signing of the Declaration of Independence so the *Music Shop* cast was free. Al, Peace and I saw the fireworks at nearby Piedmont Park, but other than that, I spent a long, boring weekend at home.

That certainly put me in a more receptive mood for the call I received Monday morning from a former school friend, Laura Towers. Although our lives had not paralleled, Laura and I kept in touch. I'd sent flowers on the recent birth of her second child, so her first words were, "Fanny, you were an angel to send the beautiful flowers...thank you, thank you...I'm back on my feet and Julian Towers the Third is thriving."

She sounded so contented and happy that once again I wondered why my life's pattern was so different from that of most of my girlhood contemporaries. If I hadn't bolted out of the corral after too early a marriage, I'd probably have a sibling for Al by now. My time would be spent lounging at the Piedmont Driving Club's pool and in doing volunteer work. At least I'd know where I was, if not who I was. Instead I'd spent precious years darting down first one road and then another, with little to show for it.

Laura's cheerful voice coaxed me away from melancholy thoughts, and after I'd inquired about the well-being of her husband, she continued, "A thank-you for flowers wasn't the only reason I called. I'm offering you an invitation that may change your life. Julian is on a committee of Atlanta businessmen who want to welcome some Lockheed executives. They're here from California to open the old Bell Bomber plant...remember...that plant out near Marietta where they made planes during the war."

"Sure, I remember, but I can't imagine how that's going to change my life. All I know about planes is that I don't like to fly in 'em."

"Oh, be serious, you won't have to do anything but come to the party we're giving on Friday night for those executives...and guess what, Fanny...*one of them's a bachelor.*"

Laura gave that last announcement with as much pride as if she'd discovered the eighth wonder of the world.

"Oh, Laura," I groaned, "here it comes. My poor faithful friends have worked so hard to marry me off...never fear though, hope is on the horizon."

I caught myself in time. I didn't want the news about John to leak out before I notified WLWA and Laura would find it impossible to keep my confidences to herself.

Laura quickly picked up on my last remark. "What do you mean, hope is on the way? Fanny, I'm dying to know...who is it?"

"Ah me, let's see. How about Gary Cooper?...Laura, I only meant while there's life, there's hope."

"No you didn't, you had that same hedging tone of voice when you were stalling in Miss Martin's Latin class. What's 'hope's' name. I know it isn't Bob."

She didn't wait for an answer, for which I was grateful. "Never mind, we'll get it out of you at the party. If you don't feel like chatting with our bachelor find, we won't make you."

"Okay, I may not...I'm only coming to see you, Julian, and new baby...but in case I do speak to him, what's the man's name?"

"It's kind of an odd one, Kearton...Reginald Kearton. Julian says he's quite nice—for a *Yankee.*"

Once I'd met the 'Yankee', I had to agree. He *was* quite nice— so nice in fact, that later, I happily changed my name from Fran Adams to Fran Adams Kearton.